"*Jesus Skeptic* is a different kind of book. It examines the positive social impact of those who believe in Jesus. That impact is widespread and far greater than most people realize. Moving from one area to another, Dickerson documents that influence and then looks deeper into what and who is behind it. This is a fascinating read that may just surprise you."

Dr. Darrell L. Bock, *New York Times* bestselling author
and senior research professor of New Testament studies
at Dallas Theological Seminary

"My hometown of Portland, Oregon, is filled with wonderful people, especially millennials, who gravely misunderstand who Jesus is and have little understanding of the ways his followers are making our city and the world a better place. My friend John S. Dickerson has written a much-needed book to help alleviate that! The story of the church, of the community of people filled by the Spirit of Jesus for more than two thousand years, is a story of radical love and justice that has shaped education and healthcare, catapulted scientific inquiry, helped to abolish slavery, and led the way in protecting human rights. Understanding this impact can encourage wavering believers and soften the hearts of many skeptics."

Kevin Palau, president of the Luis Palau Association

"As with his other work, Dickerson's words are extremely insightful and relevant."

Dr. Jim Denison, CEO of Denison Forum and author
of *How Does God See America?*

"This generation isn't simply asking, 'Is Christianity true?' They want to know, 'Is Christianity *good*? Does the faith actually promote human rights, alleviate suffering, and enable humanity to flourish?' In *Jesus Skeptic*, John Dickerson provides a compelling answer to these pressing questions. He leads readers on a lively tour through the ancient world, demonstrating Christianity's positive impact at key moments in history. This book is a remarkable accomplishment. It is sweeping in scope yet deeply personal. Dickerson, a reporter and pastor, reveals Christianity's impact on history—then zooms in to explore what Christ means for each person. The evidence Dickerson offers will enlighten believers and non-believers alike. In the introduction, he writes that skeptics 'are safe here.' That's true—but their skepticism is definitely in danger."

Drew Dyck, contributing editor at CTPastors.com
and author of *Your Future Self Will Thank You*

"Only John Dickerson could so artfully weave history, politics, pop culture, and personal stories in a way that is both educational and entertaining. As a devout agnostic, I thoroughly enjoyed learning about a different perspective—presented in a thoughtful, engaging, and enlightening way."

Amy Silverman, award-winning journalist, editor,
and author of *My Heart Can't Even Believe It*

"Many scholarly works make points and arguments for Christ and Christianity similar to those John Dickerson makes here; however, his book seems more readable and engaging than most. The length seems ideal for the book's intended audience—not so short as to appear inconsequential, yet not so lengthy as to be uninviting. It is well worth reading!"

Dr. Hugh Ross, astronomer, pastor, and president
of Reasons to Believe

"My good friend John S. Dickerson has unearthed his biggest story ever as an investigative reporter. *Jesus Skeptic* is an eye-opening and desperately needed resource in a world of revisionist history. Honest skeptics as well as parents and pastors will find facts—not opinions—to answer their most challenging questions about

Jesus's life, teaching, and impact in history. I highly recommend this book."

Chip Ingram, author of *Why I Believe* and teaching pastor
at Living on the Edge

"More than ever we need an articulate and detailed study of the importance and impact of the Christian faith that is not charged with emotions but is loaded with evidence. I am pleased to recommend John's work to you, knowing that it will surprise you and draw you into the greater narrative of God's unfolding mission within history. If you are a skeptic, this book is especially for you, and John's arguments and research will intrigue you and invite you further into dialogue with history's most significant person, Jesus."

Ed Stetzer, executive director of the Billy Graham Center

Praise for John Dickerson

"Few writers can gather, process, distill, and apply a host of facts with the precision of John S. Dickerson."

John McCandlish Phillips, former *New York Times* journalist

"I am a believer in John's ability to hold readers in his thrall, to tell simple and uplifting human stories, and to share his eloquent hopes."

Ken Auletta, *New Yorker* media critic, Pulitzer Prize judge,
and bestselling author

skeptic Jesus

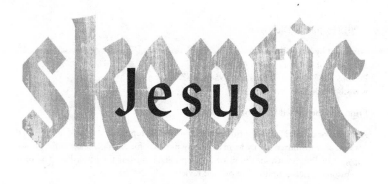

Jesus Skeptic

A Journalist Explores the Credibility
and Impact of Christianity

JOHN S. DICKERSON

BakerBooks

a division of Baker Publishing Group
Grand Rapids, Michigan

© 2019 by John S. Dickerson

Published by Baker Books
a division of Baker Publishing Group
PO Box 6287, Grand Rapids, MI 49516-6287
www.bakerbooks.com

Printed in the United States of America

Library of Congress Cataloging-in-Publication Data
Names: Dickerson, John S., author.
Title: Jesus skeptic : a journalist explores the credibility and impact of Christianity / John S. Dickerson.
Description: Grand Rapids : Baker Books, a division of Baker Publishing Group, 2019.
Identifiers: LCCN 2019015096 | ISBN 9780801078088 (pbk.)
Subjects: LCSH: Jesus Christ—Influence. | Apologetics. | Jesus Christ—Historicity.
Classification: LCC BT304.3 .D53 2019 | DDC 239—dc23
LC record available at https://lccn.loc.gov/2019015096

19 20 21 22 23 24 25   7 6 5 4 3 2 1

To all who seek to find
meaning, identity, and significance.
May you find what you seek.

Contents

Part 3: The Most Influential Person

Preface

You and I have something in common. We are both searching for the same things in life. We seek to answer basic questions about ourselves.

Who am I? The question of identity
What am I worth? The question of value
Where will I belong and be safe? The question of belonging
Why do I exist? The question of purpose

Your quest to find meaningful answers to these questions is really what this book is about. At least, that's how it started for me.

As I moved through high school and college and then into my career as an investigative news reporter, I met people who were trying to answer these questions in every possible way—from fame and fortune to drugs and achievement.

As a reporter, I spent intimate moments observing the daily routines and emotions of millionaires, billionaires, celebrities, and professional athletes. I had the same access to heroin addicts, victims of trauma, prison inmates, and dehydrated immigrants stumbling across the Mexican border into Arizona.

In all those people, I noticed a universal hunt.

We all hunger to answer these same questions: *Who am I? What am I worth? Where will I belong and be safe? Why do I exist?*

I have seen that a person's answers to these questions will shape the course of their life—for better or worse—leading either to a life of freedom and joy or to a life that seems continually smaller and emptier.

How you choose to answer these basic questions will define your internal sense of peace, significance, and fulfillment.

I have seen firsthand that a person can be a world-famous millionaire but still be restless and unfulfilled if they do not have good answers to these questions. I have also seen that a person can be poor and unknown but entirely fulfilled and happy if they have good answers to these universal questions.

My work as an investigative reporter gave me a front-row seat to the many ways people attempt to find meaning and significance. I met millionaires who were depressed and impoverished missionaries who were deeply fulfilled. In this kaleidoscope of human experience, I found one thing at the core of the most fulfilled, stable, and heroic people I met. Time after time, these people found their identities, value, and purpose in a person I could not see—a man called Jesus Christ.

From NBA team owners to Grammy-winning musicians to doctors volunteering in poverty to humanitarian aid workers, I kept meeting people I wanted to be like. I wanted what they had in their internal lives, their behind-the-scenes lives. These people consistently claimed to find identity, purpose, and peace in one place—a "relationship" with a real God who relates to them through Jesus. Across different cultures and situations, this Jesus repeatedly surfaced as the center of the most centered people I met.

I struggled to understand how people could find such meaning and purpose in someone they could not see with their eyes, touch with their hands, or hear with their ears. I was not sure that a

God existed at all, let alone that Jesus was that God. At times, I wondered if these well-intentioned people had been duped into believing a myth.

Even if Jesus was a myth, the recurring evidence of changed lives was something I had to consider. So many of these people I admired were believers in this Jesus, and they demonstrated peace, significance, joy, and selflessness—all qualities that are exceptional across the human spectrum.

In time, I learned that one out of three people alive today claims to follow Jesus. This makes Jesus the most followed person in the history of the world by a large margin.

For all these reasons, I set out to consider this Jesus. I wanted to know if he actually lived, I wanted to read what he actually said, and I wanted to measure how his followers have impacted humanity.

Could this Jesus provide significant answers to the universal quest for security, identity, and purpose?

Could Jesus's way of life set people on a path of freedom, achievement, peace, and significance?

Because I am an investigative reporter, I applied a factual and skeptical approach to investigate Jesus. The result is a book that includes a library of images and hundreds of irrefutable facts. It is a resource that is unlike anything I encountered in my study of Jesus. I wanted to summarize academic and historical records in a way that makes this information available for anyone.

You will see that I never took off my skeptic's hat as I considered the history, evidence, and impact of Jesus. Instead, I measured Jesus with the same tools used in my award-winning news investigations.

This journey has taken me more than ten years and has covered everything from ancient manuscripts to modern individuals who claim to be radically transformed. In all of it, I found the life and story of Jesus to be notable. For anyone who hungers to answer the universal questions of self and existence, this Jesus and his movement are worthy of consideration.

And so this book in your hands—*Jesus Skeptic*—is ultimately about you. It is about your journey to find your identity, your purpose, and your security. May you find each, and may you experience a life of freedom, purpose, and significance.

Introduction

I f you are a skeptic who does not believe in God, you are safe here. If you were raised as a Christian but are no longer sure what you believe, you are safe.

If you like Jesus but not the church, this book is a safe place for you.

If you are tired of Christianity being defined by bigots and political parties, you are safe too.

I have been all these things and more.

What follows is my own ten-year investigation into how Jesus and his followers have impacted our world. I call it *Jesus Skeptic* because that is how I began my investigation—as a professional skeptic, a research journalist.

In my news career, I have gathered evidence and facts to build dozens of investigations. I have exposed the lies and abuses of powerful people. I have used the power of the pen to fight for the rights of racial minorities, women, immigrants, and many others.

My news investigations have earned some of the highest journalism honors in the nation—including an award given by Christiane Amanpour of CNN, Tom Brokaw of NBC News, and executives from NPR and the *New York Times*.[1]

As important as those investigations were, I believe the findings of this book are even larger in scope because this book investigates the validity of the largest movement in world history—the movement that today claims one out of three people worldwide, the movement of Jesus's followers, often known as Christianity.

I aim to conclude whether the teachings of Jesus have anything meaningful to offer to you, to me, and to modern progressive society. As a research journalist, I committed to reach conclusions about Jesus from evidence rather than from opinion.

I set out to answer questions such as:

Did Jesus actually exist?

Can Jesus's teachings actually provide peace, identity, and fulfillment today?

Do Jesus's teachings block social justice and human progress—or do Jesus's teachings further those causes?

This book is unique. I am a millennial-generation journalist investigating Christianity's record on matters of social justice, human rights, racial equality, and human dignity. This book presents numerous irrefutable artifacts and images rather than a collection of opinions or feelings. In the following pages, you will discover stories and facts that you never knew about Jesus and the people he inspired.

Jesus's followers have occupied key places in history, often turning up in my research where I least expected to find them. One example is Frederick Douglass, who escaped slavery a decade before the Civil War and then spent his life fighting to end slavery in the United States. Douglass's story is so inspiring that I now have his picture hanging on my office wall.

After physical and racial abuse, Douglass had every right to spend the rest of his life isolated, angry, and bitter about the injustices that had been done to him. But, instead, Douglass channeled his anger into a fearless, positive, and tireless fight to end slavery and secure human rights for millions of others.

Long before the Civil War, Douglass traveled the country, speaking to packed auditoriums in the Northern states. He described to white audiences the horrors of slavery in the South. Pro-slavery mercenaries frequently showed up to kill Douglass. On more than one occasion, pro-slavery activists attempted to burn down lecture halls where he spoke.

Figure 0.1. Frederick Douglass.

Yet Douglass continued to fearlessly declare his case against slavery. As I read Douglass's writings, I was surprised to discover that he cited the words of Jesus as formative for his own identity and also as his moral authority for declaring slavery evil. In Douglass's own account of his life, he described his deeply held Christian faith.

Here is an excerpt from Douglass's autobiography, in which he described his conversion to Christianity.

> In my loneliness and destitution, I longed for someone to who I could go, as to a father and protector. The preaching of a white Methodist minister, named Hanson, was the means of causing me to feel that in God, I had such a friend.
>
> I consulted a good colored man named Charles Lawson, and in tones of holy affection he told me to pray, and to "cast all my care upon God." This I sought to do; and though for weeks I was a poor, broken-hearted mourner, traveling through doubts and

fears, I finally found my burden lightened and my heart relieved. I loved all mankind, slaveholders not excepted, though I abhorred slavery more than ever. I saw the world in a new light, and my great concern was to have everybody converted. . . . The good ole man had told me that the "Lord had great work for me to do," and I must prepare to do it.[2]

(Note: As with every quotation in this book, the source information can be found in the notes section at the back of the book. In addition, the images and evidence in this book can be searched and shared at JesusSkeptic.com.)

Douglass became one of the most unstoppable forces to end slavery in the United States and then around the globe. By his own account, his journey was as much a spiritual quest—motivated by the message of Jesus—as it was a humanitarian quest.

Douglass's life story—written by his own hand—is what I refer to as "Primary Evidence." This evidence speaks directly and un-equivocally about Jesus's impact on Douglass's life and person.

Primary Evidence is the most tamper-proof, bias-proof type of information we can use in any investigation. It allows us to see for ourselves what key people in history believed about Jesus. We can learn from their writings what motivated them to make the world a better place. We will review a kaleidoscope of Primary Evidence in the pages of this book.

On our journey, I will share more about my career as an investigative reporter, my own exploration of Jesus's impact on society, and the impact this project has had on my search for personal identity and purpose. But first, I want to give you a sneak peek at the quality of Primary Evidence we will be investigating in this book.

PART 1

Skeptics Welcome

one

A Dead Body

My stomach turned when I saw the bruises on the dead body. As an investigative reporter, I had documented death, but I had never seen anything like this.

At least a dozen pockmarks were scattered—like hail damage—along the side of the human corpse. The chest and torso looked as if they had been beaten repeatedly with a baseball bat. One massive bruise of yellow, black, purple, and blue the size of a pizza wrapped around the man's upper body.

Juan Farias's face was in even worse condition: swollen lips, blood in the mouth and nostrils. A deep gash sliced into the cartilage on his nose. Another bruise spread across his forehead.

I compared these autopsy photos to a picture taken when Farias had entered the county jail. Juan Farias had been unbruised and uninjured when he had walked into the jail.

In the first moments of my investigation, when I held those autopsy photos, I suspected Farias had been beaten to death while in the county jail. But I needed more evidence to either confirm or disprove my hunch.

As a reporter, I needed to dig deeper to learn *who* had beaten to death Farias, a Mexican immigrant who had died in an Arizona jail. Had he died due to abuse from jail guards? Or had he gotten into a fight with other inmates? Was the death of Farias—a racial minority and an immigrant—part of a larger pattern of abuse in that jail? I needed more evidence.

No one else in the world was asking about Farias's death. And so it was my job, as a journalist, to draw attention to it, to learn the truth behind his death, to seek justice.

I contacted the county medical examiner, asking for a written autopsy report on Juan Farias's dead body. I requested more photos. I filed multiple public records requests with jail authorities and began contacting relatives and witnesses.

A growing stack of data revealed an unsettling story: the evidence suggested that jail guards had beaten Juan Farias to death, even after he had been handcuffed and posed no threat to them.

With further research, I uncovered an apparent cover-up by jail officials. Videos, photos, and written reports all indicated that jail guards had surrounded Farias, struck him repeatedly, soaked him in pepper spray, fastened a Hannibal Lecter–style "spit mask" over his face, and then sat on his chest during a beating that dragged on for the better part of an hour.[1]

To find the truth about Farias's death, I had to uncover evidence from inside the jail. I had to file legal records requests with county authorities multiple times and ways. I had to search court records. My newspaper even had to file a lawsuit against the sheriff who oversaw the jail.

Eventually, I secured Primary Evidence. Primary Evidence is what I am always looking for in any serious investigation. It enables us to see the difference between opinions and reality.

In the case of Juan Farias's death, the Primary Evidence included the following:

- witness statements that guards had written after Farias died
- twenty-five hundred pages of paperwork
- employment logs from inside the jail
- Farias's autopsy and photos from the county medical examiner
- video security footage from inside the jail, and much more

The resulting investigation exposed a scandal of injustice, corruption, and abuse in one of the nation's largest jails.

Uncovering the truth makes my heart sing. It is why I doggedly work to conduct investigations such as the one just described. Nobody in a position of power stood up for Juan Farias during his life, but at least I could stand up for him in his death by writing the truth of his story for thousands of people to read.

My investigation into the jailhouse murder of Juan Farias is just one of my award-winning investigations.[2] There are many others, including the unveiling of a $990 million financial scam and a medical doctor who performed surgeries while high on cocaine.

Those investigations affected lives and deaths, laws and lawsuits. But none of them are as broad in scope as the inquiries of this book. This is an investigation into the largest social movement in human history—Christianity. And this investigation is unique. We will measure if the people who follow Jesus make the world a worse or better place. We will measure if Jesus's existence is a matter of myth or fact.

Primary Evidence

For this investigation into Christianity, I have applied the same standard of Primary Evidence that I use in my news investigations. With a topic as broad as Christianity, we could easily line up ten "experts" who call Christianity "the best thing in world history," and then, the next day, we could find another ten "experts" who declare Christianity "the greatest evil in history." Clearly, the opinions of "experts" can contradict one another when it comes to complex matters. But just as with the best news investigations, Primary Evidence is clear and convincing if we take the time to view it.

The following wealth of Primary Evidence about Jesus's followers speaks clearly and has never before been compiled in one place. The evidence tells a compelling story about Jesus's impact on social justice and human progress.

In this chapter, I want to give you a sample of the quality of Primary Evidence we will see on our journey. My aim in this chapter is not to present any conclusions but rather to provide some examples of the evidence that exists for a serious investigation of Christianity.

Sample Primary Evidence regarding Jesus's Existence

When I investigated whether Jesus actually lived, I was surprised to find fifteen ancient writers from the time of Jesus who wrote about his existence and early followers. None of these writers were Christians, and none of their writings are in the Bible. These writers were Jewish, Roman, and Greek, and they did not believe that Jesus was God (as Christians do).

The outlined section on the page in figure 1.1 is one instance in which the ancient writer Flavius Josephus wrote about Jesus.[3] Josephus described Jesus as a dynamic teacher who was crucified by a ruler named Pilate. He wrote that Jesus was followed by spiritual disciples, reportedly resurrected from the dead, and was believed by his followers to be the Messiah (the Jewish concept of God on earth to rescue humanity).

Josephus is one of many ancient witnesses—outside the Bible and outside Christianity—who wrote about Jesus existing as an actual person. Here is an English translation of Josephus's ancient account:

Figure 1.1. Copy of a page written by Flavius Josephus, a Jewish historian who lived during the same era as Jesus. Josephus was not a Christian.

At this time there was a wise man who was called Jesus. His conduct was good and [he] was known to be virtuous. And many people from among the Jews and the other nations became his disciples. Pilate condemned him to be crucified and to die. But those who had become his disciples did not abandon his discipleship. They reported that he had appeared to them three days after his crucifixion, and that he was alive; accordingly he was perhaps the Messiah, concerning who the prophets have recounted wonders.[4]

These ancient accounts—outside the Bible—surprised me, and I will walk through several of them in chapter 13. For now, I present this as a preview of the quality of Primary Evidence we will use in our investigation. Rather than asking an internet forum if Jesus existed, we can look at historical artifacts and make a fact-based conclusion—just as I would do with any news investigation.

Figure 1.2. On this coin, "Hadrianus" is inscribed next to a silhouette of the head of the Roman emperor Hadrian. In ancient written records, Hadrian's secretary Suetonius[5] referred to Jesus's followers and described a movement started by a Jew named Jesus (Christus or Christ).

Each of the ancient writers who wrote about Jesus presents unique Primary Evidence. For example, two emperors (from the era when Jesus lived) discussed Jesus and his early followers with their advisors. Today we have not only those ancient writings but also coins bearing the faces of those emperors.

This is the sort of Primary Evidence we will consider when we investigate whether Jesus actually existed.

Sample Primary Evidence regarding Christianity and Human Rights

Where better to start an investigation into human rights than with Martin Luther King Jr. (MLK)? MLK is perhaps the most famous advocate of racial equality and human rights in history. When I studied the Primary Evidence about MLK's beliefs (his documented writings and recorded speeches), I found that MLK credited Jesus and Christianity for his beliefs about human equality and for his motivation in the struggle for equality.

Figure 1.3. Martin Luther King Jr.

28

Here are two historically verified quotations from MLK. Each is Primary Evidence.

> Jesus still cries out in words that echo across the centuries: "Love your enemies; bless them that curse you; pray for them that despitefully use you." This is what we must live by. We must meet hate with love. Remember . . . if I am stopped, this movement will not stop, because God is with the movement. Go home with this glowing faith and this radiant assurance. [said after a bomb was thrown into his house in Alabama on January 30, 1956][6]

> If one is truly devoted to the religion of Jesus he will seek to rid the earth of social evils. The gospel is social as well as personal.[7]

Figure 1.4. Masthead of the popular anti-slavery newspaper *The Liberator*, which circulated before, during, and after the Civil War.

In the decades leading up to the American Civil War, anti-slavery newspapers such as *The Liberator* swayed the minds of millions of people, convincing the nation to uproot slavery at any cost. The men and women who printed these anti-slavery newspapers and who wrote the articles within them were strongly Christian. We do not need an expert to tell us whether these people were anti-Christian or pro-Christian because we can read their words for ourselves. Consider also the following details in *The Liberator* masthead shown in figure 1.4:

- The ribbon along the bottom reads, "Thou shalt love thy neighbor as thyself." This is a quotation from Jesus, as recorded in the Christian Gospels.[8]
- The coin in the middle of the logo features Jesus standing between a black man and a white man. The men are kneeling on equal footing, with the Christian cross in the background.
- Around the edge of the coin is written, "I come to break the bonds of the oppressed." This is another saying of Jesus, also taken from the Christian Gospels.[9]

This physical *Liberator* newspaper, which we can hold in our hands today, is Primary Evidence about the impact of Jesus and his followers on the overthrow of slavery.

The samples of Primary Evidence we have considered in this chapter are real manuscripts; real, historic people; and real, tangible artifacts. This is a preview of the quality of Primary Evidence we will consider together.

Our investigation will not be a collection of opinions and hunches. Instead, we will examine undeniable artifacts that we can view with our own eyes. As we gather and examine this evidence for ourselves, we can discover for ourselves the impact of Jesus's movement on the world.

two

Suspicions about Christianity

I t sounds like a scene from a movie, but it actually happened to me in Phoenix, Arizona.

While I was investigating a corrupt politician, a spooky, unmarked police cruiser began following me as I drove around town. This intimidating, all-black patrol car belonged to the Selective Enforcement Unit, an SS-like division that the local sheriff used for special projects.

When I went to interview survivors of jail abuse and the relatives of inmates who had died in jail, a few of these menacing police cruisers occasionally tailed my car. The drivers never turned on their police lights or pulled me over, but the message was clear: "We are watching you."

My colleagues and I continued our investigation. Then one night these same unmarked sheriff's cars surrounded the house of my editor. Selective Enforcement Unit officers jumped out of the cars carrying guns and wearing bulletproof vests. They stormed the house and arrested my editor in the middle of the night.

My editor's arrest prompted an outcry from the *New York Times* and other national news outlets.[1] As a result, my editor was soon released. Years later, my editor won a lawsuit against the sheriff's department because the arrest was found to be illegal intimidation and retaliation for our news investigations.

I tell you that story because it illustrates a reality I have learned as an investigative reporter: wherever there is a powerful story, there are powerful people who want to suppress the truth.

I believe the same to be true with this book. **I believe there are people who do not want you to see the evidence in this book.**

There are people who do not want you to think for yourself about the impact of Jesus's life and movement. Many thought-leaders today have reached their own conclusions about Christianity, and they are not open-minded toward or tolerant of evidence that may contradict their bias.

But just as with my news investigations, I remain committed to announcing the facts and the truth. My aim as a reporter is to present facts so that justice is served and humanity improves. My aim here is to present the truth so that you can decide for yourself what to believe.

When it comes to Christianity, my ten-year investigation has convinced me that my generation of Americans—millennials, born in the 1980s and 1990s—has been largely denied the truth about Christianity's influence and record on social justice. We have been told the negative moments in Christian history, and we have been told the positive moments from other world belief systems. But we have not been exposed to the whole truth of the Christian record so that we can decide for ourselves whether Jesus's teachings and movement would be helpful to our personal lives and to the positive society we want to build.

In these pages, we will examine indisputable evidence about Jesus and his global movement in order to determine the following:

- whether the Jesus of Christianity lived at all
- why Christianity continues to give purpose to one out of three people alive today
- whether the Christian message moves people toward social progress and human rights or toward bigotry and backwardness
- whether followers of Jesus have blocked or enabled modern progress, equality, tolerance, science, and education

My aim is not to tell you how to think but, very simply, to show you the artifacts, the evidence, and the record.

Whether we like it or not, Jesus's movement has become the largest movement in human history.

Out of about 7 billion people in the world, 2.3 billion believe the spiritual and historical claims of Jesus to be true.[2] These people sincerely believe that Jesus lived and then rose from the dead. They believe that Jesus is God and will return to set up a kingdom of peace and prosperity. Today more people adhere to Christianity than to any other single belief system. As a result, any educated person should be informed about Jesus, his claims, and the measurable impact his followers have had on society.

The Jesus story is either among the greatest scams ever perpetrated or among the greatest news ever told. On this journey, we aim to discover which is more likely.

If you are skeptical about religion, you should know that I am too. I am a skeptic by nature. In fact, my work as an investigative journalist is the work of a professional skeptic.

I was only twenty-four years old when the Arizona Newspaper Association named me "Journalist of the Year."[3] A better name for that award would have been "Skeptic of the Year," because my investigations all grew out of my suspicions.

In those early years of reporting, I uncovered a credit card debt relief agency that was actually scamming debtors and driving them deeper into financial disaster. I also uncovered a modeling agency that was scamming parents with false promises about their children becoming famous—charging $10,000 for a few portrait photos.

I conducted those and many more significant investigations because:

- I am naturally skeptical of people in power.
- I am driven to uncover lies and abuses.
- I am driven to help people who are not in a position of cultural power.
- I believe that when things sound too good to be true, they often are.

I tell you this about myself to assure you that if you are skeptical about Jesus, Christians, or Christianity—well, you are in good company. If you feel suspicious about religion or about what the Christians in your life stand for, I share your skepticism about all those matters.

Here are some questions that prodded me to investigate Jesus and Christianity for myself.

Why is it that Christianity is so prevalent? Why are there so many crosses on necklaces and buildings? Why are there so many Christian fish emblems and bumper stickers on cars?

If the truth about the most influential person in history has been concealed from me, would I want to know it?

If foundational truths about the world have been deliberately hidden from me, would I want to know it?

If the truth about Jesus and Christianity could be known through Primary Evidence (rather than opinion), would I want to see that evidence for myself and decide what to believe for myself?

If one belief system consistently surfaced—across centuries—in which human rights and equality were promoted, would I want to know so that I could use that system in today's fight for human rights and equality?

I wanted to know the answers to these questions. So I set out to dig up irrefutable facts about Jesus and Christianity.

In the end, the clarity and the quantity of this evidence astounded me. Never in all the investigations I had conducted had a mountain of evidence piled so high or pointed to such a clear conclusion.

At times, this evidence challenged my own biases and prejudices. Other times, the evidence made me furious that people of power had convinced me to believe the opposite of the historic record.

I expect you will also be surprised by some of these irrefutable facts, many of which may have been hidden from you as well.

three

Keystone Species

The Importance of a Keystone Species

When I visit California, one of my favorite things to do is drive to the Pacific Ocean near Moss Landing and watch the sea otters play in the water.

California sea otters have to be among nature's cutest animals. They backstroke through the water, and it is not uncommon for a backstroking otter mommy to set a pup on her chest as she swims. If that wasn't cute enough, otter families often hold hands as they nap, swim, or float in lazy formations.

But don't let their cuddly appearance fool you. When these easygoing sea otters dive underwater, they get a lot done. In fact, marine biologists have learned that California's entire ocean ecosystem depends on the sea otter.

When sea otters are present in an area, other ocean life thrives— from plankton all the way up to great white sharks and whales. But when sea otters are absent, life deteriorates for all species. Marine biologists call sea otters a "keystone species" because all other ocean life rises or falls on them.[1]

Figure 3.1. Otters holding hands.

We humans learned the hard way about the keystone importance of sea otters. In Monterey Bay, California, sea otters were hunted to near extinction in the 1920s. Without sea otters, a massive area of the ocean became lifeless and stagnant. In the 1970s, researchers figured out why this happened when they discovered the link between sea otters and the ocean ecosystem.

Looking beneath the ocean surface, researchers discovered that many ocean creatures come to Monterey Bay to feed on massive underwater forests of sea kelp. Sea kelp are giant seaweed trees that can be as large as 175 feet tall under water.[2] The forests of sea kelp stretch on for miles in some areas, providing food for thousands of ocean creatures.

A particular sea urchin eats this kelp and destroys it, leaving no food for the small animals at the beginning of the food chain and thereby destroying the entire ecosystem.

In Monterey Bay, only one predator can stop the sea urchin and thus save these underwater forests. You guessed it; it's the cuddly California sea otter. Sea otters feed on the sea urchins— keeping them from destroying a vital food source and devastating the ecosystem.

When zoologists reintroduced sea otters into Monterey Bay, the ecosystem roared back to life. It is now thriving again, and hundreds of species of ocean creatures journey to Monterey Bay to feed and to mate. Researchers have even tracked great white sharks and orca whales who swim thousands of miles to Monterey Bay to feast on its rich food supply. This is all the result of the cuddly looking sea otters. Such is the power of a keystone species.

Figure 3.2. A sea otter feeding on a sea urchin.

During my ten-year investigation into Christianity's impact, the Primary Evidence continually surprised me. I reached a point when—looking at hundreds of pieces of evidence—I found myself wondering, *Could Christianity be a keystone species for human society? Could it be that society improves in fundamental ways when Christians are present?*

I remember the moment this question struck me. I was driving past a well-known Arizona hospital named St. Joseph's. The hospital is named after a Christian saint. I knew of half a dozen other Christian-named hospitals, including St. Mary's, St. Francis, and St. Vincent, all started by Jesus's followers but all happy to care for atheists, Muslims, Hindus—people of any or no religion.

Then my mind skipped to one of the best hospitals in the nation. It has the word "Presbyterian" in its name (a Christian denomination). I began recalling other leading hospitals with words such as "Baptist," "Methodist," and "Franciscan" in their names (these are also Christian groups). *Was it a coincidence that all these hospitals had Christian names?*

I decided to investigate the founders of these leading hospitals. *How many of the leading hospitals were started by Christians?* Here's what I found among the top ten hospitals.[3]

The Top Ten Hospitals in the United States

Rank	Hospital	Founders	First Doctors
1	Mayo Clinic (Rochester, MN)	Christian[4]	Christian educated
2	Cleveland Clinic (Cleveland, OH)	Christian[5]	Christian educated
3	Johns Hopkins Hospital (Baltimore)	Christian[6]	Christian educated
4	Massachusetts General Hospital (Boston)	Christian[7]	Christian educated
5	University of Michigan Hospitals (Ann Arbor)	Christian[8]	Christian educated
6	UCSF Medical Center (San Francisco)	Christian[9]	Christian educated
7	UCLA Medical Center (Los Angeles)	Christian[10]	Christian educated
8	Cedars-Sinai Medical Center (Los Angeles)	Jewish[11]	Christian educated
9	Stanford Health Care-Stanford Hospital (Stanford, CA)	Christian[12]	Christian educated
10	NewYork-Presbyterian Hospital (New York)	Christian[13]	Christian educated

Primary Evidence revealed that nine of the top ten hospitals in the United States were started—many as Christian charities—by Christians who were motivated by the teachings of Jesus to care for the poor. One of the top ten was started by a Jewish group, and its first doctors were trained at Christian-founded medical schools. (I will reveal the Primary Evidence about these founders and their hospitals in chap. 8.)

From covering healthcare as a reporter, I knew full well that, no matter how you may feel about Christians or Jesus, if you are having a heart attack or major surgery, you want to be in one of these ten best hospitals.

I wondered, *Has anyone else realized that without Christians none of these top ten hospitals would exist as we know them?*

The irony, of course, is that many of us who are most educated in America today have been led to believe that Christianity is bad for society—that it hinders human progress. I wondered, *What if the facts show the exact opposite of what we have been told to believe?* Whatever the facts showed about Jesus's impact, I wanted to see the evidence for myself.

Could Christianity Be a "Keystone Species" That Improves Humanity?

Experts did not realize that California sea otters were a keystone species until the otters were hunted to near-extinction and the entire ecosystem fell apart.

In the United States and Western Europe, more than 70 percent of the population has identified as "Christian" for the majority of the last four hundred years. We say that a fish doesn't know what water is because water is all they have ever known. In a similar way, we who have been born into American or European culture have a difficult time understanding what a society without Christian influence would actually look like. Christian assumptions and values have influenced us more than we realize—through the hospitals where we were born, the names many of us bear, our education system, our inherited rights, our assumptions about human dignity, and much more.

I also noticed the "sea otter effect" of Christianity when I studied global data on women's rights. To my surprise, the countries with the best women's rights all have predominately Christian populations. And the countries with the worst women's rights are where Christianity has been outlawed or is socially punished. (The statistics in the following tables came from non-Christian researchers.)

Percent of Christians in the Ten Best Nations for Women's Rights

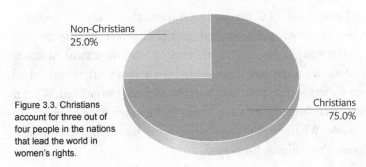

Non-Christians
25.0%

Christians
75.0%

Figure 3.3. Christians account for three out of four people in the nations that lead the world in women's rights.

Percent of Christians in the Ten Worst Nations for Women's Rights

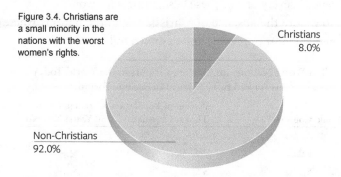

Figure 3.4. Christians are a small minority in the nations with the worst women's rights.

Christians 8.0%

Non-Christians 92.0%

According to the World Economic Forum, here are the ten nations that lead the world in women's rights.

Ten Best Nations for Women's Rights in the World Today
as ranked by the World Economic Forum[14]

Rank	Country	Percent of Population That Is Christian	Christian Culture > 50 Years? Yes/No
1	Iceland	85%	Yes[15]
2	Norway	77%	Yes[16]
3	Finland	70%	Yes[17]
4	Sweden	65%	Yes[18]
5	Ireland	87%	Yes[19]
6	Rwanda	84%	Yes[20]
7	Philippines	93%	Yes[21]
8	Switzerland	73%	Yes[22]
9	Slovenia	78%	Yes[23]
10	New Zealand	48%	Yes[24]

On average, Christians make up 75 percent of the populations in the nations that lead the world with the best women's rights, including matters such as equal pay, the right to vote, the right not to be sold into marriage, and a striving toward equal rights in all areas. It turns out that Christianity has had significant cultural influence in every one of these best cultures for women.

Now, note the absence of Christianity in the nations where women are most oppressed and devalued today.

Ten Worst Nations for Women's Rights in the World Today
as ranked by the World Economic Forum

Rank	Country	Percent of Population That Is Christian	Christian Culture > 50 Years? Yes/No
1	Yemen	0.2%	No[25]
2	Pakistan	2%	No[26]
3	Syria	5%	No[27]
4	Chad	44% (but persecuted)	No[28]
5	Iran, Islamic Republic	0.2%	No[29]
6	Jordan	2%	No[30]
7	Morocco	0.1%	No[31]
8	Lebanon	38% (but persecuted)	No[32]
9	Mali	2%	No[33]
10	Egypt	5%	No[34]

Christians are a stifled minority in the nations with the worst records for women's rights. Most of these nations have outlawed Christianity—giving us a picture of the ocean without the sea otter. None of these worst cultures for women's rights have had a significant Christian influence on social norms. In these nations, women are still denied education rights and voting rights. In some instances, women are even denied the right to drive a car. Many still practice the horrific ritual of genital mutilation for young girls. In some, girls are still sold into marriage. Even worse, in some of these cultures, a woman gets physically punished if she is found "guilty" of being raped by a man.

No matter how much you may respect other global cultures, if you have a daughter, sister, or mother, you do not want her living in one of these societies.

As a father of young daughters, I realized something profound. Regardless of what I personally believed about Christianity, I wanted my daughters to grow up in a Christian-influenced society because, statistically, they would have far more rights, more education, and better equality in a nation that was largely and historically influenced by Christianity than in a nation that was not.

That conclusion was not a matter of opinion but of statistics.

We do not need to be religious to acknowledge the facts. In fact, we would be foolish to deny such facts simply because we have a bias or a prejudice against religion or against Christianity specifically.

At this point in my journey, I began to consider that perhaps Christianity had widespread implications for society—for medicine, for women's rights, and for other areas too.

As I compiled hundreds of pieces of Primary Evidence, patterns began to emerge. I began to see—in the evidence—a pattern of social improvement where Christians saturated culture. The Primary Evidence suggested that this correlation was not a coincidence; it revealed specific human rights champions and innovators who initiated these human advances. And as I read the writings of these champions and innovators, people such as Martin Luther King Jr., I repeatedly discovered that they cited the words of Jesus and the Christian Bible as their motivation.

I found Jesus's followers and ideas where I least expected them—often as the spark beneath world-changing improvements in areas such as science, the ending of open slavery, the founding of universities, and much more.

As my mountain of evidence grew, I needed to formulate a research method that would lead me toward concrete, factual conclusions about Christianity's impact on humanity. In the end, I chose a research method that I also used for one of my most complex news investigations. (I describe this research method in appendix C.) The research revealed a pattern—built from Primary Evidence—about

Christianity's measurable impact on humanity. *Could this connection between Jesus's followers and human rights be a coincidence?* I wondered.

In the following chapters, I will show you evidence that has never before been compiled in one place—irrefutable images and quotations that taken together created a mosaic of facts that challenged some of my deeply held assumptions.

PART 2

Measuring Christianity's Impact on Society

four

The Scientific Revolution

I am the way and the truth and the life.

Jesus, as quoted in the historically verified Gospel of John[1]

After years of research for this project, with hundreds of pieces of evidence, I struggled with how to present the findings in this part of the book.

Should I summarize what all the findings mean up front? Or will spoiling the ending remove the element of discovery and surprise that I myself so enjoyed as I gathered this Primary Evidence?

In the end, I decided to go with the oldest rule in journalism: start with the unexpected.

Of all the advances that have benefited our modern world (modern hospitals, universities, science, the end of open slavery, public education, and so forth), the area where I least expected to find serious Jesus followers was science.

After all, *aren't Christianity and science incompatible? Don't they contradict each other?*

My findings about the role of Jesus's followers in the Scientific Revolution were completely unexpected. As you will see below, this is not a matter of opinion or guesswork. Here the Primary Evidence was overwhelming, convincing, and entirely unexpected. The scientists who ushered us into the modern world wrote about Jesus with a passion that today is reserved for musicians writing love songs.

My favorite thing about this book in your hands is that you don't have to take my word for any of these conclusions. You will be able to read the writings of these scientists for yourself in this chapter.

If we recall middle school science, we remember that world-famous scientists such as Isaac Newton, Johannes Kepler, and Blaise Pascal unlocked the secrets of the universe during a time known as the Scientific Revolution. If not for their world-changing advances, we might still be living in the days of the pioneers—with no electricity or modern lifesaving technologies.

So foundational is the work of Isaac Newton that Albert Einstein once said this about Newton's contribution to our modern world: "In the beginning, God created Newton's laws of motion together with the necessary masses and forces. This is all; everything beyond this follows from the development of appropriate mathematical methods by means of deduction."[2]

During the Scientific Revolution, Newton and his peers threw open doors of knowledge that had been locked for thousands of years. They unlocked the secrets of the universe so that every scientist and inventor who followed could build upon their work—from the Wright brothers and Thomas Edison to Einstein.

Our modern homes, hospitals, heaters, lights, air-conditioning, and phones are all the end result. The technologies, conveniences, and lifesaving tools that separate us from the Dark Ages did not happen by accident. They were not inevitable; they were the result of a specific season of scientific breakthrough.

This revolution in science was led by specific people, including Isaac Newton, Johannes Kepler, and Blaise Pascal. These three—and many of their peers—have something else in common. Primary Evidence reveals that each of these scientific founders was a devout follower of Jesus and devoted to his teachings. I found the Christian faith of the scientific founders not by asking any one expert but by reading the writings of the founders themselves, in which they described their own beliefs and motivations.

Newton, Kepler, and Pascal were so devoted in their beliefs about Jesus and their faith that they each wrote personal prayers and Christian Scripture passages in their journals. Those Primary Evidence documents remain to this day, and we will investigate some of them below.

Pascal actually kept a poem about Jesus in his coat pocket. In it he wrote, "This is eternal life, that they know you, the one true God, and the one that you sent, Jesus Christ."[3] (You can see a picture of this poem in fig. 4.9.) Pascal, of course, remains among the most important scientific innovators in human history.

Newton wrote thousands of pages about Jesus and the Christian Bible, and you can read them today. They include lines such as this one from his personal journal: "Christ gave himself for me."[4] (I have compiled some of these Primary Evidence writings below and at JesusSkeptic.com.)

The clear Christian faith of the scientific founders contradicts a deeply held false stereotype. Many in our day have been told that science and Christianity have always been at odds, and I must admit that the Primary Evidence here surprised me.

After a careful examination of the Primary Evidence, it became clear to me that followers of Jesus played an irrefutable role in launching the Scientific Revolution, which in turn unleashed the technology of our modern world.[5] Also of significance: every founder of the Scientific Revolution whom I studied was educated at Christian-founded universities such as Cambridge and Oxford.

Let's continue by defining the term "Scientific Revolution."

The Scientific Revolution was a unique time in human history when the mysteries of the universe were unlocked by a relatively small group of people, in one focused part of the world, during one precise window of time.

The Scientific Revolution took place during a time of spiritual revival and intense Christian belief known as the Protestant Reformation. The Protestant Reformation took place when followers of Jesus began reading and applying the Bible for themselves rather than merely trusting the dogma of priests in the formal church. It was when sincere followers of Jesus attempted to return the faith to a pure expression of what Jesus had taught and to cleanse the church of corruption, evil, and politics.

Accepted dates for the Protestant Reformation are 1517 to 1648. Interestingly, accepted dates for the Scientific Revolution are 1543 to 1687. It is no coincidence that the Scientific Revolution followed on the heels of the Protestant Reformation and took place in the same part of the world. Because of the Protestant Reformation, society was open to increased reading, learning, and independent thought, all of which grew out of Christian-founded universities and church schools. This era—which also overlapped with the Renaissance—was an age of skeptical inquiry in Europe birthed out of these Christian-founded universities, which we will study in chapter 7.

During the Protestant Reformation, a population that was majority Christian was now reading the Bible and thinking for themselves. In the sciences, the dogma handed down from the Greeks and some nonbiblical church traditions were now open to questioning. The refining of ancient science developed into a rigorous method, formalized by thinkers such as Francis Bacon. Bacon once wrote, "It is true that a little philosophy inclineth man's mind to atheism, but depth in philosophy bringeth men's minds about to religion."[6] Like a great majority of the key figures in the Scientific Revolution, Bacon was a committed Christian.

We should not assume that the knowledge of the Scientific Revolution was inevitable. After all, humans had been rubbing sticks together and experimenting with rocks and metals for ages and ages without ever reaching the avalanche of discoveries that Bacon, Newton, and the other founders of the Scientific Revolution ignited.

Scientists from the Scientific Revolution Whose Writings Show Their Belief in Jesus as God

As we will see from the Primary Evidence that follows, if we remove Christian influence from world history, then we lose the Scientific Revolution. Evidence shows that many influential scientists of the past were devout followers of Jesus.

Isaac Newton

You probably know Isaac Newton best from pictures showing him with an apple falling from a tree. Newton is the gravity guy. He defined the Laws of Motion, including

Figure 4.1. Isaac Newton.

51

gravity. If you don't like my conclusion that modern science would not exist as it does without Newton, then take it up with Albert Einstein. He is the one who planted that idea in my mind.

Figure 4.2. Replica of Isaac Newton's telescope.

Newton undoubtedly ranks among the most important scientists in history. Some would argue that he is *the* most influential because of what he unlocked. It was as if the secrets of science were locked in a cabinet that many smart people tried to break into for thousands of years. Then Newton suddenly unlocked the cabinet. Since then, everyone after him has been able to play with what was inside.

Newton was a physicist. He was a mathematician. He was an astronomer and inventor. And he was a prolific writer.

Newton created calculus (making high school much harder for the rest of us). He did not get assigned calculus homework—he invented it. Newton also invented the generalized binomial theorem. He did all of this before he finished his undergraduate university studies.

Like the other founders of the Scientific Revolution, Newton was educated at a Christian-founded college. He graduated from Trinity College, which is one division within Cambridge University, one of the original Christian "seed" universities. (I will explain the Christian seed universities, which gave birth to the modern university, in chap. 7.)

Figure 4.3. Title page of a book written by Isaac Newton in 1686.

If you are scientifically oriented, you may enjoy reading some of Newton's writings for yourself. Whenever I spend time reading his writings, I realize how small my mind is compared to the mind of this once-in-history thinker. Here is a glimpse of Newton's writings. This is not from one of his religious texts but from one of his famous physics texts, *Principia*.

> This most beautiful system of the sun, planets, and comets could only proceed from the counsel and dominion of an intelligent and powerful being. This being governs all things, not as the soul of the world, but as the Lord over all, and on account of his dominion, he is wont to be called "Lord, God."[7]

Here Newton uses a Greek word for "almighty" or "universal ruler." What you will see if you really look at the writings of Newton and the writings of many other great scientists of the Scientific Revolution is that they were not incidentally Christian. They were not accidentally Christian. They did not just happen to be Christian. Their entire way of seeing the world and the universe was through the lens of Jesus as God, a real being in whom they firmly believed. They believed Jesus to be a God who is good and who works with order and predictability.

According to their own writings, it was this belief in Jesus that they used as a foundation to map out the universe and to unlock the secrets of science—things no other human had been able to unlock in the ages before them.

Newton was so obsessive about the Bible that he would often study Bible predictions (or prophecies), and he would study them in every original language available. That included Hebrew, Latin, Syriac, and Greek. Newton would study these Bible writings and then make vast mathematical calculations based on them.

It has been estimated that Newton wrote more than four million words of theology (theology is the study of God). To put that number into perspective, consider that this entire book is about

65,000 words. So Newton wrote more than fifty-seven volumes the size of this book on the subject of God and the Bible.

Figure 4.4 shows just one of the thousands of pages Newton wrote about the Christian God. Because he was educated at a

Figure 4.4. Isaac Newton often combined his study of God with his study of science, as seen in this page from his journal. The world-famous scientist wrote more than four million words about God.

Christian university, Newton could read and write in the ancient languages in which the Bible was originally written. On this page, you can see the distinctive Hebrew language, which Newton wrote in his own handwriting as he studied God in the Christian Bible.

The National Library of Israel has scanned and digitized about seventy-five hundred pages of Newton's theological writings. You can search them and read them for yourself by following the URL in the endnote.[8] Thousands of additional pages Newton wrote about theology and science can be accessed at the Newton Project.[9]

Newton believed that the Bible speaks into our physical and spiritual world. He believed this so deeply that he often took physical measurements from the Old Testament temples and wrote out charts of those measurements, applying them to the universe.

Newton believed that Jesus is God and that Jesus will return as the literal Christ to set up a new kingdom on earth (as all sincere Christians believe). Newton was so certain of this that he made calculations predicting the year he believed Jesus would return to earth—the year 2060. All of this is documented in *Observations upon the Prophecies of Daniel, and the Apocalypse of St. John* (1733).[10]

This all may sound goofy to you. But somehow from all these studies and predictions came Newton's groundbreaking scientific works, which even the most anti-Christian scientist must admit unlocked the door to modern science as we know it.

Here are three quotations from Newton's personal writings:[11]

This is life eternal that they might know the onely true God, & Jesus Christ whom thou hast sent. John 17.3

Jesus Christ the same yesterday & to day & for ever.

We are in him that is true, [even] in his son Jesus Christ. This is the true God.

We don't have to ask experts what Newton believed about Jesus. We can read it with our own eyes. Newton's writings demonstrate his belief that Jesus of Nazareth is God, who died on the cross for the sins of the world, who literally rose from the dead, and who will return to repair the human condition.

Newton's thoughts and notes reveal a sincere student of the Christian Scriptures. He was clearly a person who read the Bible over and over again, seeking to connect the truths within it, seeking to make sense of the universe from God's point of view. Here are some additional quotations from Newton's writings:[12]

Christ is called light also. John 1.4, 5, 7, 8, 9. & 3.19 & 8.12 & 12.35, 36, 46.

(Note: The numbers in each of these quotes from Isaac Newton are chapter and verse references to various books of the Bible. For example, "John" refers to the book of John; "1.4" refers to chapter 1, verse 4 of that book. To compile all these references about Jesus from physical copies of ancient texts—without a computerized search—Newton would have needed to spend countless hours reading the Bible.)

Christ the only begotten Son of God in respect of his miraculous birth of the Virgin by divine power without a father. Acts 13.32,

33, 34. Psal 2.7. Heb 1.4, 5. Luc 1.32, 35. Mark 13.33. John 1.34, 49. & 6.69 & 9.16, 33, 35. & 10.35, 36 & 11.27 & 13.3. Heb. 3.6.

The Jews did not expect their Messiah to be more then [sic] a man, yet freely called him the Son of God. Christ did not magnify his divinity before his passion yet freely called himself the Son of God. See Matt. 24.33. & 26.63 & 27.54.

To this end Christ both died & rose & revived that he might be lord both of the dead & living.

Christ died for our sins.

Christ hath loved us & hath given himself for us, an offering & a sacrifice to God for a sweet smelling savour.

These are direct writings from Newton's journal.

He was such a student of the Christian Scriptures that he often visited the various libraries at Oxford and Cambridge to leaf through ancient Bible documents. (The libraries at Oxford and Cambridge contain many thousands of ancient manuscripts of the books that today make up the Christian Bible.)

Oftentimes, Newton spread out ancient Christian writings in Arabic, Ethiopian, Greek, and Hebrew alongside one another in order to verify the accuracy of the Christian Scriptures and to interpret them.[13]

Johannes Kepler

Whether or not you know Johannes Kepler's name, you know the gist of his Laws of Planetary Motion—describing how the earth orbits around the sun,

Figure 4.5. Johannes Kepler.

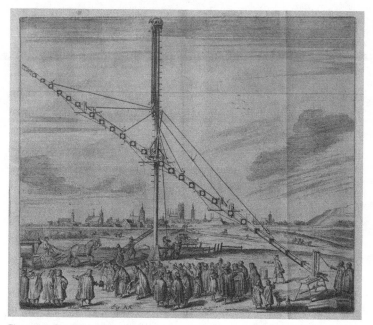

Figure 4.6. The Kepler telescope.

the moon around the earth, and so on. Like Newton, Kepler is an undeniable key figure in the Scientific Revolution.

If you wear eyeglasses, you can thank Kepler.[14] He invented eyeglasses, the pinhole camera, and the Kepler telescope. Galileo invented a telescope, but Kepler improved significantly on the design by switching some of the lenses.

Kepler began his studies as a theology student, hoping to be a pastor or priest, but he showed such brilliance in his math classes that his professors switched him to math. Kepler's writings reveal that he continued to be a devout believer in Jesus as God, even as he made world-changing scientific discoveries.

Kepler wrote in *Mysterium Cosmographicum*, "Before the universe was created, there were no numbers except the Trinity [Father, Son, and Holy Spirit], which is God himself. For the line and the plane imply no numbers. Here, infinitude itself reigns. Let us consider therefore the solids."[15] Clearly, God and science were interwoven in the mind of this scientist who helped unlock the mysteries of science.

Later in my investigation, when I studied the words of Jesus, I found a verse in the Bible where he claims to be "the light of the world."[16] How interesting that through telescopes, eyeglasses, lenses, and other advances, followers of Jesus have literally given light to so many in the world. The lights by which we now see exist physically because of the scientific contributions made by followers of Jesus such as Johannes Kepler.

Blaise Pascal

Scientific founder Blaise Pascal also had a devout faith in Jesus, as revealed in his own Primary Evidence writings.

Pascal is a world-famous mathematician, physicist, and inventor. He made monumental contributions to geometry and the understanding of pressure and vacuums. Scientists today—all around the world—still use a scientific measurement called a "pascal." Pascal's mechanical calculator (see fig. 4.8) is considered by many to be the first computer in history. It predates other early mechanical computers by more than a century.

Pascal built his calculator by hand—physically pounding or shaping each piece of metal to create this gear-driven mechanical computation device (or computer). In a world in which people still chopped firewood and burned coal for heat, a world where electric appliances had not yet been invented, how many people could have had the intellect to

Figure 4.7. Blaise Pascal.

Figure 4.8. Pascal's calculator.

envision and then create a mathematical calculation machine—
and one that actually worked?

This is the way this innovator's mind worked.

This same innovator wrote about his Christian faith in multiple
places, including his books titled *Pensées* and *Lettres Provinciales*,
both of which disprove the stereotype that Christianity and science
are incompatible.

The most remarkable piece of Primary Evidence regarding Pas-
cal's devotion to Jesus is a handwritten poem that Pascal authored.
When he passed away, he had a copy of it inside his coat pocket.
Pascal wrote it in French and Latin. Below it is translated into
English.

> GOD of Abraham, GOD of Isaac, GOD of Jacob
> not of the philosophers and of the learned.
> GOD of Jesus Christ.
> My God and your God.
> Forgetfulness of the world and of everything, except GOD.
> He is only found by the ways taught in the Gospel.
> Grandeur of the human soul.
> Righteous Father, the world has not known you, but I have
>   known you.

59

Joy, joy, joy, tears of joy.
This is eternal life, that they know
   you, the one true God, and the
   one that you sent, Jesus Christ.
Jesus Christ.
Jesus Christ.
I left him; I fled him, renounced
   him, crucified.
Let me never be separated from
   him.[17]

These are not the words of someone who was passively a Christian or who claimed to be a Christian merely because doing so was convenient. These are the yearnings of someone who deeply believed that Jesus is God and has the power to provide peace, identity, purpose, security, and eternal life.

Figure 4.9. Copy of Blaise Pascal's "Memorial," a passionate poem he kept with him that includes the line "This is eternal life, that they know you, the one true God, and the one that you sent, Jesus Christ."

Above, as Primary Evidence, is a picture of this original poem written by Pascal's own hand in French (see fig. 4.9).

If you're skeptical by nature, like me, you may think: That just sounds too good to be true for the Christians. They've got Blaise Pascal and Isaac Newton. How can the Christians have such smart people on their side?

Robert Boyle

Robert Boyle is known as the father of modern chemistry. In his writings, he strongly argued that the principles and methods of chemistry must be applied to the study of the natural world and to medicine, which became a cornerstone for modern chemistry. However, Boyle is also well-known in the field of physics for various discoveries about the physical characteristics of air, including Boyle's Law (that the volume of a gas decreases with increasing pressure and vice versa), and the relationship between air and the propagation of sound.

So much of our modern life—from plastics to medicines—resulted from Boyle's breakthroughs in the fields of both chemistry and physics.

Boyle was also a sincere Christian who used science to support Christianity throughout his career. In addition to his scientific contributions, Boyle was known for his many theological writings.

Figure 4.10. Robert Boyle.

His book *The Christian Virtuoso*, published in 1690, argues that faith in Jesus promotes a greater mind, leading to better scientific understanding. Boyle wrote that studying nature as a product of God's handiwork is a religious duty and that through such study,

God's goodness and overarching existence are illuminated.

Boyle gave money to missionary societies and other organizations to promote the spread of Christianity and the translation of the Bible into other languages. Upon his death, he designated a portion of his estate to be used for a lecture series that explores the

Figure 4.11. Robert Boyle, the father of modern chemistry and the creator of Boyle's Law, wrote frequently about his Christian faith. This book, *The Christian Virtuoso*, argues that faith in Jesus promotes a greater mind, leading to better scientific understanding.

relationship between Christianity and the natural world. These lectures, now known as the Boyle Lectures, continue today, and you can watch videos of recent lectures online.[18]

Like Newton, Kepler, and Pascal, the father of modern chemistry was also a devout believer in Jesus as God.

John Ray

Naturalist John Ray was the founder of our modern understanding of biology and zoology. He was the first person to define the species of animals and to decipher the meaning of the rings inside a tree trunk. He was also an artist.

Ray viewed theology (the study of God and God's relationship to the world) as intertwined with science. And both he and Isaac Newton credited their scientific break-

Figure 4.12. John Ray.

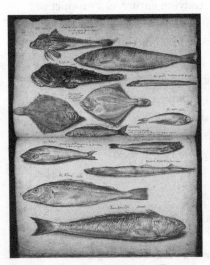

Figure 4.13. Drawings of fish by John Ray.

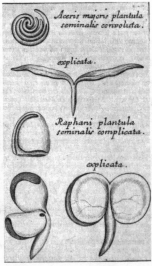

Figure 4.14. One of John Ray's many drawings. According to Ray's books, which survive to this day, he was a devout follower of Jesus.

throughs to their belief in Christ as God. Devout Christians like these launched the Scientific Revolution, and as a result the Industrial Revolution and the modern way of life we know today with electric appliances, antibiotics, and modern medicine.

Like Newton, Blaise Pascal, and Robert Boyle, John Ray wrote entire books about Jesus in addition to his books about science.[19] One book is titled *The Wisdom of God Manifested in the Works of the Creation.* Another of his books, *Three Physico-Theological Discourses* (1713), further demonstrated his belief that the best science grows out of Christian understanding.

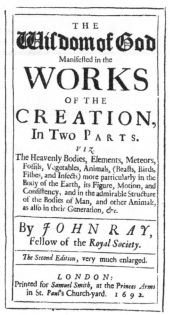

Figure 4.15. John Ray's book titled *The Wisdom of God Manifested in the Works of the Creation.*

Other Christians Who Led Scientific Breakthroughs

Sociologist Rodney Stark explored the journals and personal artifacts of the fifty-two most influential scientists who launched the Scientific Revolution. (That list of the fifty-two most influential scientists was chosen by a secular group.) **He found that 98 percent of the founders of the Scientific Revolution were committed Christians.** They studied creation because they believed it was a way to study the God who had made everything. Within that 98 percent, more than half were devoted believers, like Newton and Pascal, who wrote about Jesus in their personal journals and writings. Only 2 percent of the fifty-two most influential scientists were not Christians.[20]

**Founders of the Scientific Revolution
Who Were Christian vs. Non-Christian**

Christian	98 percent
Non-Christian	2 percent

The number of influential scientists from this time in history who were devout Christians is so significant that I could write an entire book on the topic with hundreds of pages of Primary Evidence. If you are science-oriented, I encourage you to read their writings for yourself and allow these brilliant minds to speak for themselves regarding their belief in Jesus.

Other sincere followers of Jesus who changed the world with their scientific breakthroughs include:

Carl Linnaeus	Lise (Elise) Meitner
George Ohm	Michael Faraday
George Washington Carver	Robert Grosseteste
Gottfried Leibniz	Tycho Brache
Henrietta Swan Leavitt	William Harvey
John Dalton	William Kelvin
Joseph Lister	William of Ocam
Joseph Priestley	

Very simply put, the Primary Evidence demonstrates that the most influential founders of modern science were Christians. These are not cherry-picked examples; rather, they are symbolic of the Christian greenhouse of thought in which the seeds of the Scientific Revolution and modern science were planted and nurtured. These people of faith routinely credited their Christianity as the reason for their breakthroughs in discovery.

Which leads us to the question *Why does this matter?*

Implications for Today

The discoveries of the Scientific Revolution became the foundations of modern life, including modern medicine, the Industrial Revolution, atomic physics, and the Information Age. If these specific scientists were somehow removed from world history, then you and I would likely be living in a world that does not understand planetary motion, calculus, basic physics, the circulation of blood in the human body, germ theory, or Newtonian physics, among other things.

Therefore, whether or not we personally believe the claims of Jesus to be true, we would be ignorant to act as if Christianity does not matter to the world.

When I first viewed the Primary Evidence about Christianity and the Scientific Revolution, it challenged my assumptions. It turns out that today's believers in Jesus stand intellectually alongside Isaac Newton, Johannes Kepler, Blaise Pascal, and many of the others who launched modern science. To hint then that Christianity is for the stupid not only is biased against today's believers but also is an ignorant suggestion. Unless I wanted to claim to be smarter than Isaac Newton and Blaise Pascal, I needed to stop suggesting that faith in Jesus was anti-intellectual.

As for my personal journey, I was astounded to see the role of Christian belief in the lives of scientists whom I had admired and learned about earlier in my life. Among their writings, I found one quotation from Jesus that was repeated by both Newton and Pascal. Each of these brilliant people wrote it down using pen and parchment (copies of which still exist today as Primary Evidence): "This is life eternal that they might know the onely [sic] true God, & Jesus Christ whom thou hast sent."[21]

If these men were right about planetary physics and calculus, I wondered, *what if they were also right that there is an "eternal life" and that this eternal life is found by knowing Jesus Christ, the man who claimed to be God?*

Newton and Pascal both clearly believed this in the deepest way possible. If there is such an eternal life, then they may be watching us, even now, from that dimension. If that eternal life exists, perhaps they are lighting the way toward it for us.

As Pascal wrote:

> Grandeur of the human soul.
> Righteous Father, the world has not known you, but I have known you.
> Joy, joy, joy, tears of joy.
> *This is eternal life, that they know you, the one true God, and the one that you sent, Jesus Christ.*
> Jesus Christ.
> Jesus Christ. . . . Let me never be separated from him.[22]

Christians Improving Society Today

The Story Continues:
Science

Francis S. Collins
Director of the National Institutes of Health
and Leader of the International Human Genome Project

As I learned about the Christian faith of history's scientific greats, I wondered if any leading scientists today believe that Jesus is God. I found more than a few, but here is one who stood out from the crowd.

Physician-geneticist Francis S. Collins is ranked among the top practical scientists of our time. He shares the same faith in Jesus as Blaise Pascal, Isaac Newton, and the other scientists whose primary writings we considered.[23]

Collins leads an international team of scientists to decode human DNA. He has also revolutionized modern methods to

screen genes for disease. Collins currently serves as director
of the National Institutes of Health, the largest supporter of
biomedical research in the world. He also serves on prestigious
medical and scientific boards and has won numerous awards for
his scientific work.[24]

Collins views science and belief in God as fully complementary. In fact, he reads our own DNA "instruction book" as God's
language for all living things.[25] Collins has written several books
on science, medicine, and Christianity, including the *New York
Times* bestseller *The Language of God: A Scientist Presents Evidence for Belief*.

Collins began his scientific career as a self-professed atheist. He began questioning his atheism in medical school after
encountering patients who clung firmly to their Christian faith
while battling terminal illnesses, life-altering diseases, and other
sufferings. Collins realized that in viewing faith as an irrational
myth, he had rejected it without collecting any data about what
he was rejecting. That premature rejection of Christianity was,
he concluded, contrary to his own scientific training.[26]

This prompted Collins to research the evidence for faith in
Christ. He began reading the writings of Oxford scholar C. S.
Lewis, among other notable Christian thinkers. Collins's research revealed that there is a rational basis to believe that God
exists.

"The idea that you would arrive at faith because it made
sense, because it was rational, because it was the most appropriate choice when presented with the data, that was a new
concept," he recalls.[27] Collins struggled with this conclusion
until the age of twenty-seven, when he personally chose to believe in Jesus as God, or the Christ.

Collins describes how scientific research of DNA led him to
his faith in Christ:

> [A] search to learn more about God's character led me to the
> person of Jesus Christ. Here was a person with remarkably
> strong historical evidence of his life, who made astounding

statements about loving your neighbor, and whose claims about being God's son seemed to demand a decision about whether he was deluded or the real thing. After resisting for nearly two years, I found it impossible to go on living in such a state of uncertainty, and I became a follower of Jesus.[28]

Collins says that despite his initial reluctance to share his faith with his scientific colleagues, his pursuit of medical genetics emboldened his Christian beliefs.

Some would say that [genetics] would be the most godless of all possible disciplines, because if misused, it tends to take the wonders of humanity and reduce it to the language of this organic chemical called DNA. Certainly, to many outside perspectives, the idea of both starting down a path towards that branch of science and becoming a convicted believer didn't seem like a very compatible circumstance. I think they have turned out to be intensely compatible.[29]

As leader of the International Human Genome Project, Collins has the job of reading and decoding "the 3.1 billion letters of the human genome." As he has studied the code written into all of humanity, he has come to see "DNA, the information molecule of all living things, as God's language, and the elegance and complexity of our own bodies and the rest of nature as a reflection of God's plan."[30]

In his own words, Collins puts it this way: "I have found there is a wonderful harmony in the complementary truths of science and faith. . . . The God of the Bible is also the God of the genome. God can be found in the cathedral or in the laboratory. By investigating God's majestic and awesome creation, science can actually be a means of worship."[31]

Life before Jesus's Influence

As I considered whether Jesus could be the answer to my questions about identity (*Who am I?*) and purpose (*Why do I exist?*), I was surprised to find that thinkers such as Isaac Newton found Jesus to be their answer to these questions.

These brilliant minds were living proof that looking to Jesus to answer the deep questions about ourselves is not anti-intellectual, ignorant, or foolish.

In the previous chapter, we saw Primary Evidence in the writings of some of the founders of the Scientific Revolution. Those writings revealed that the people who unlocked the mysteries of science shared a common belief in Jesus as God.

Would you be surprised to learn that I found similar evidence among the people who did the following?

- created the university and college systems as we know them
- created the modern hospital and modern medicine
- ended open slavery
- created public education as we know it
- launched the Scientific Revolution (as we saw in the previous chapter)

The quality and clarity of the Primary Evidence in each of these areas astonished me.

The significance of these innovations is not merely about history or education. These advances are the difference between a world in which we shiver in the cold at night and a world in which we sleep in the warmth of modern heating. They are the difference between a world in which people are bought and sold and a world in which people can openly fight for equal rights. These innovations shaped our modern world, making it exponentially better than the world most people experienced throughout history.

In this chapter and the next, we will put these ideas into perspective—again using documents and facts.

Let's start by asking this question: *What would life be like today if Jesus had never lived?*

Let's compare our way of living today to the average human life before Jesus lived (or in some instances, before Jesus's teachings affected a region or culture). If we can understand what life was like before Jesus, then we can begin to measure if Jesus's ideas have made human existence better or worse in the regions of the world where Jesus's followers have influenced society.

To start, let's build a basic understanding of what life was like before Jesus. (In my news investigations, I call this step "baselining," and I further explain it as an investigative technique in appendix B.)

The Surprisingly Difficult Existence of Most People throughout History

As I am writing this, about 108 billion people have lived on planet Earth from the start of human history until now.[1] Of these 108 billion, about 7 billion are alive today. So, in rough figures, everyone alive today makes up about 6 out of every 100 people who have ever lived on the planet.

We in the Western nations (Western refers to Europe and its off-shoots such as the United States, Canada, and Australia) account for the wealthiest, healthiest, freest, and most educated people of all the 108 billion people who have ever lived.

If we simplified all the people who ever lived down to a group of 100 people, we who live in America or Europe today would be the top 2 out of that 100. We have a longer life span, better health-care, better education, more access to clean water and food, more freedom, and more prosperity than any other people in history.

Within the United States, we sometimes hear about the "1 percenters"—those few people who hold an inordinate amount of the world's wealth today. In the scope of human history, everyone living in America or Europe today is among the top "2 percenters" of all humanity. We enjoy far better lifestyles and length of life than 98 out of 100 people in all of history. We live on average twice as long as people throughout world history lived.

From mobile phones, toilets, and heated and cooled homes to medicine, education, freedom, individual rights, and leisure time, much of what we assume as "normal" in our lives has only ever applied to 1 or 2 percent of the people who have ever lived. So what was life like for the other 98 percent?

A little confession here regarding my own ignorance. As I began to research life conditions before Jesus lived, I was surprised to discover how uninformed I had been about the difficulty of life for most people who preceded us. (I was also surprised to learn the difficulties people still face in less-developed parts of the world, which happen to be the regions where Christianity has not shaped society.) Most people in history suffered through plagues, famines, epidemics, wars, and deaths that I have only ever seen acted out in movies.

Of the 108 billion people who have ever lived, about 106 billion never had (or do not presently have) access to the education, healthcare, freedom, clean water, and electricity that we think of as normal.

Because we have been born into a society in which these benefits are normal, we struggle to understand how difficult life was before these innovations and therefore fail to comprehend how fundamentally these innovations have improved our world. We tend to falsely impose our modern rights and way of life onto ancient humanity. We tend to imagine ancient people as cleanly bathed, drinking fresh water, and enjoying basic human rights and other modern realities that simply did not exist in their time.

So what was life like for most people throughout history?

To grasp what daily life was like for the majority of our human neighbors, let's imagine ourselves living during a different century of world history (pick any era from history). Visualize yourself living perhaps under an Egyptian pharaoh, in an Aztec tribe in Central America, under a Roman emperor, or in an African tribe.

Now, on average, here is what your life would look like under those circumstances.[2]

- You have never taken a warm shower.
- You do not have any social media accounts or YouTube because you do not have a phone—nobody does.

- You do not have electricity or heat.
- You have watched siblings and other relatives die in your home during your childhood.
- If you are one of the fortunate who have lived past age ten, you will likely not survive past your late forties.
- No matter your race or skin color, there is a good chance you are a slave. (This was true on every continent; between one and seven out of every ten people in the ancient world was a slave.)[3]
- If you are a female, you are not allowed to own land.
- Whether male or female, you do not know how to read and do not have access to learn how to read.
- You have no dental care and will lose many of your teeth by your thirties.
- You eat whatever food you can grow in the ground, harvest from your animals, or barter for by trading.
- You physically pull water up from a well dug in the ground or carry it from a lake, stream, or river.
- You live without modern plumbing, and you often have dysentery (diarrhea) because human waste contaminates the water supply, but you and your neighbors do not understand how to prevent this.
- You often do not have enough food.
- You have one, two, or at most three sets of clothes.
- You routinely feel severe hunger pains due to unpredictable famines. There are no metal irrigation pipes for farm fields, no pump machines for wells, no tractors, and no modern fertilizer for crops.
- You watch relatives and loved ones die from sickness, disease, and epidemics that you do not understand. Many in your tribe or society associate these sicknesses with evil

spirits because there is no understanding of basic germ theory, disease, or hygiene.

- You likely believe the world is flat and have not been taught elementary-level science.
- You believe there are gods or spirits that control people and their health randomly and unpredictably. Your society may require the sacrifice of crops or even of babies and children to please these imaginary gods.
- Other than furs, fires, and rudimentary structures, you have no protection from the cold, the wind, or the heat.
- You are not allowed to vote because there is no voting. Democracy as we know it has not yet been invented. (Greek democracy is an exception if you chose to live in Greece. However, women were not allowed to vote in Greece's democracy, and the Greeks often voted about matters we would consider barbaric and inhumane today—for example, whether to rape and kill the wives and children of the city they just defeated or to keep the women and children as slaves.)
- You work with your hands from sunrise to sunset, digging in a field, herding animals, gathering food, serving as a soldier, or toiling at a trade such as weaving, woodworking, or metallurgy—whether as a slave or a free person.
- If female, you will likely be sold to a husband and have no say in whom you will marry. Your husband will likely be decades older than you, and there is a chance he will have additional wives to bear children for him.
- If female, your husband sees your value primarily for sex and childbearing. Some exceptions exist, but you are likely to be treated more as a slave than what we would consider a spouse or equal today.

- If female, you are likely treated as lower class and inferior, as property.
- You live with a sense of fear and dread regarding government authority because, in most cultures, the ruler (king, Caesar, pharaoh, chief) can kill you on a whim with no recourse.
- You live in a brutal, bloody, and violent society.
- You smell and see death regularly.
- You do not have a doctor with a scientific understanding of medicine.
- If you are not a slave, you are likely a peasant and will remain that way, with no chance of breaking into a higher class. The few people who are born into the higher classes use their power to make sure low-class people cannot access their way of life. They tax you, eat the food you grow, and use you to enable their affluent lifestyle.
- Wars, battles, and violent hostilities are normal. Your city or home may be pillaged or destroyed at some point in your lifetime. If not, you are likely a soldier who pillages and destroys other people's homes, in which case you will eventually die on a battlefield—more likely from an infected wound than from an actual sword or spear.
- You do not have access to eyeglasses or contacts because they do not exist.
- You do not have access to antibiotics, hospitals, or medicines of scientific usefulness because they do not exist. Other than alcohol and rare instances of opiates or other natural drugs, you have no serious pain relievers.
- If you are female, you will have as many children as physically possible, because this is your perceived value as a

woman and because such a small percentage of children survive.

Now breathe.

Welcome back to the modern era.

I apologize if that exercise made you feel as if you were walking through a Halloween haunted house or an episode of *The Walking Dead*. I assure you that I did not invent these realities. Such was the way of life for the vast majority of people in human history.

Our lives today are radically better and easier than that average existence. And so the questions become:

Who changed society in such fundamental ways?

What motivated the people who instigated global advances such as modern farming, modern medicine, and the end of open slavery?

Did these innovators share a common belief system, or were these improvements random and sporadic?

The reality is that if we removed a few foundational advances from the last thousand years, we would be living in the same darkness described above. Some of those key advances include:

- university education
- modern hospitals and medicine
- the end of open slavery
- literacy

In the following chapters, we will examine Primary Evidence to see specifically who initiated each of these world-changing benefits.

Primary Evidence Showing What Life Was Like before Jesus's Teachings Spread around the Globe

As I researched life for an average person in history, I learned that when we rewind history, we tend to falsely impose our modern rights and way of life onto ancient humanity.

Physical artifacts and accomplished historians agree that life was bleak and difficult for most people before our time. The world was a violent and brutal place ruled by a few powerful people and their armies.[4]

One example of the violence is human sacrifice. Human sacrifices—in which women, children, or men were sliced open or burned to death to appease imaginary spirits or gods—have been documented on every continent, including North America.[5] The pottery shown in figure 5.1 is from Italy before Christian influence redefined culture in that region. It shows Neoptolemus sacrificing Polyxena after the capture of Troy.[6]

In 2018, archaeologists found a mass grave of more than two hundred children who were sacrificed in South America only five

Figure 5.1. Italian pottery depicting human sacrifice.

hundred years ago—again, before the culture was influenced by followers of Jesus.[7] To put that into perspective, about the same time that Puritan Christians were creating public education by teaching both boys and girls to read the Bible and the *New England Primer*, other cultures were still cutting the hearts out of their children and offering them to imaginary gods.

Similarly, about one thousand years ago, a culture in Central America was practicing a religion in which they would publicly skin humans and wear the human skins as ritualis-

Figure 5.2. Central American pottery depicting human sacrifice.

tic garb.[8] Incidentally, across the Atlantic Ocean, this was about the same time that the first universities were being established by Christians as additions to cathedral churches.

Archaeologists have also found Primary Evidence of mass human sacrifices in what is today Missouri, Illinois, Oklahoma, Mexico, and across the Americas. These sacrifices date back to centuries before Jesus's followers had influenced the Americas. The pottery in figure 5.2 shows a human sacrifice in Central America.[9]

Today, in areas of the world where Christianity has not yet influenced societies, some human sacrifices still take place in remote places.[10] The point of these graphic illustrations is that slavery and human sacrifice have existed in dozens of civilizations, and that Christian influence has often been the cultural force that has ended both human sacrifice and slavery.

Correlation Does Not Mean Causation

Clearly, then, life after Jesus is much better than it was before Jesus, and life has improved most measurably in the heavily Christian regions of the world. But these facts alone do not mean that Jesus gets the credit for the advances of the last two thousand years. After all, Jesus isn't the only influential figure born between that brutal old world and our new, modern world.

To learn who deserves credit for the better world we live in, we must discover who actually led the advances that lifted humanity out of its brutality. We need to study specific world-changing advances (such as the five we have identified: the Scientific Revolution, universities, medicine, the ending of open slavery, and literacy). We need to discover who led these advances, and we need to examine Primary Evidence that reveals what motivated these world-changers to improve humanity as they did.

Let's be curious together.

Here are some of the questions I asked as I explored the Primary Evidence in these five areas:

Who led these dramatic changes in the trajectory of humanity?

Can we know the specific names, faces, and stories of the people who led these advances that have lifted us from darkness to light?

Among the people who led these advances, is there a common belief system? Were most of them Muslim, atheist, Hindu, Christian, Buddhist, or something else?

Were Jesus's followers mere observers while humanity improved itself? Or were Jesus's followers the ones leading the improvements in social justice and well-being?

Finally, can we know from Primary Evidence what motivated the people who launched the world-changing innovations that have so improved human life?

six

Seeds, Trees and Fruit

My wife, kids, and I used to live in California. We enjoyed the sunshine and a backyard that had both an orange tree and a lemon tree. The two trees produced dozens of oranges and lemons year-round. The fruit was delicious, organic, and fresh. Our young children would load up their red Radio Flyer wagon so full of oranges and lemons that they couldn't even budge the wheels.

In the summer months, I would set my toddler up on the kitchen counter, and she would help me make fresh orange juice and lemonade, all with the fruit from our own trees in our own backyard. It was a lot of fun.

We always enjoyed eating the fruit from those trees. But one day I realized something significant about the fruit we were enjoying. I realized that I never once did anything to care for those trees. I never watered them. I never fertilized them. Yet I got to enjoy the fruit from them.

I realized that I had no idea who had planted the seeds, watered them, and taken care of them—possibly before I was even born. When the trees were seedlings, I was not the one who had straightened them upright with a pole so they could stand vertical during windstorms. I did none of the work. (In high school, I worked a few summers in an apple orchard, so I have a sense of how many years of hard labor it takes to produce a successful fruit tree. They don't happen by accident.)

There I was enjoying all the fruit from those trees, but I had not planted them. I enjoyed the benefits, even though all the hard work had been done by others long before me.

That day, standing in the kitchen with fresh lemonade sweet on my lips, I realized that those fruit trees were a picture of the society we have inherited. Sure, our society in America is far from perfect. We all know its flaws. We know its broken, bloody history, including injustice, prejudice, and ongoing inequality. Just like my backyard in California was not perfect, our "yard" is not perfect in America or in other Western nations. But if we are honest, our society does have a number of healthy trees that have produced fruit we enjoy, even though we did not plant the seeds.

What kind of seeds and trees and fruits am I referring to?

I am referring to things such as modern hospitals and universities. If you travel to Africa, Haiti, or other less-developed parts of the world, you can see firsthand how unique our streets, hospitals, schools, homes, laws, and other social norms really are.

81

Even developing nations such as Brazil and India have far lower average standards of life when it comes to healthcare, personal wealth, economic stability, and education. Other developing nations such as China have areas of widespread poverty that neighbor areas of relative wealth, but all those areas lack freedom of information and expression that we consider normal.

Every global culture has its own unique beauty and features, to be sure, but the reality is that if you need to have open-heart surgery, you want to be in a hospital that has been influenced by the medicine of the West. And the best hospitals are typically connected to a Christian-founded university.

These modern hospitals in our society didn't develop by accident. Somebody planted the seed. The same is true of the "trees" that have produced our laws, our courts, our cars and phones, our economy, our universities, our scientific advances, and so much more that raises our way of life above the historical average.

In the previous chapter, we considered just how above average our lifestyles are compared to the historical average. In this chapter, we will consider the specific innovations that have created these improved, modern lifestyles.

These innovations are like seeds.

Because we were taught to read as children (another fruit that was planted by someone else before we were born) and because we have access to more information than any other people in history (thanks to universities, education, and internet resources), we can actually rewind history. We can look back in time as few people before us could. We can see who planted the seeds that have so improved our lives.

As a journalist, I know that the best investigations are specific. And so we will be asking specific questions for each of these seeds that have benefited the world:

Who planted this seed?
When was this seed planted?

Where was this seed planted?
Why was this seed planted?

We can know as fact—not opinion—who specifically planted these seeds of human improvement. Take, for example, the vaccines that have prevented disease for entire nations and have now saved more than an estimated five hundred million lives. We know the name of the person who invented the first vaccine, and we even know what motivated him. When we study modern medicine in chapter 8, we will see exactly who planted this seed and why.

The reality—if we consider our society in comparison to average human history—is that we have been born into a sprawling grove of fruit-producing trees. *Where did all these trees come from? What is it that makes life in the United States so different from life today in Africa, Venezuela, or India?*

I am grateful that my generation is eager to spread our wealth to other parts of the world. I am grateful to be part of a generation so eager to take our fruit and use it to make the world a better place. This is a noble desire. I believe we can best spread these innovations and improvements to others if we understand where they came from, if we understand how these seeds were planted in the first place.

For example, we can study the people who worked to end slavery so that we can better strive toward racial equality in our time.

We can study the people who created public education so that we can better strive toward equality of education in our time.

By tracing these fruits down to their roots—by taking the time to learn who planted the seeds—perhaps we can learn how to plant our own seeds in a way that will better society for our global neighbors and our children.

Consider this: two hundred years ago, slavery was a norm in the majority of the world. Today it is illegal almost everywhere—and

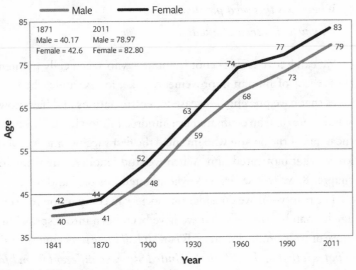

Figure 6.1. Life expectancy graph.

certainly everywhere that Christianity has had major cultural influence.

Or consider this: just two hundred years ago, the average life expectancy was about forty-one years of age. Today it is nearly twice that, especially in the nations that have adopted Western medicine and science (see fig. 6.1).[1]

Within the last two hundred years, human health has flourished. The same is true of literacy (the ability to read) and so many other trees in the orchard that we call our society or culture.

To discover who is responsible for these advances, we can look at specific fruit. We can trace our fingers down the trees to their roots and can factually pinpoint the women and men who planted the seeds that produced the fruit that now benefits us.

In the next chapters of this book, we will use Primary Evidence to answer the following questions:

Who planted the seed of the modern university—from which science, medicine, and so much more eventually sprouted?

Who planted the seeds of the modern hospital and modern medicine?

Who planted the seed to end open slavery—even after it had been a global norm for thousands of years?

Who planted the seed of social literacy—so that we know how to read these words?

(We already looked at who planted the seed of the Scientific Revolution—forever improving humanity with lifesaving and wealth-building technology—in chap. 4.)

We can trace each benefit that we enjoy down to its roots. We can uncover through Primary Evidence not only who planted each seed but also why.

I was frequently surprised by the overt Christian faith of so many people who improved humanity—but please don't take my word for it. I will show you their writings.

Having processed all this evidence, I still struggle to comprehend the immense scale at which followers of Jesus have shaped the positive features in our world. The cascading effect of these contributions is staggering and nearly impossible to fully grasp. Yet I am convinced that even a child can grasp and appreciate the following Primary Evidence, if considered with an open mind.

Like an electric cord that has been buried in the dirt, when you grab onto the little bit that sticks above the dirt and you begin pulling and walking, you will find that the cord continues. These findings are connected, and they do seem to lead to a power source.

What follows is Primary Evidence demonstrating an undeniable track record of the light, life, and freedom that have flourished where Jesus's followers have put his words into action in human society.

Because the teachings of Jesus were so frequently cited by these world-changers, I will begin each chapter with a historically verified quotation from Jesus.

Feel free to disagree with my conclusion that Jesus's follow-ers have made the world a better place. There was a time when I disagreed with it too. But that was before I saw the evidence.

Let's open our minds and discover what motivated some of the most noble and notable world-changers of all time.

seven

Universities

Then you will know the truth, and
the truth will set you free.

Jesus, as quoted in the historically
verified Gospel of John[1]

When Jesus spoke again to the
people, he said, "I am the light of
the world. Whoever follows me
will never walk in darkness, but will
have the light of life."

Gospel of John[2]

Almost two thousand years ago,
Jesus claimed that his truth would
set people free. Soon his followers
began establishing monastic schools so
that they could train others in the truth,
freedom, and life that they believed Jesus
provides.

Those monastic schools later gave birth to cathedral schools and then to overtly Christian universities, such as Oxford, leading to the modern university as we know it today. In this chapter, I will show you the progression from Jesus to the monastic schools, to the cathedral schools, to the first universities, to the modern university.

Of all the human improvements we will study, the university may seem to be the most boring at first glance. But it is, in fact, the most essential, for from this seed sprang the advances in technology, human rights, worldview, and social change that produced the modern era.

Universities trained the innovators who planted the other "seeds" we are studying. Together, these innovators lifted humanity from darkness to light. Without universities, there would have been no graduates to create public education or abolish slavery or create the modern hospital or create the thousands of other offspring universities that now dot the world, educating millions of people every year. Each of these innovations came from specific people who were trained by the early Christian-founded universities.

The Beginning of the University

University education as we know it is not just another form of education (which the world had known for thousands of years), but it is a very specific type of education rooted in a culture shaped largely by followers of Jesus.

Early Christians standardized this education system in an effort to spread the ideas of Jesus to farther regions and to following generations. As soon as three hundred years after Jesus's birth, early Christians had formed the first schools in Christian monasteries. The focus of these schools was teaching the Christian Scriptures. In time, math, logic, and other courses were added to complement the study of Jesus.

About five hundred years after Jesus's birth, the monastic schools gave birth to cathedral schools, which followers of Jesus operated in dozens of European cities. These Christian cathedral schools educated children in the ways of the church and in basic literature, drawing from the curriculum of the monastic schools. The cathedral schools formed the spine of what we today call K-12 education. In fact, some Christian cathedral schools from the AD 500s remain in existence today.[3]

Figure 7.1. An entrance to the King's School, Canterbury, a Christian cathedral school founded in AD 597 that has been in continual operation ever since.[4] Early Christian schools such as this one laid the foundation for modern education as the world knows it today.

Around AD 1000, Christian cathedrals (church buildings) in Europe began offering further education for the graduates of their cathedral schools.[5] This gave birth to a unique learning institution called the "universita." *Universita* is a Latin word meaning "the whole, total, or universe." The universita—as you may guess—was the seed that would grow to become our modern university today.

This was a dramatic fork in the road for humanity. Outside Christianity, most ancient learning was what we would today call propaganda. It consisted of rote memorization and emphasized conformity. In the universita, students were encouraged to think for themselves, to ask challenging questions, and to form their own ideas. This freedom of independent thought was revolutionary and eventually gave birth to revolutionary ideas such as the Protestant Reformation and Western democracy, and other historic revolutions.

The universita—expressing the Christian idea that all people are made in the image of God—created an environment in which every person could think for himself or herself rather than simply being commanded by an authority to believe certain ideas or behave a certain way. This freedom was not incidental. It originated from the Christian teaching that at the very beginning of the Christian story, God gave Adam and Eve freedom either to live God's way or to reject God's way and choose a path that led to death.[6]

For thousands of years, other civilizations had temples and places of learning, but the Christian universita became something different. It transformed education from rote memorization into intellectual exploration.[7] It incubated mental stimulation, gave students permission to question, and introduced the scientific method into the classroom.[8] The proof of these claims is in the results, for only the students of the Christian universities went on to launch the Scientific Revolution.

In the early AD 1000s, Christian-founded universitas such as Oxford began multiplying across Europe, emerging from Christian cathedrals in dozens of cities. Search for the world's oldest universities, and you will find that all the early universities were Christian, including those in Paris, Perugia, Rome, Madrid, Bologna, Salamanca, and Siena.

It is an incontrovertible fact of history that these universities and their graduates began to do the following:

- launch additional universities across Europe, creating the modern college and university system as we know it
- lay the foundation for the scientific method, which would lead to the Scientific Revolution and modern medicine
- lay the foundations for societies in which all people would be taught to read
- train the people who would implement laws requiring public education for all
- train the people who would write the constitutions of Western democracies

- train the people who would found additional universities, whose graduates would:
  - create modern hospitals, which still lead the world in medical care
  - abolish slavery in Europe and the United States
  - invent the first vaccine, which has saved hundreds of millions of lives
  - identify and harness electricity
  - launch the Industrial Revolution
  - begin the fight for women's rights, and much more

Based on the foundational belief that God is good, predictable, truthful, and orderly, these Christian learning centers taught that everything in the universe can be explored, tested, and dissected.[9] Classrooms filled with students who had already learned the basics in their cathedral schools (think elementary to twelfth-grade education) could now add layers of scientific, mathematical, medical, and theological exploration to their education.

Oxford University

One thousand years before the founding of Oxford, Jesus claimed, "I am the light of the world. Whoever follows me will never walk in darkness, but will have the light of life."[10] This idea of God's truth as "light" and life without God as "darkness" permeated the foundation of the Christian university. We find it in the enduring motto of Oxford, which reads, "The Lord is my light." In Latin, this reads *Domminaus Tio Illumea*.

Oxford's founding motto is not just an overtly Christian idea; it is actually a quotation from the Christian Bible, which reads, "The LORD is my light and my salvation."[11] The three crowns on the Oxford crest represent the three parts of the Christian

Godhead: God the Father, God the Son (Jesus), and God the Holy Spirit.

To this day, many historians and educators still refer to education as "the light of learning"—a nod to Oxford's motto and to Jesus's two-thousand-year-old claim that "whoever follows me will never walk in darkness, but will have the light of life."[12]

No movement of humans is perfect. Throughout history, some who have claimed to be Christian have committed evils—as have people from all major world cultures. Yet despite those exceptions, the last thousand years have demonstrated that where Christian-founded university education spreads, advances in science, human rights, and medicine tend to follow close behind.

Such university education is a light that has lifted humanity out of the darkness in such practical ways as inventing the light bulb, eyeglasses, and medical breakthroughs that have doubled our average life expectancy.

Looking to God as provider and director was the principle on which Oxford was founded. For hundreds of years, seeking God in the Christian Scriptures remained core to the most influential universities in the world, both in Europe and in the United States. These Christian-founded universities remain the top universities in the world today, ranked in the top ten in such practical matters as science, medicine, and technology.

Oxford—and the universities it spawned—helped to perpetuate what historians and sociologists once called "Western civilization." Western civilization includes many basic human rights that we see as normal today but that were not normal in other world cultures throughout human history. Principles such as freedom of speech, human dignity, freedom from slavery, women's rights, personal property ownership, and the world-changing concept of Western democracy all can be linked to these universities and the graduates whose minds were shaped in their classrooms.

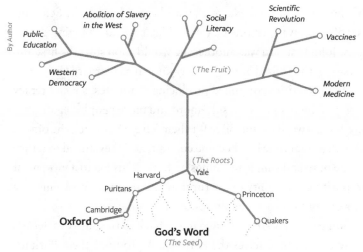

Figure 7.2. Graduates from Christian-founded universities initiated these specific advances.

In future chapters, we also will see that, time and again, the workers who led the fight against slavery and for other social justice breakthroughs were educated at Oxford or at one of its Christian-founded offshoots, such as Cambridge, Harvard, and Yale.

The light of the Christian Lord, as Oxford's motto phrases it, began to shine into the darkness of ignorance. Scientific learning commenced. Independent thought flourished. Compassionate ethics leaped forward. Brave ideas about human rights, human dignity, and human equality took root, eventually shaping the foundations of future societies. (We will see many specific examples in the following chapters.)

Cambridge University

In 1209, faculty from Oxford University started another Christian-founded university: Cambridge. Graduates from Cambridge would soon change the world in multiple ways. You will recognize some of their names. Isaac Newton, who helped launch the Scientific Revolution, was just one of Cambridge's world-changing graduates. John Harvard was another; he would soon start the first university in the United States—today known as Harvard University.

As universities continued producing graduates, social literacy began to increase. As a result, more and more people began reading Jesus's words in the Bible for themselves. Many felt the official church at that time had become corrupt, and they aimed to return to the pure and simple teachings of Jesus. This led to a movement to purify Christianity of corruption and political involvement, a movement known as the Protestant Reformation.

Some who said they wanted to get back to the purity of Jesus's words called themselves the Puritans. A group of these Puritans who were graduates of Cambridge University soon traveled to the New World of North America, where they forever shaped American history and culture.

Harvard University

The Puritan graduates of Cambridge University who traveled across the Atlantic to North America named their new city Cambridge, after the university they had attended. (Today that city is Cambridge, Massachusetts.) Their first priorities were to:

- stay alive
- build homes and livelihoods
- build a church
- establish a basic government
- create a university so that their children could read the Bible

That group of pastors, including John Harvard, successfully founded the first university in North America—Harvard. Like

Yale, Princeton, and most of the leading state universities, Harvard began as a seminary to train ministers or pastors.

As seen in figure 7.3, these words from the founders of Harvard remain etched in stone on a gate leading into Harvard University:

> After God had carried us safe to New England, and we had builded [sic] our houses, provided necessaries for our livelihood, reared convenient places for God's worship, and settled the civil government, one of the next things we longed for and looked after was to advance learning and perpetuate it to posterity, *dreading to leave an illiterate ministry to the churches when our present ministers shall lie in the dust.*[13]

In other words, they arrived and the land was completely undeveloped. It was thick forest. Many of them had died on the difficult journey, and they soon realized that those who could read and understand the Bible would die in time. As a result, they felt an urgency to train the next generation to read the words of Jesus,

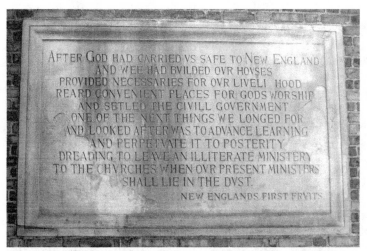

Figure 7.3. Stone etching, declaring God's ministry as the purpose for Harvard University.

which they believed led to life and an ideal society. That is why they created Harvard University—a descendant of Cambridge, Oxford, and the cathedral schools—with lineage tracing all the way back to Jesus.

Today Harvard is ranked as one of the top universities in the world. Its graduates have been presidents and world leaders and have led the world in scientific and health innovation. Harvard also boasts the largest academic and private library in the world.[14] Harvard has informed and shaped our definition of what a college or university is.

That early group of Puritans (who had graduated from Cambridge) gave their lives and fortunes to establish Harvard as a Bible-training university. One of them—John Harvard—died in his thirties. He willed his Christian library and all his assets to help the university.

If you go to Harvard today, you can see the crest shown in figure 7.4 that is still in the stonework there. The crest contains Latin words that mean "Truth for Christ and the Church."[15] The

Latin word for truth, *veritas*, is spread across three Bibles. Like the three crowns on Oxford's crest, the three Bibles represent God the Father, God the Son (Jesus), and God the Holy Spirit. The Latin words *Christo et Ecclesiae* ("for Christ and the Church") unravel in a scroll. *Ecclesiae* is the exact word that Jesus used when he said, "I will build my church, and the gates of hell shall not prevail against it."[16]

In the early days, the "Rules and Precepts" for all students stated, "Let every student be plainly instructed,

Figure 7.4. Harvard crest.

and earnestly pressed to consider well the main end of his life and studies is to know God and Jesus Christ, which is eternal life (John 17:3) and therefore to lay Christ in the bottom as the only foundation of all sound knowledge and learning."[17]

> 2. Let every Student be plainly instructed, and earnestly pressed to consider well, the maine end of his life and studies is, *to know God and Iesus Christ which is eternall life*, Joh. 17. 3. and therefore to lay *Christ* in the bottome, as the only foundation of all found knowledge and Learning.
> And feeing the Lord only giveth wifedome, Let every one feriously fet himfelfe by prayer in fecret to feeke it of him *Prov* 2, 3.
> 3. Every one shall fo exercife himfelfe in reading the Scriptures twice a day, that he shall be ready to give fuch an account of his proficiency therein, both in *Theoretticall* obfervations of the Language, and *Logick*, and in *Practicall* and spirituall truths, as his Tutor shall require, according to his ability ; feeing *the entrance of the word giveth light, it giveth underftanding to the fimple*, Pfalm. 119. 130.

Figure 7.5. Sample text of Harvard University's "Rules and Precepts."

Figure 7.5 shows an image of that original text from 1643, which you can find online at the URL in this endnote.[18] You can also physically examine that original text in multiple libraries across the country.

This belief is why Harvard Yard has a Christian church at its center.[19] It is just one of many chapels that were built for Christian Scripture reading and prayer throughout the university's history.[20]

Harvard's Christian roots are not an anomaly among the world's

Figure 7.6. Holden Chapel, Harvard University.

Figure 7.7. Memorial Church, Harvard University.

leading universities. Nearly every leading university in the world was founded by Christians, as will be shown below.

Yale University

Like Harvard, Yale was also founded by a group of pastors who said, in today's language, "We are going to start a Bible-training institution so that our children will have pastors and our society will have Christian understanding." Here is how the founders of Yale worded it in their day: "A sincere regard to and zeal for upholding and propagating the Christian Protestant religion, wherein youth should be instructed." And their goal: "through the blessing of almighty God, for public employment, both in the church and civil state."[21] (Study Yale's founding charter at JesusSkeptic.com.)

Princeton University

Like Harvard and Yale, Princeton University was also founded as a Bible school by devout Christians. "Three of them were graduates of Yale: Jonathan Dickinson, pastor at Elizabethtown; Aaron Burr, pastor at Newark; John Pierson, pastor at Woodbridge. The fourth, Ebenezer Pemberton, pastor of the Presbyterian Church in New York, was a graduate of Harvard."[22]

Princeton's original charter and earliest documents cite "the grace of God," "being Protestants," and the school being a "Seminary of Piety and good literature . . . a foundation for the future prosperity of Church & State." Its founding document quotes Christian Scripture in referring to this good institution's reward as "a Crown that fadeth not away" (a quotation from the New Testament referring to eternal reward in heaven).[23] Also mentioned is the aim to "promote the Kingdom of the great Redeemer" (Jesus Christ) by making the institution "a seminary of true religion" (a reference at the time to Christianity).[24]

Offspring Universities

The Primary Evidence reveals that Harvard, Yale, and Princeton had explicitly Christian foundations. And they are not alone.

Following is a list of the first nine universities founded in North America. Most are still regarded as the best universities in the nation and even in the world. All nine were founded by specific Christian groups. Each group listed to the right is a specific brand or denomination of Christianity.

The First Nine Universities in North America

University	Founding Group
Harvard University	Puritan Congregationalists
College of William & Mary	Church of England
Yale University	Puritan Congregationalists
Princeton University	Presbyterians
Columbia University	Church of England
University of Pennsylvania	Church of England
Brown University	Baptists
Rutgers University	Dutch Reformed
Dartmouth University	Puritan Congregationalists

In fact, you can continue down this list, and here is what you will find. Back when people with axes were literally clearing trees to build the first university buildings, 167 of the first 182 colleges and universities in North America were started by Christians with the express purpose to teach people to read the Christian Scriptures.[25] And from those colleges and universities came every other major university and college in the United States today.

Harvard, Yale, Princeton, and the other early American universities became the mothers and fathers of places such as Stanford, MIT, the University of Chicago, and state schools such as the University of Michigan and Penn State, which were founded by graduates from the first seed universities.

Pick any of the highest-ranked universities in the world today, and if you dig through its history, you will find that its founder was a pastor, reverend, minister, or priest; that the university was founded by devout Christians; or that the university's founders, first presidents, or early faculty were graduates of one of the Christian-founded colleges listed above.[26] Very often the first presidents of today's state universities studied the Bible in seminary at Yale or Harvard. In other words, they had trained to be pastors or ministers.

This is true of Berkeley in California, which started out as a Christian college founded by Congregationalist pastor Henry Durant, who was educated at Yale and who later served as the first president for the entire California university system. Search any university you admire in the United States, and you will likely find that its founders were in some way connected to these early Christian universities.

The Western world from which universities emerged was so influenced by Christianity that for hundreds of years this transcontinental culture was referred to as "Christendom."

The Impact of Christian Universities

If we were to remove universities from American history, we would not have American law. We would not have innovations such as the light bulb, the computer, the automobile, the airplane. We would not have Western democracy, modern medicine, modern hospitals, or modern agriculture.

And without these contributions, we would be back in a world where many children die by age ten, where most people do not know how to read, and where life expectancy is only thirty to forty years.

Here is the bottom line. If you remove Christians from this era of human history, then you no longer have Harvard, Yale, Princeton, and their educational offspring, all of which have literally shaped modern university education as we know it and whose graduates have collectively benefited human life in ways we cannot fully comprehend or measure.

These institutions shaped presidents, scientists, writers, thinkers, lawmakers, abolitionists (who fought against slavery), and suffragists (who fought for women's right to vote).

Some may argue that the invention of the university was inevitable. They may suggest, "Well, if the Christians didn't start universities, somebody else would have." However, history proves that argument wrong, and here is how. Human history dates back thousands and thousands of years. In all that time, nothing like the modern university was ever created by any other group.

If we want to be strongly skeptical, we could say, "In enough time, someone else would have done it." But that is not unlike saying, "In enough time, pigs will fly." I would rather learn about flight from the Wright brothers. (Incidentally, their father, who taught them their love for science and book learning, was Bishop Milton Wright, a seminary president and Christian pastor.)

When we can see Primary Evidence with our own eyes, then we do not have to trust an expert who claims either that "Christians are evil" or that "Christians are good." On the matter of education, the record is clear: Christianity has been good for the world as it relates to education.

Primary Evidence demonstrating the role of Christianity in the founding of the seed universities is literally etched into the stone around many of these university campuses. Today you can visit Harvard University and find a stone and brick entrance that reads, "Open ye the gates that the righteous nation which keepeth the truth may enter in." These words are from the Christian Scriptures, specifically the Old Testament book of Isaiah,[27] one of the prophetic books that most predicted what Jesus would accomplish.

The Evidence Is Compelling

Let's change this scenario slightly to put it into perspective. Let's consider if just one of these world-leading universities had been started by followers of Muhammad or Karl Marx or some other thought-leader. That would be notable for that group. In the same way, it would be notable if followers of Jesus had started just *one* of the leading universities in the world. Instead, we have seen that every one of the "who's who" among the original world-class universities was founded by Christians.

As a researcher, that is a significant finding I cannot ignore. It moves me toward a fact-based conclusion about whether Christianity is good for the world at large.

If you still doubt the influence of Jesus's followers and ideas in launching these world-changing colleges and universities, then consider this objective ranking of the top ten universities in the world by the Center for World University Rankings.[28] For each one, I sought to determine if its founders were:

- non-Christian
- overtly Christian (the school was founded for the purpose of Bible training)
- Christian (key founders were graduates of an overtly Christian institution)

The results are striking.

The Top Ten Universities in the World

Rank	University	Founders
1	Harvard University	overtly Christian/Christian[29]
2	Stanford University	Christian[30]
3	MIT	Christian[31]
4	Cambridge University	overtly Christian/Christian[32]
5	Oxford University	overtly Christian/Christian[33]
6	Columbia University	overtly Christian/Christian[34]
7	University of California, Berkeley	overtly Christian/Christian[35]
8	University of Chicago	overtly Christian/Christian[36]
9	Princeton University	overtly Christian/Christian[37]
10	Yale University	overtly Christian/Christian[38]

Is there a single top ten university in the world today that was not founded by Christians? No, there is not. And eight out of the top ten were started to train students in the Christian Bible.

Are the founders or founding motivations of these schools complicated or contested? No, they are not. The Primary Evidence is irrefutable, and the documents can be studied by anyone. Written purpose statements such as the following can be found for each of these universities.

Purpose: "dreading to leave an illiterate ministry to the churches when our present ministers shall lie in the dust"[39] (Harvard, ranked number one in the world).

Purpose: "upholding and propagating the Christian Protestant religion"[40] (Yale, ranked number ten in the world).

Purpose: "the promotion of Christian education, under Baptist auspices, in North America"[41] (University of Chicago, ranked number eight in the world).

Visit Stanford University today (ranked number two in the world), and you will see that the entire campus is built around a Christian cathedral. This was the requirement of founder Jane Stanford, who, like so many in the 1800s, viewed higher education as intertwined with Christianity.

The record of Christians establishing the world's modern education system is undeniable. The amount of evidence on this matter is far more overwhelming than the conclusive evidence I found for any of my news investigations. When it comes to the establishment of the modern university, the evidence that Christianity has improved humanity is astounding.

What was surprising to me as a researcher was that most young Americans have no awareness of this today. I found myself wondering, *Why has this basic piece of history and human improvement been concealed from my generation?*

These ten universities have been—and remain—the most influential places of learning in the world. As seed institutions, their graduates and policies have impacted literally thousands of other universities, and they continue to do so.

Whether we love Christianity or loathe it, this is a fact of Christianity's influence on human progress. If we are honest students of reality, then we must acknowledge such Primary Evidence.

By tracing artifacts and records through history, it becomes clear that Christian universities provided the intellectual foundations of science, medicine, education, Western democracy, the principles of human equality and justice as we know them, and much more. That record will be demonstrated in the Primary Evidence compiled in the following chapters.

These Christian universities and their offspring trained the women and men who instigated world-changing social advances, which have bettered humanity for hundreds of years.[42]

Christians Improving Society Today

The Story Continues:
Education

Jonathan and Susan Kopf
Missionaries to the Hewa Tribe of Papua New Guinea

Primary Evidence reveals that today's prestigious universities grew from Bible-training seminaries. If we trace the roots back far enough, these universities have roots as early as the AD 400s, when monastic schools were established to teach the reading of Scripture.

Every year followers of Jesus travel into remote parts of the world—where language is not yet written and where literacy does not yet exist—to tell people about Jesus and his way of life. These missionaries often establish rudimentary schools, hospitals, and orphanages. Indeed, many leading hospitals and schools in developing nations began this way.

During our lifetime, the seeds for a future university, literate society, and healthcare have been planted by Jesus followers who have taken basic nursing training and an alphabet, reading program, and Bible training to a tribe of people who had never before had a written language.

In the early 1990s, Jonathan and Susan Kopf were living the American dream. They had a comfortable home, a profitable business that was providing well, and a comfortable lifestyle in the mountains of Arizona. Back then, Jonathan says, "we were into the groove of the American dream, thinking about how much money we could make and retire early."

That is when they say God began tugging on their hearts. As a devout follower of Jesus, Jonathan says that God would not let him be satisfied with the American dream. "I realized that I was living full-time for myself really, to make a living, to make a retirement, to be secure, to be comfortable . . . all those kind of things." Jonathan says he was convicted by the words of Jesus in Matthew 6:33: "Seek first [God's] kingdom and his righteousness, and all these things will be given to you as well."

"I realized I wasn't matching up to that," Jonathan says. "I was seeking first my kingdom, my financial status, my comfort, whatever. It was all about us. And over time, we realized, 'We've got to make a break.'"

They heard of remote tribes in the undeveloped back reaches of the jungle on the remote island of Papua New Guinea north of Australia—an area without electricity or any modern way of life and where cannibalism still occurs.

Motivated by their faith in Jesus and his teachings, the Kopfs sold their business and abandoned the American dream in order to follow Jesus into the jungle. They genuinely believed that Jesus loved these people who had never even heard the word

"Jesus." They determined to do everything in their power to show and then tell the love of God.

The Kopfs eventually joined Ethnos 360 to train as missionaries to Papua New Guinea and in 1999 moved there. While living there, they learned about the Hewa Tribe in the rugged mountains of central Papua New Guinea. At that time, the Hewa had very little contact with the outside world. For roughly seven years, the tribe had been asking for missionaries to come and live among them. This is common in developing parts of the world, as Christian missionaries so frequently bring healthcare, education, and modern tools.

In 2000, the Kopfs and another family relocated to a village to live with the Hewa people. They began learning the Hewa language so that they could teach the indigenous people how to read. Doing so meant creating an alphabet and writing the tribe's language for the first time in history.

Over the past eighteen years, the Kopfs have been translating the Bible into the Hewa language, developing lessons to teach the Bible, and planting churches. They also started a literacy program to help the Hewa people learn to read and write.[43]

Every year hundreds of missionaries around the world invest their lives in helping illiterate people groups learn to read. The Kopfs have now given almost thirty years of their lives to this endeavor.

Hospitals and Modern Medicine

The blind receive sight, the lame walk, those who have leprosy are cleansed, the deaf hear, the dead are raised, and the good news is proclaimed to the poor.

Jesus, as quoted in the historically verified Gospel of Matthew[1]

I have come that they may have life, and have it to the full.

Jesus, as quoted in the historically verified Gospel of John[2]

Survey the leading hospitals in any large American city, and you will find Christian words in the names of these institutions that provide lifesaving care to millions of Americans. Their names often include Christian denominations such as Presbyterian, Baptist, Methodist, or Franciscan. They also sometimes bear the names of Christian heroes such as St. Joseph, St. Vincent, or St. Mary, among many others.

Why are so many hospitals named like this? And why are there no world-leading hospitals named after Karl Marx, Confucius, or Muhammad?

The reason so many leading hospitals bear Christian-themed names is because Christians planted the seeds of modern medicine. This would be a bold claim if not for the Primary Evidence. We can trace modern medicine all the way back to its founders to see that this is not a matter of opinion but irrefutable fact.

As I explored the origins of modern medicine, I was surprised to find devout Christians at nearly every turn. Not only were devout Christians central to hospitals that bear Christian names, but many other well-known hospitals, such as Johns Hopkins and the Mayo Clinic, were also started by devout Christians and by doctors who were trained at Christian universities.

When we considered the world before the impact of Jesus's followers, we learned that for most of history, the average human life expectancy was thirty to forty years. Today in the developed world, we can expect to live to about age eighty. We will live twice as long as most people in history. This jump in life expectancy has occurred just within the last two hundred years.

This increase in life span was due in large part to the knowledge produced by specific universities, which produced specific medical breakthroughs that we can measure and document. These medical breakthroughs have now spread to the rest of the world, thankfully. But we can see with clarity where they began.

We can get to the root of modern medicine by answering one simple question: *What people and institutions led the way in the medical breakthroughs that have produced this doubling of human life expectancy?*

The Primary Evidence we will examine reveals that the seeds that produced the modern hospital and modern medicine were planted by devout Christians who were motivated by their sincere Christian beliefs.

Early Seeds

As early as the second century, historians began documenting how followers of Jesus frequently cared for the orphans, the widows, and the poor. This was unusual behavior in that period of history. Many people in ancient cultures were so consumed with the difficulties of daily life that they did not go out of their way to care for the many lepers, diseased, injured, weak, or dying in society.

For example, second-century historians described how pagans would throw their unwanted or deformed babies in the river because they did not want them. Describing many societies before Christianity, the ancient philosopher Seneca wrote how the Romans destroyed children who were born with flaws: "We destroy monstrous births, and we also drown our children if they are born weakly or unnaturally formed; to separate what is useless from what is sound is an act, not of anger, but of reason."[3] This ancient Roman approach of drowning imper-

Figure 8.1. Seneca.

fect children is representative of many ancient cultures, which terminated or ignored their sick, weak, and poor.

At a time when unwanted babies were thrown into the river to drown, the early Christians were mocked for wading out into those waters to rescue them. They would then adopt these deformed, rejected, and unwanted children.[4] By doing so, these early Christians were following Jesus, who described his work in this way: "The blind receive sight, the lame walk, those who have leprosy are cleansed, the deaf hear, the dead are raised, and the good news is proclaimed to the poor."[5]

The early Christians (or Jesus followers) were also taking literally Jesus's words that his movement existed "to give life" and that his followers were to care for "the least of these."[6] In a letter to early Christians, Jesus's brother James wrote that the religion of Jesus is "to visit orphans and widows in their affliction."[7]

In the ancient world—and for hundreds of years following—followers of Jesus sacrificed themselves in caring for the sick, the poor, the unwanted, and the outcasts of society.[8] This became so common that the term "Christian charity" remains to this day, describing orphanages, hospitals, and other care centers that help the unfortunate, the poor, and the outcasts of society.

Historical records reveal that Jesus's followers venerated, made heroes of, and looked up to the Christians who cared for the poor and the sick. As a result, more Christians were inspired to give their lives to nurse the sick and help the poor.

According to one respected historian who specializes in the history of modern medicine, this care for the poor was the seed from which modern nursing and hospitals grew.[9] Below I will show Primary Evidence that aligns with this expert's conclusion.

How Modern Hospitals Came to Be

Christian hospitals existed as early as AD 400, long before modern medicine.[10] These early Christian hospitals were crude by our scientific standards today, but they were places where anyone who was sick, poor, or hungry could go to receive God's love and care through actions.

For Christians, the care of the sick and the poor is a good work that will be eternally rewarded. It is an act of following Jesus, who said, "Whatever you did for one of the least of these brothers and sisters of mine, you did for me."[11] Jesus described eternal rewards in heaven for his followers' earthly sacrifices to help the hurting.

Followers of Jesus view the washing of feet as symbolic of serving others. On the night before Jesus was crucified, in a final dramatic act with his disciples, Jesus knelt down and washed their feet. Those sandaled feet were dirty from walking in an arid, ancient, Near Eastern climate. Jesus knelt down and acted as a servant. He washed twenty-four feet that night. In the midst of doing so, Jesus—whom his disciples believed to be God—said, "If I then, your Lord and Master, have washed your feet; ye also ought to wash one another's feet."[12]

Jesus taught that we enter the path to greatness by serving others. He taught a vision for human greatness that included serving "the least of these" and physically helping those in need. Jesus cast a revolutionary vision. Then the early church started to live out that vision.

So where do hospitals come from?

One medical historian, a professor at the University of California, San Francisco, in his book *Mending Bodies, Saving Souls: A History of Hospitals*, traces modern hospitals back to early Christian care centers. He writes this about the early Christians: "Joining this religion, the Christians, ensured membership in a dedicated network of believers, whose family values protected orphans and widows, and whose nursing services were eagerly sought."[13]

Before formal nursing services existed, early Christians went out of their way to nurse anyone who needed care. When earthquakes, fires, or epidemics produced injuries and suffering, most people fled the area. The Christians instead ran toward the difficulty, caring for the injured and the sick.

Christianity became the basis for a new social solidarity, and Christian healthcare began transforming into a real movement.

This movement continued in cathedral hospitals throughout the Middle Ages. Then during the Scientific Revolution (which grew from the Christian cathedral schools), science developed next door to these crude hospitals, and the two started to intermingle. This was the beginning of modern medicine as an actual scientific practice.

As compassionate as the earliest Christian hospitals were, it was the knowledge gained during the Scientific Revolution (also launched by Christians) and in the universities (also started by Christians) that moved Christian hospitals from mere centers of compassion to places of scientific learning and advancement.

The end result was eventually the modern hospital.

Edward Jenner—Father of Immunology

Christians were engaged in caring for the sick even while they were launching the Scientific Revolution and a new understanding of germ theory and viruses and bacteria. One such person was Edward Jenner, who is considered the father of immunology. He created the first vaccine. His invention has now saved the lives of hundreds of millions of people.

In the one hundred years before Edward Jenner discovered and created the first vaccine, 400 million people died from smallpox. There are 320 million people in the US right now, so that gives you a sense of how destructive epidemics used to be. Throughout history, epidemics would routinely wipe out entire families and cities.

To this day, scientists marvel at how Jenner created the first vaccine. This

Figure 8.2. Edward Jenner.

was before plastic and modern hypodermic needles (which we now use to inject vaccines). Jenner somehow invented the first vaccine using glass and handmade instruments. He then started to vaccinate the public against smallpox, and it became evident even within his lifetime that his discovery would save many lives.

Jenner is often cited as having saved more human lives than any other person in human history.[14] UNICEF estimates that 9 million lives are saved every year because of Jenner's invention of the vaccine,[15] resulting in billions of lives saved.[16] To put that figure into perspective, consider this: the total number of people living in the United States and Russia is less than 550 million.

This is a massive population of people whose lives have been saved by Edward Jenner, including us and our ancestors. The reason we do not die from measles, smallpox, the Black Plague, and dozens of other civilization-reducing diseases is Edward Jenner's vaccine. My point here is that Edward Jenner laid a foundation block in modern medicine. Today we don't even worry about those terrible diseases because of his work.

Jenner was a devoted Christ follower who read his Bible regularly. Toward the end of his life, Jenner said, "I am not surprised that men are not grateful to me, but I wonder that they are not grateful to God for the good which he has made me the instrument of conveying to my fellow creatures."[17]

Much like Isaac Newton and Blaise Pascal, Edward Jenner did not believe he was a smart, gifted person who happened to be a Christian. Instead, he believed, "I am a follower of Christ. I am a tool in the hands of God. And as I follow God with my gifts to help the poor and the sick, God will use me as an instrument to convey his good to my fellow creatures" (my paraphrase).

(Incidentally, the other scientist frequently cited as saving more lives than any other person, Norman Borlaug, was also a devout Christian, raised in the Lutheran denomination.)[18]

Florence Nightingale—Nursing Innovator

Another founder of modern medicine is Florence Nightingale, a nursing innovator who created the layout of modern hospitals.

Not only did Nightingale create the various wards and divisions within hospitals, but she also pioneered the use of charts and statistics within medical care. As Primary Evidence, consider one of Nightingale's hand-drawn charts in figure 8.5.

This was a first. Nightingale was tracking causes of death in a unique and groundbreaking way—the way we now think of as normal

Figure 8.3. Florence Nightingale.

in scientific medicine. She took statistical data in medicine to a new level.

Nightingale was also a sincere Christian, and in one of her books, *Suggestions for Thought*, she wrote, "Christ, indeed, came

Figure 8.4. *The Mission of Mercy: Florence Nightingale Receiving the Wounded at Scutari* by Jerry Barrett.

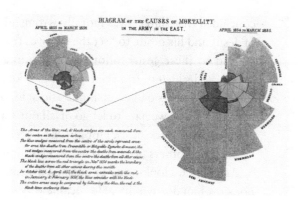

Figure 8.5. Mortality chart drawn by Florence Nightingale.

into the world to save sinners, to wash them with his blood, to deliver men from sin and its consequences," which are sickness and death. She adds that Christ came into our world "to establish the kingdom of heaven with him," that is, a kingdom where sickness is healed.[19] Nightingale describes helping the sick as Christ's mission on earth and thus her mission.

Nightingale's entire life was motivated by this twofold belief: Jesus came to "save sinners" and then to motivate those saved sinners to make the world a better place.

Johns Hopkins—Innovator of the Modern Hospital

You have probably heard of Johns Hopkins Hospital because it is a global leader in medical research. Johns Hopkins Hospital has ranked as the number one hospital in the world for twenty years straight.[20] The founder of Johns Hopkins was a devout Christian who was raised as a Quaker, a popular movement of Christianity during the early years of the United States.

The boy who would grow up to become the famous Johns Hopkins was raised by Christian parents who, long before slavery had been outlawed, determined that slavery was evil. They had gathered with their Christian brothers and sisters one Sunday and had concluded that slavery was morally wrong—based on the words of Jesus and his desire to "set the captives free."

And so these Jesus followers—including Johns Hopkins's parents—decided to free their slaves. Hopkins was a teenager at this time, and his dad came home and said, more or less, "Son, to follow Jesus, we have to let go of all our slaves. We need to let them be free." Previously, Hopkins had been in school, but now he and his brothers needed to work their family's fields.

As a result, Hopkins never finished his education, but that did not slow him down in life. He became very successful in business and was a natural entrepreneur. By the end of his life, he had built a significant fortune. He was unmarried and did not have children, and as a follower of Christ, he asked, "What do I want my life and legacy to be about?"[21]

Hopkins decided that he wanted to help former slaves, he wanted to help the sick, and he wanted to educate those who could not afford to pay for school. These were the very things he had been taught to do as a young boy growing up in a Quaker Christian home. So in his will, Hopkins split his fortune. One half went to an orphanage for African American orphans. The other half was divided to create two institutions: a hospital and a university. He wrote into his will his vision for the first-ever research hospital. It would work with a university to do research in science and medicine, even as it cared for the sick.

The motto of Johns Hopkins University is, "The truth will set you free." This is a quotation from Jesus as recorded in the Christian Bible.[22] Johns Hopkins Hospital—one of the most important and influential research hospitals in world history—was founded on a Christian Bible verse and funded by a devout Christian who hoped to help the poor, the sick, and the hurting.

Johns Hopkins Hospital has been so foundational in the establishment of the modern hospital that it is almost impossible to have a serious discussion about modern health advances without referring to it. So many of the hospital structures we think of as normal today were innovations of Johns Hopkins—things such as doctoral residents and the making of rounds.

On a broader level, the idea of a modern research hospital, where academic research takes place simultaneously with the care of patients, grew out of Johns Hopkins. This hospital is undeniably one of the seeds from which modern hospitals and healthcare have grown, and the Primary Evidence reveals that this seed was planted by a Christian.

The Mayo Clinic's Christian Foundation

The majority of the most respected hospitals in the world were started by Christian founders and by doctors who were educated at Christian-founded universities. The world-famous Mayo Clinic is an example.

One of the Mayo Clinic's founders was a Catholic nun named Mother Mary Alfred Moes, who had given her life in Christian charity to help the poor and the sick. Without the Christian influence of Mother Mary and the Sisters of Saint Francis (Catholic women who devoted their lives to follow Jesus in serving the poor), the Mayo Clinic as we know it today would not exist.[23] Mary Moes was born into a wealthy family in Europe. However, after being transformed by Jesus's teachings, Moes left a comfortable life and inheritance to sail across the Atlantic so that she could serve the poor and the Native Americans on the American frontier.

Motivated by her Christian care for the sick and the poor, Mother Mary convinced a local doctor—William Worall Mayo—that if he opened a hospital to care for the poor, she and her Christian sisters would act as nurses to care for the injured and sick there. Maybe, she suggested, Dr. Mayo could attract other physicians to work alongside them. She would provide the nurses if he could attract other doctors. As a result, Dr. Mayo moved

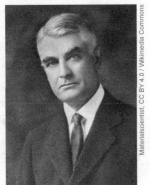

Figure 8.6. St. Mary's Hospital at the Mayo Clinic.

Figure 8.7. William James Mayo.

from being a sole practitioner to establishing a regional hub of medical care. So influential was Mary's role in the founding of the Mayo Clinic that a building there is named after her (see fig. 8.6).

The Mayo family continued to shape American medicine for generations. I could write an entire chapter on the impact of Christianity on the Mayo family. For example, William James Mayo trained at the University of Michigan, which was founded by a pastor and a Catholic priest. As with most of the early state universities, the first president of the University of Michigan was a pastor and a seminary graduate, John Monteith, who was also a devout abolitionist in the fight to end slavery. Monteith worked alongside a Catholic priest, Gabriel Richard, who also had a vision for a Christian learning institution in that area.

Another early framer of the Mayo Clinic, Charles Horace Mayo, was also trained in medicine at a Christian university, known today as Northwestern University. The nine founders of Northwestern University were all Methodist Christians; they actually knelt in prayer as they dedicated Northwestern University to Christ. They gave the school two mottos, both taken from the Bible: "Whatsoever things are true"[24] and "The word full of grace and truth."[25]

Figure 8.8. Father Gabriel Richard.

Figure 8.9. Dr. Charles Horace Mayo.

Figure 8.10. Northwestern University was founded by a group of Christian ministers. In the university's crest, note the Bible in the middle. The writing is New Testament Greek and is a quotation from the Bible: "The word full of grace and truth," a reference to Jesus from John 1:14. Like Yale, Princeton, Harvard, and nearly every other leading university in the Western world, Northwestern was first established to teach the Bible.

Like many of the world's most influential, innovative, and lifesaving hospitals, the Mayo Clinic would not exist today if not for Christian universities, Christian-influenced charity, and Christian founders such as the devout nun Mother Mary Moes.

The Christian Roots of the Top Hospitals in the United States Today

We began this chapter with an observation. In any major American city, the best hospitals tend to have Christian terms or figures in their names, such as St. Vincent, Baptist, Presbyterian, Methodist, St. Joseph, Franciscan, and so forth.

But what about the leading hospitals that don't have overtly Christian names?

As we saw with Johns Hopkins and the Mayo Clinic, oftentimes these leading hospitals were also started by Christians. In addition, the majority of the significant hospitals in the United States were first staffed by doctors who graduated from Christian-founded universities, from Harvard and Yale to state schools such as the University of Michigan, the University of California, Indiana University, and dozens of others that were also started by pastors and graduates of the seed Christian universities.

Below is a list of the top ten hospitals in the United States, as ranked by *U.S. News & World Report*.[26] I researched these top ten hospitals to discover which hospitals were founded by Christians and which hospitals' first doctors were trained at Christian-founded universities.

The Top Ten Hospitals in the United States

Rank	Hospital	Founders	First Doctors
1	Mayo Clinic (Rochester, MN)	Christian[27]	Christian educated
2	Cleveland Clinic (Cleveland, OH)	Christian[28]	Christian educated
3	Johns Hopkins Hospital (Baltimore)	Christian[29]	Christian educated
4	Massachusetts General Hospital (Boston)	Christian[30]	Christian educated
5	University of Michigan Hospitals (Ann Arbor)	Christian[31]	Christian educated
6	UCSF Medical Center (San Francisco)	Christian[32]	Christian educated
7	UCLA Medical Center (Los Angeles)	Christian[33]	Christian educated
8	Cedars-Sinai Medical Center (Los Angeles)	Jewish[34]	Christian educated
9	Stanford Health Care-Stanford Hospital (Stanford, CA)	Christian[35]	Christian educated
10	NewYork-Presbyterian Hospital (New York)	Christian[36]	Christian educated

Many of these top ten hospitals in the United States today are also revered as the top in the world. Ten out of ten began with medical doctors who were trained by Christian universities, and nine out of ten had Christian founders who declared their Christian faith as their motive for establishing the hospital (such as Johns Hopkins, the Mayo Clinic, Massachusetts General, and others).

What about the next best hospitals?

Let's also consider the hospitals ranked eleven through twenty in the United States. Six echo the same theme.

- Duke University Hospital, founded by Christian Methodists and Quakers
- Vanderbilt University Hospital, founded by Christian Methodist-Episcopalians
- UPMC Presbyterian, founded by Christian Presbyterians
- University of Pennsylvania-Penn Presbyterian, founded by Christian Presbyterians
- Brigham and Women's Hospital, founded by three Christian hospitals that had grown out of Harvard
- Northwestern Memorial, founded by Christian Methodist, Lutheran, and Episcopal denominations

As a researcher, I found this theme of Christian beginnings so common among the top twenty hospitals that I would venture the following guess: if someone were to examine the top one hundred or even top five hundred hospitals in the world, they would find that a majority had Christian founders.

More Seeds

We have seen the overwhelming influence of Christianity in founding the most influential hospitals. Many of the best-ranked hospitals were founded by Christian pastors, ministers, nuns, doctors, or priests as houses of charity. The majority were enabled by Christian donations and were staffed by doctors who had trained at Christian universities.

These are seed hospitals in the sense that they have created countless medical breakthroughs and have immeasurably improved medicine at the hospitals that have followed them across the country and around the world. They have spread lifesaving medical advances across the globe. In this sense, each of these leading hospitals has planted its own seeds of lifesaving innovation, which have led to further medical advances and hundreds, perhaps thousands, of other hospitals.

While we do not have the space in this book for an examination of European hospitals, the reality is that identical research can be done on the leading European hospitals to demonstrate the same inextricable role that Christianity played in planting the seeds of the modern hospital around the globe.

It is a fact of medical history that today's medical advances originated from these institutions. It is also a fact that the knowledge and discoveries from these Christian-founded institutions have now been freely shared and have spread to other parts of the world. As a result, in the last century, there has been a global adoption of these medical advances, thus planting the seeds for continued medical innovation around the world.

Consider this final finding in my research on the leading hospitals in the United States today.

Three Primary Seeds in American Medicine

Of the three oldest hospitals in the United States (each of which remains in the top twenty today), all three were started by overtly Christian organizations for Christian purposes of charity.

These hospitals began as Christian charities because, back in the 1800s, there were no hospitals as we know them today. The best (and most expensive) doctors only made house calls, which meant that only rich people could afford to see a doctor. The poor had to go without doctors. And so Christians—motivated by Christ's teaching to "care for the least of these"—began building hospitals where the poor could receive the medical care they could not afford. This was the birth of today's hospital.

For example, Harvard University's Massachusetts General Hospital was instigated by John Bartlett, a Christian pastor who served as chaplain for a charity to the poor in Boston known as the Almshouse.[37] Like Mother Moes at the Mayo Clinic, it was Reverend Bartlett who cast the vision to a group of doctors to begin practicing in one place so that they could care for many impoverished people in one place.

Christian pastors cast the vision for these hospitals. Christian donors supported these hospitals, providing the bricks and beds. And Christian universities provided the medical faculty and first doctors for these hospitals.

The three oldest hospitals in the United States were each started by Christians, and each remains a leader in the innovation of modern healthcare practices.

- Pennsylvania Hospital—founded in 1751 by Quaker Christian Dr. Thomas Bond and Benjamin Franklin, also a Christian;[38] ranked number fourteen in the nation today.
- New York-Presbyterian Hospital—founded in 1771 by Episcopal Christian Samuel Bard;[39] ranked number ten in the nation today. (Note: Founder Samuel Bard established an Episcopal church even while he led some of the earliest medical schools in the history of the United States.)
- Massachusetts General Hospital—founded in 1811 by Rev. John Bartlett, who was motivated by Christian charity for the poor; ranked number four in the nation today.

The conclusion for any honest investigator is clear. If you have a deadly medical condition, you want to be in a hospital that was founded by Christians or Christian-trained doctors.

The Primary Evidence reveals an overwhelming Christian presence in the founding of the modern hospital and modern medicine as we know them today.

Christians Improving Society Today

The Story Continues:
Medicine and Healthcare

Dr. Tom Catena
Catholic Missionary at Mother of Mercy Hospital, Sudan

Followers of Jesus founded the best hospitals in the United States, and they have been taking the developments of modern medicine to the "ends of the earth." On every populated continent, you can now find leading hospitals that were established by Christian founders or missionaries and are staffed by Christian-educated doctors. Dr. Tom Catena is just one example.

A Muslim chief referred to Dr. Tom Catena as "Jesus Christ" because, like Jesus, he heals the sick, makes the blind see, and helps the lame walk.[40] Although he would not claim to be Jesus, Dr. Tom, as his patients call him, credits Jesus as his role model and the motivation behind his challenging and dangerous work.[41]

Dr. Tom is the only doctor serving more than a half million people in the war-torn Nuba Mountains in the southern part of Sudan, Africa. For decades, civil war has ravaged this isolated and dangerous country. Residents faced daily bombings until recent years, when economic sanctions were lifted against Sudan. One bomb landed within miles of Dr. Tom's home and the hospital where he works. Almost no humanitarian relief has been provided to the Nubans since the fighting started. There is not enough food and virtually no knowledge of modern medicine.[42]

Dr. Tom's 435-bed Mother of Mercy Hospital is the only healthcare facility in the region. The hospital typically has no electricity or running water. Dr. Tom and his team treat up to 400 patients a day and perform more than 2,000 surgeries a year (many of which he learned to perform on the job). Many patients walk for seven days to receive treatment at Mother of

Mercy Hospital. Dr. Tom also treats a community of lepers.[43] He is on call 24/7 and earns around $350 per month.[44]

Dr. Tom has lived in Sudan since 2007. A native of upstate New York, Dr. Tom earned a degree in mechanical engineering from Brown University but felt called to missions as a follower of Jesus. Realizing that there were limited opportunities with his background, Dr. Tom went to medical school so that he could pursue missions. He volunteered at a hospital in Kenya for six years before moving to Sudan and establishing Mother of Mercy Hospital.

Dr. Tom says that Christ's mission is also his mission—to serve the least of these, the poorest of the poor. He says that faith in Christ drives his desire and willingness to stay and serve the people of Sudan, despite the overwhelming challenges and personal dangers he faces daily.

"I've been given benefits from the day I was born," Dr. Tom is quoted as saying in the *New York Times*. "A loving family. A great education. So I see it as an obligation, as a Christian and as a human being, to help."[45]

nine

The Evil of Slavery

Here is my servant, whom I uphold,
> my chosen one in whom I delight;

I will put my Spirit on him,
> and he will bring justice to the nations.

> > ancient Hebrew prediction
> > of the Messiah, as recorded
> > by the prophet Isaiah[1]

Thou shalt love thy neighbor as thyself.

> Jesus, as quoted in the historically
> verified Gospel of Mark[2]

Jesus said he came "to set the oppressed free."

> Jesus, as quoted in the historically
> verified Gospel of Luke[3]

The Reverend Martin Luther King Jr. is, without a doubt, among the most influential and successful advocates of racial equality and human rights. A survey of his sermons, speeches, and writings makes clear that King was motivated and shaped by the teachings of Jesus Christ and the Christian Bible.

Figure 9.1. Martin Luther King Jr. at a rally.

Here are a few historically verified quotations demonstrating how the teachings of Jesus shaped Martin Luther King Jr. (MLK) in his fight for racial equality and human rights. In many cases, video and audio recordings of these statements exist.

> Suppose the teaching of Jesus should be accepted by competing nations of the world, particularly Russia and America. They would no longer compete to see which could make the bigger atom bombs, or which could best perpetuate its imperialism, but which could best serve humanity. This would be a better world.[4]

> I want to say that we are not here advocating violence. We have never done that. I want it to be known throughout Montgomery and throughout this nation that we are Christian people. We believe in the Christian religion. We believe in the teachings of Jesus. The only weapon that we have in our hands this evening is the weapon of protest. That's all.[5]

> If we are wrong, Jesus of Nazareth was merely a utopian dreamer that never came down to Earth. If we are wrong, justice is a lie, love has no meaning. And we are determined here in Montgomery to work and fight until "justice runs down like water, and righteousness like a mighty stream." (The final sentence is actually

a paraphrased quotation from the Christian Bible, which MLK referred to frequently.)[6]

Slavery was officially outlawed in the United States before MLK was born, but he shared the vision of the abolitionists, based on the biblical idea that all people are created equal. MLK continued the unfinished fight for fair and equal treatment of all races. Primary Evidence reveals that Jesus's life and teachings were central to MLK's motivation and his fearlessness in the face of death.

Primary Evidence also indicates that those who started the fight for racial equality by striving to end slavery were, like MLK, sincere followers of Jesus. This includes both African American and Caucasian activists who worked together to end slavery. Some of these activists were former slaves themselves.

Former Slaves in the Fight to Abolish Slavery

In this chapter and the next, we will examine specific people who ended the practice of open and legal slavery—both in the United States and around the world. These figures are well known and well documented in the overthrow of slavery. What is less known is their beliefs about God and Jesus. As I studied the writings of these heroes, I was surprised to find the theme of Jesus. But don't take my word for it. Let's let these heroes speak for themselves.

Harriet Tubman

After escaping from slavery, Harriet Tubman, a follower of Jesus, often risked her life to venture back into the pro-slavery states in the South to help slaves escape to the North via the Underground Railroad. The Underground Railroad was a network of safe places, mostly churches and the homes of Christians, where escaped slaves could find refuge on their journey to freedom in the North.

So strong was Tubman's faith in the personal God of Christianity that she was known to verbally ask direction from God about which way to flee while being pursued. The following historically verified quotation from Tubman includes a prayer for her slave master.

> "Oh, dear Lord, change dat man's heart, and make him a Christian." . . . I went to the horse-trough to wash my face, and took up de water in my hands, I said, "Oh, Lord, wash me, make me clean." When I took up de towel to wipe my face and hands, I cried, "Oh, Lord, for Jesus' sake, wipe away all my sins!" When I took up de broom and began to sweep, I groaned, "Oh, Lord, whatsoebber sin dere be in my heart, sweep it out, Lord, clar and clean;" but I can't pray no more for pore ole master.[7]

This quotation from Tubman was eye-opening for me. I had often been taught that many of the white Southerners who owned slaves were Christians. However, in Tubman's case, it is clear that her slave master was not a Christian, while she herself was a Christian. Tubman regularly prayed that her master would convert to Christianity, believing that the act would improve both his life and hers.

At the end of her life—after risking her freedom to usher hundreds of other slaves into the North—Tubman still had

Figure 9.2. Abolitionist and women's rights advocate (suffragist) Harriet Tubman escaped slavery and then fought against slavery until it was made illegal in the United States. Tubman was a devout Christian who frequently prayed aloud to Jesus and believed his claims to be God.

a high view of God. In her final words, as documented in her formal obituary, Tubman referred to the many Christian churches that were stops of refuge along the Underground Railroad: "Give my love to all the churches. . . . 'I go to prepare a place for you, and where I am ye may also be.'"[8]

The last words she spoke were from Jesus. Shortly before his crucifixion, Jesus said to his followers, "When I go and prepare a place for you, I will come again and will take you to myself, that where I am you may be also."[9]

Harriet Tubman was a devoted follower of the teachings of Jesus, deeply believing him to be the real God, the Savior of the world, and the path to genuine freedom, not only in this life but also in eternity. The same was true of another heroic abolitionist, also a former slave, Frederick Douglass.

Frederick Douglass

Like Tubman, Frederick Douglass also escaped from slavery. After such abuse and inhumane treatment, Douglass had every right to spend the rest of his life angry and bitter about what had been done to him. Instead, Douglass was able to channel all that anger into a fearless fight for human good and freedom. Douglass declared a biblical case against slavery, arguing from God's nature and from the Christian Scriptures.

Figure 9.3. Frederick Douglass, abolitionist, was a devout Christian who—like Tubman—credited Jesus's teachings as the motivation for his humanitarian work.

It turns out that the vast majority of abolitionists—both white and black—shared Douglass's Christian faith. These are the men and women who moved the nation to oppose slavery, and the Primary

Evidence reveals they were routinely motivated by the teachings of Jesus and the Christian Bible.

Alongside his fellow abolitionists, Douglass stirred the nation to rise against slavery. In his autobiography, Douglass described his conversion to Christianity at the age of thirteen, when he was still a slave.

> In my loneliness and destitution, I longed for someone to who I could go, as to a father and protector. The preaching of a white Methodist minister, named Hanson, was the means of causing me to feel that in God, I had such a friend. I consulted a good colored man named Charles Lawson, and in tones of holy affection he told me to pray, and to "cast all my care upon God." This I sought to do; and though for weeks I was a poor, broken-hearted mourner, traveling through doubts and fears, I finally found my burden lightened and my heart relieved. I loved all mankind, slaveholders not excepted, though I abhorred slavery more than ever. I saw the world in a new light, and my great concern was to have everybody converted. . . . The good ole man had told me that the "Lord had great work for me to do," and I must prepare to do it.[10]

Tubman and Douglass represent countless former slaves who claimed to find spiritual freedom in Jesus and who then gave their lives as activists to end slavery. Some others from American history include Sojourner Truth, Booker T. Washington, and many others listed at the end of chapter 10.

The Global Scope of Slavery

When Jesus was born—over two thousand years ago—slavery was a global norm. In fact, about 40 percent of the world's population were slaves during Jesus's lifetime.[11] In my initial research, this was surprising to me.

Because of my American-centric education, I once had the impression that slavery was created and perpetrated only in the United States, from the 1600s until the Civil War. I have since learned how ignorant I was about the evils of slavery and its history in most major civilizations.

While slavery is an ugly and heinous part of America's history, the unpleasant reality is that it was a global norm among many civilizations, dating back thousands of years before the United States existed.

Many of the earliest Christians were slaves, including Onesimus, who is thought to be the slave of Philemon of the New Testament. Another famous follower of Jesus, Saint Patrick, for whom the St. Patrick's Day holiday is named, was also a slave in Ireland over a millennium ago.

Ancient artifacts and writings reveal that slavery was common among the majority of world cultures, including Greek, Roman, Egyptian, American indigenous, Irish, Viking, African, Arab, and Asian cultures. Historians who specialize in the history of slavery confirm that slavery was the horrific norm rather than the exception throughout human history.[12]

"In her cross-cultural and historical research on comparative captivity, Catherine Cameron found that bondspeople composed 10 percent to 70 percent of the population of most societies, lending credence to Seymour Drescher's assertion that 'freedom, not slavery, was the peculiar institution.'"[13]

One definitive work on world slavery states, "In the ancient Near East, as in Asia, Europe, Africa, and the preconquest Americas, various forms of slavery and servitude almost certainly emerged long before they were systematized by laws or legal codes."[14]

The following list does not include all examples of slavery throughout history, but even this limited list provides some context regarding humanity's long history with the evil of slavery.

Slavery throughout History

Empire	Estimated Number of Slaves
Ancient Rome	1.5 million[15]
Muslim World	17.95 million (from the 1100s to the mid-1900s)[16]
Ottoman Empire	2.5 million[17]
Crimean Khanate	1 to 2 million[18]
Barbary Coast	1 to 1.25 million[19]
Qing Dynasty	2 million[20]
India	8 to 9 million in 1841[21]

As for America's ugly history with slavery, we have almost exact figures. Below are calculations, made from actual ship manifests, of the number of Africans who were enslaved and shipped to the Americas during the colonial era.

African Slaves Transported by European Countries to the American Colonies[22]

Country	Number of Slaves Transported
Portugal (modern Brazil)	4.65 million
Spain (modern Cuba)	1.6 million
France (modern West Indies)	1.25 million
Holland	500,000
Britain	2.6 million
British North America (modern United States)	300,000
Denmark	50,000
Other	50,000

So common was slavery in world history that well-known ancient thinkers like Aristotle often justified it as the natural order of humanity.[23] What is unique and notable for the United States is not that slavery existed but that slavery was eventually overthrown so definitively and permanently.[24]

As the *Oxford Research Encyclopedia* puts it:

The history of American slavery began long before the first Africans arrived at Jamestown in 1619. Evidence from archaeology and oral tradition indicates that for hundreds, perhaps thousands, of years prior, Native Americans had developed their own forms of bondage. This fact should not be surprising, for most societies throughout history have practiced slavery. In her cross-cultural and historical research on comparative captivity, Catherine Cameron found that bondspeople composed 10 percent to 70 percent of the population of most societies, lending credence to Seymour Drescher's assertion that "freedom, not slavery,

Figure 9.4. Painting depicting an American plantation with African slaves.

Figure 9.5. Engraving depicting Arab slave traders and their captives.

was the peculiar institution." If slavery is ubiquitous, however, it is also highly variable. Indigenous American slavery, rooted in warfare and diplomacy, was flexible, often offering its victims escape through adoption or intermarriage, and it was divorced from racial ideology, deeming all foreigners—men, women, and children, of whatever color or nation—potential slaves. Thus, Europeans did not introduce slavery to North America. Rather, colonialism brought distinct and evolving notions of bondage into contact with one another.[25]

Primary Evidence suggests that the evil of slavery existed during most eras of human history. It was a norm in Mayan culture, Egyptian culture, Roman culture, Arab culture, Greek culture, and hundreds of others. The enslaving of half or more of the population was a horrific norm all around the world for thousands of years.[26]

Even Jesus was born into a world where slavery was accepted by the dominant governments of his time. Within such a world, Jesus predicted that his movement would break the bonds of slavery—a prediction that seemed impossible in the time of Roman rule, when nearly half of Rome's population were slaves. Jesus's prediction must have seemed laughably impossible for so many centuries that followed—as slavery continued to infect most global cultures.

Understanding the global scope of slavery does not lessen the evil perpetrated in the United States and other countries. Yet grasping how "normal" slavery was in human history does enable us to better

Figure 9.6. Pottery circa 520 BC depicting slaves gathering olives in ancient Greece.

appreciate the overthrow of slavery in the United States and England, thanks to the fearless work of abolitionists, many of whom were guided in their work by the teachings of Jesus.

The abolitionists we consider in this chapter and the next achieved a definitive overturning of slavery—such as the world had never before seen.

The Christian Idea of Abolishing Slavery

As mentioned above, billions of people in world history were born into cultures that accepted slavery—and billions of people never successfully challenged the assumption that slavery was a normal part of human existence.

Two thousand years ago, Jesus planted the seed of an idea: "breaking the bonds of the oppressed" and "setting the captives free." As the early followers of Jesus began to spread to other countries, they began implementing this concept.

In the biblical letter of Philemon, Paul the Apostle—a first-generation Christian leader—wrote to a slave owner. The recipient of the letter had a slave whom he had purchased before becoming a Christian. Paul wrote to him to say that now he must no longer treat the man as a slave but rather as a brother: "No longer as a slave, but better than a slave, as a dear brother. He is very dear to me but even dearer to you, both as a fellow man and as a brother in the Lord."[27]

These teachings of Jesus and his early followers inspired Christians to fight against slavery. Long before the Civil War, anti-slavery Christians made and distributed coins in the United

Figure 9.7. This coin, distributed by anti-slavery Christians in England and America, contains references to the New Testament Bible on both sides: "Am I not a man and a brother?" (from Philemon 16) and "Whatsoever ye would that men should do to you, do ye even so to them" (Matthew 7:12 KJV).[28]

Figure 9.8. Masthead of the popular anti-slavery publication *The Liberator*, which circulated before, during, and after the Civil War. As its name suggests, *The Liberator* existed to argue for the freedom of slaves and the ending of slavery.

States and England that bore the same Bible verse from Philemon 16 (see fig. 9.7).

The anti-slavery newspaper *The Liberator*, which still exists, is also Primary Evidence of abolitionists' Christian beliefs. Study the details of the logo in figure 9.8 and you will find common Christian themes.

First, the ribbon along the bottom reads, "Thou shalt love thy neighbor as thyself."[29] This is a quotation from Jesus taken from the Christian Bible. The central theme of the abolition movement in the United States was this: Because Jesus said to love our neighbors as we love ourselves, we cannot tolerate slavery in our land.

The coin in the middle of the logo shows Jesus standing between a black man and a white man, and the men are kneeling on equal footing with a cross in the background. This is a visual of what the abolitionists believed—that God sees all people as equal and that we must treat people equally because we will give account to a higher power.

Around the edge of the coin, it says, "I come to break the bonds of the oppressed."[30] This is another quotation from Jesus, also taken from the Bible. Interestingly, this second quotation from Jesus was a prediction—and a bold prediction at that.

137

To determine whether Christianity has helped or harmed the world in relation to slavery, I set out to study the lives and motivations of those who led the cultural revolution to overthrow slavery.

My questions as an investigator included the following:

Who were the specific people who acted to overthrow open slavery by making it illegal in the modern world?

What motivated the specific people who acted to overthrow open slavery?

In the next chapter, I will share Primary Evidence about more specific cultural revolutionaries who worked to overthrow slavery in the United States, England, and the world. (Note: The images in these chapters can be searched for and shared at JesusSkeptic .com, along with many additional resources.)

ten

The End of Open Slavery

> The Spirit of the Lord is on me, because he has anointed me to proclaim good news to the poor. He has sent me to proclaim freedom for the prisoners and recovery of sight for the blind, to set the oppressed [or slaves] free.
>
> Jesus, as quoted in the historically verified Gospel of Luke[1]

*I*f open and "legal" slavery was so common around the world for thousands of years, how did it end? Who are

139

the specific people who uprooted it in the United States? How did national laws around the world move from pro-slavery to anti-slavery?

Through Primary Evidence, we can trace the abolition of slavery all the way down to its roots to see who planted the seeds that led to the end of open slavery.

Those Who Fought to End Slavery

Let us consider the specific people who are known to have ended open slavery and examine what each group or individual believed about Jesus. As with all conclusions in this book, we will examine Primary Evidence for our conclusions about the people who ended the practice of legalized slavery.

As a preview, consider the titles of these influential anti-slavery books. Each of these books turned millions of people against slavery.

- *The Bible against Slavery*[2]
- *Letters on Slavery*[3]
- *Real Christianity*[4]
- *The Guilt of Slavery and the Crime of Slaveholding, Demonstrated from the Hebrew and Greek Scriptures*[5]
- *God against Slavery*[6]
- *My Bondage and My Freedom: A Narrative of the Life of Frederick Douglass, an American Slave* [7]
- *A Condensed Anti-Slavery Bible Argument*[8]
- *The Wrongs of American Slavery Exposed by the Light of the Bible and of Facts*[9]

I have provided source information in the endnotes so you can read these books for yourself. But don't stop there! There is so much more evidence about the specific people who overthrew thousands of years of open slavery.

The Quakers

The Quakers were a devout group of Christians who wrote the first known anti-slavery literature in the Americas, dated 1688 (see fig. 10.1). Long before the United States formally became a nation, the Quakers were declaring the evil of slavery and calling for its end.

The Quaker document is one of the earliest written documents declaring universal human rights for all people. It repeatedly

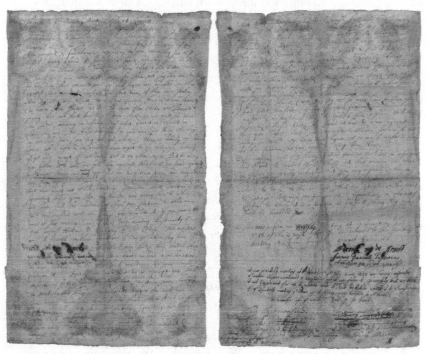

Figure 10.1. Quaker Christians called for the end of slavery in "The 1688 Germantown Quaker Petition against Slavery."[10]

quotes Jesus from the Bible: "Do unto others as you would have them do unto you" (also known as the Golden Rule).[11]

As Quakers and other Christians began campaigning to outlaw slavery in America, the message spread to England—where other Quakers were becoming aware of the slave trade to the American colonies.

The role of the Quakers is so central to the abolition of slavery that one cannot make a serious study of abolition without stumbling across the word "Quaker" time and again. Led by the Quaker-Christian idea to "do unto others as you would have them do unto you," English Christians produced and distributed metal coins with biblical quotations on both sides.

The Quakers joined forces with Christians of other denominations to lead a historic campaign to uproot and end slavery in all British territories, including the colonies in the Americas. In fact, today's word "campaign," as in a "political campaign" or "campaigning for social change," was birthed out of this great social organization by Christians in Britain. One student of history states:

> The British abolitionists—William Wilberforce, Granville Sharp, Josiah Wedgwood, Thomas Clarkson and others—who led the decades-long campaign to end slavery in the empire developed powerful arguments against slavery. They chronicled its horrors. They defied Christians to square chattel slavery with the compassion they saw as essential to their religion. And they campaigned, hard—campaigned like nobody had before, with slogans, pamphlets, children's books, buttons, petitions and medallions produced to a scale befitting the institution they sought to vanquish: Slavery.[12]

Another example of the hundreds of documents that the Quaker Christians wrote—both in England and in America—insisting on the end of the slave trade is shown in figure 10.2. The document, written in 1783 by 273 Quaker Christians, petitioned Britain to outlaw slavery in all its territories, declaring that slavery contradicts "the Gospel"[13] and that "a nation professing the Christian Faith should" work with God's "principles of humanity and justice" to see slavery as "a cruel treatment of this oppressed race."[14]

Figure 10.2. Excerpt from the Quaker petition to Britain against slavery.[15]

Thomas Clarkson

Three years after the Quaker petition to Britain, a young Christian man wrote an award-winning essay at the influential Cambridge University. His name was Thomas Clarkson, and in his essay, he cited Paul the Apostle and the case of Onesimus in the New Testament.

In the essay, Clarkson wrote:

> The benevolent apostle, in the letter which he wrote to *Philemon*, the master of *Onesimus*, addresses him to the following effect: "I send him back to you, but not in his former capacity, *not now as a servant, but above a servant, a brother beloved*. In this manner I beseech you to receive him, for though I could *enjoin* you to do it, yet I had rather it should be a matter of your *own will*, than of *necessity*.
>
> . . . *Onesimus*, when he was sent back, was no longer *a slave*, . . . he was a minister of the gospel, . . . he was joined with *Tychicus* in an ecclesiastical commission to the church of the *Colossians*, and was afterwards bishop of *Ephesus*. If language therefore has any meaning, and if history has recorded a fact which may be believed, there is no case more [clear than the opposition of slavery].[16]

Then Clarkson imagined a conversation with an African slave being shipped across the Atlantic. The imaginary European attempts to explain Christian charity and nobility to the trafficked slave:

> *Christianity* is the most perfect and lovely of moral systems. It blesses even the hand of persecution itself, and returns good for evil. But the people against whom you so justly declaim; are not *Christians*. They are *infidels*. They are *monsters*. They are out of the common course of nature. Their countrymen at home are generous and brave. They support the sick, the lame, and the blind. They fly to the succour of the distressed. They have noble and stately buildings for the sole purpose of benevolence. They are in short, of all nations, the most remarkable for humanity and justice.

The slave then responds:

> But why then . . . do they [Christians] suffer [allow] this? Why is Africa a scene of blood and desolation? Why are her children wrested from her, to administer to the luxuries and greatness of those whom they never offended? And why are these dismal cries in vain?

The European then responds that surely if the people in England understood the abuse of the slaves, they would outlaw the slave trade entirely:

> Alas! . . . can the cries and groans, with which the air now trembles, be heard across this extensive continent? Can the southern winds convey them to the ear of Britain? If they could reach the generous Englishman at home, they would

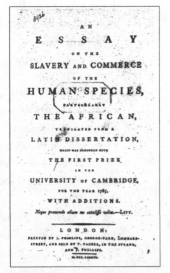

Figure 10.3. Abolitionist Thomas Clarkson gathered much anti-slavery attention in England with his essay discussing the New Testament prohibition of slavery.[17]

pierce his heart, as they have already pierced your own. He would sympathize with you in your distress. He would be enraged at the conduct of his countrymen, and resist their tyranny.

The African slave is then taken away by the slave traders, making the final point of the essay:

> But here a shriek unusually loud, accompanied with a dreadful rattling of chains, interrupted the discourse. The wretched Africans were just about to embark: they had turned their face to their country, as if to take a last adieu, and, with arms uplifted to the sky, were making the very atmosphere resound with their prayers and imprecations.[18]

Just as few people today see what goes on in the factories where most of the products we use are produced, so the majority of people in England and the United States were smoking tobacco and wearing cotton produced by slaves but had not seen the evil of slavery firsthand.

Writings such as Clarkson's began circulating in England and the United States—arguing that people who claim to be Christian must give themselves to end the evil of slavery, whether they had witnessed it with their eyes or not.

William Wilberforce

William Wilberforce was not a humanitarian. He was not a good person. He did not care about slaves. Then he became a Christian. As a Christian, he started to read the teachings of Jesus in the New Testament.

Wilberforce then wrote a book titled *Real Christianity* in which he wrote that God opened his eyes to realize the evil of slavery. He gave the rest of his life to end slavery in Britain. When Britain outlawed slavery, it controlled a sprawling empire around the world. Wilberforce's work thus spread to the British territories.

Wilberforce remains credited, more than any other individual, with ending the slave trade in the vast British Empire, including India—which had an estimated eight to nine million indigenous slaves[19] in the Hindu caste system.

Figure 10.4. William Wilberforce, a British law-maker, converted to Christianity in the 1780s, seventy-five years before the Civil War in the United States. As Wilberforce read the Christian Bible, he became convinced that slavery was an evil and an abomination. He dedicated the remainder of his life to ending the slave trade in Britain and its empire around the globe.

Wilberforce's success produced the momentum needed to complete the abolition of slavery around the world, including the United States in the 1860s and Africa in the 1890s.[20]

The Brussels Conference Act of 1890 was an international act passed by the presidents and leaders of more than a dozen Christian-majority nations at the time. It aimed to end the slave trade in African and Muslim countries by requiring nations to end the practice of slavery if they wanted to continue doing business with Europe, the United States, and Russia.[21]

Consider again the title of Wilberforce's anti-slavery argument: *Real Christianity*.[22] As the title suggests, Wilberforce argued that it was impossible to be a Christian without fighting to abolish slavery. That book and Wilberforce's advocacy ushered the world into the first era in all of known history in which open slavery was no longer a global norm.

Wilberforce once stated:

> God Almighty has set before me two Great Objects: the suppression of the Slave Trade and the Reformation of Manners.[23]

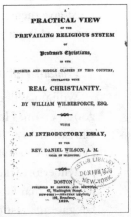

Figure 10.5. Title page of Wilberforce's book *Real Christianity*.

In his world-changing book that called all Christians to unite in ending slavery worldwide, Wilberforce asked this question:

> Is it not the great end of religion, and in particular the glory of Christianity, to extinguish the malignant passions [including slavery]; to curb the violence, to control the appetites, and to smooth the asperities of man; to make us compassionate and kind and forgiving one to another; to make us good husbands, good fathers, good friends, and to render us active and useful in the discharge of the relative, social and civil duties?[24]

The American Anti-Slavery Society

In the winter of 1833, a group of American Christians who opposed slavery gathered together at the Adelphi Building in Philadelphia. It would be a historic meeting. This group—each member concerned about the sin and evil of slavery—listened to various speakers before voting to form the American Anti-Slavery Society, a group who would lead the charge to end slavery in the United States.

The founding of the American Anti-Slavery Society was so rooted in Christianity that the charter document includes seven Christian Scripture references within a large header (see fig. 10.6). (As with all documents cited in this book, you can study a larger version online at JesusSkeptic.com.)

The one-page declaration, influentially rooted in Christian ideals, includes phrases such as the following:

- "relying solely upon those which are spiritual, and mighty through God to the pulling down of strong holds."[25]
- "Therefore we believe and affirm that . . . every American . . . who retains . . . [a slave] . . . is according to Scripture, a MAN-STEALER" (citing 1 Timothy 1:10 KJV).[26]

The signers dedicated themselves to give all they had in the fight to free the slaves, claiming:

> We shall spare no exertions nor means to bring the whole nation to a speedy repentance. Our trust for victory is solely in GOD. *We* may be personally defeated, but our principles never, TRUTH, JUSTICE, REASON, HUMANITY, must and will gloriously triumph. Already a host is coming up to the help of the Lord against the mighty.[27]

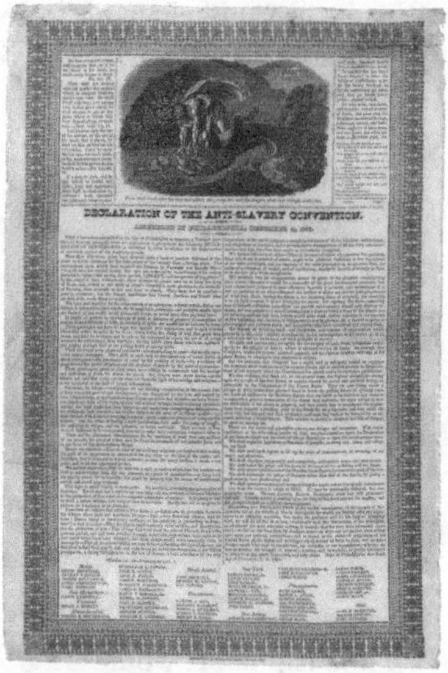
DECLARATION OF THE ANTI-SLAVERY CONVENTION.

Figure 10.6. The charter of the American Anti-Slavery Society includes seven Christian Scripture references in the header of the one-page document.[28]

Image online, courtesy Library of Congress.

The fear of God and the Christian Bible shaped the beliefs of the Americans who created the American Anti-Slavery Society. In the early days, these abolitionists faced the burning of their homes, attack from mobs, and even murder at the hands of pro-slavery mobs.

Knowing that they might face death for publicly calling slavery a sin, the sixty-two original signers of this declaration cited God's protection and stated that they were willing to give even their lives in fighting for the rights and equal treatment of African Americans. They wrote:

> We hereby affix our signatures to it; pledging ourselves, under the guidance by the help of Almighty God, we will do all that in us lies, consistently with this Declaration of our principles, to overthrow the most execrable system of slavery . . . to deliver our land from its deadliest curse—to wipe out the foulest stain which rests upon our nation . . . and to secure to the colored population of the

United States all the rights and privileges which belong to them as men, and as Americans . . . whether we live to witness the triumph . . . or perish ultimately as martyrs in this great, benevolent, and holy cause.[29]

On that historic day, almost thirty years before the Civil War, these Christian visionaries laid it all on the line.

In the Northern states, this formalized movement began spreading. Christianity was the dominant belief system, and the abolitionists' use of Christian Scripture to make their argument was akin to setting a match to dry kindling. The fire for freedom leapt to life and began to spread.

Two years after these Christians started the American Anti-Slavery Society, four hundred local chapters had sprung up. Soon that figure exploded to one thousand.

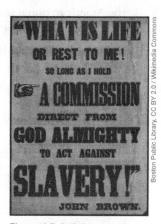

Figure 10.7. Anti-slavery poster.

Writings and gatherings such as these were the fire of cultural revolution that eventually exploded into the Civil War— the visceral opening in the fight for racial equality and the end of slavery in the United States.

The role of Christianity is inextricable not only in the lives of the founders of the American Anti-Slavery Society but also in the lives of members of the local chapters. Consider these figures regarding the society's leadership in its earliest years:

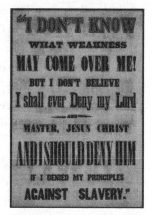

Figure 10.8. Anti-slavery poster.

- Of the local agents who represented the American Anti-Slavery

Society, 111 of the 149 (75 percent) were ordained Christian ministers.

- Of the traveling agents, the volunteers who journeyed from city to city to convince more Americans to join the anti-slavery movement, 81 of the 155 (52 percent) were ordained Christian ministers.[30]

In other words, the majority of the agents who were stirring up the American populace to uproot slavery were pastors and clergy.

Figures 10.7 and 10.8 provide additional Primary Evidence: actual posters that were circulated by the American Anti-Slavery Society.

Elijah Parish Lovejoy

As stated, the original signers of the 1833 charter of the American Anti-Slavery Society declared that they would be willing to die as martyrs for this cause. They were not being dramatic when they mentioned being killed for their public opposition of slavery.

Pro-slavery mobs routinely attacked abolitionists and burned their homes, particularly along the border states. The argument that slavery was a heinous sin and evil in God's sight did not sit well with many Southerners (particularly those hypocrite slave owners who claimed to be Christian even while they disobeyed Jesus's clear command to "set the captives free").

Just four years after the founding of the American Anti-Slavery Society, in 1837, the first abolitionist was killed by a mob of pro-slavery activists from the South. Elijah Parish Lovejoy was both a newspaper editor and a pastor. Like so many abolitionists, he used both his pulpit

Figure 10.9. Elijah Parish Lovejoy, a Christian pastor, journalist, and anti-slavery activist, was killed by a pro-slavery mob in 1837 while they were burning down his print shop.

Figure 10.10. Wood engraving of the pro-slavery mob that killed abolitionist and pastor Elijah Parish Lovejoy while destroying his printing press.

and his pen to declare slavery a sin and to call out slave owners as anti-Christian and disobedient to God.

On November 7, 1837, a pro-slavery mob attacked the building where Lovejoy was printing his anti-slavery newspaper in Alton, Illinois. This was their fourth time destroying Lovejoy's printing press. However, this time they also killed him, shooting him five times with a shotgun.

In response to death threats, Lovejoy had written, "I am governed by higher considerations than either the favor or fear of man. I am impelled to the course I have taken because I fear God."[31] On another occasion, he had declared, "I have appealed to the constitution and laws of my country; if they fail to protect me, I appeal to God, and with Him I cheerfully rest my cause. I can die at my post, but I cannot desert it."[32]

Following Lovejoy's death, his brother Owen took up the abolitionist cause for the state of Illinois and began to work alongside other Christians to end slavery in the United States.

Theodore S. Wright

Theodore S. Wright, an African American pastor and one of the original founders of the American Anti-Slavery Society, was educated at the African Free School, which had been founded in 1785 by Quaker Christians to educate former slaves. Wright volunteered his home in New York as a stop on the Underground Railroad, and he often contributed essays to William Lloyd Garrison's *The Liberator* publication.

In one contribution to *The Liberator*, Wright used the word "God" eleven times within a brief article. He wrote, "Blessed be God for the principles of the Gospel [the teachings of Jesus]. Were it not for these, and for the fact that a better day is dawning, I would not wish to live. Blessed be God for the anti-slavery movement. Blessed be God there is a war waging with slavery."[33]

Figure 10.11. In 1833, the Presbyterian minister Theodore S. Wright was among the sixty-two delegates who formed the American Anti-Slavery Society. The group included men and women, both white and black, and various Christian denominations such as Presbyterian and Quaker. Their Christian faith united them in their fight to free and dignify African Americans.[34]

William Lloyd Garrison

William Lloyd Garrison remains one of the undeniable forces in leading the anti-slavery movement. He wrote the first declaration for the American Anti-Slavery Society and published *The Liberator*, the anti-slavery newspaper that sparked the abolitionist movement. Publications like this one spread across the country long before the Civil War and planted in the consciences of the American people the idea that Christians could not tolerate slavery in any form.

Keep in mind that at this moment in history, most of the population of the rest of the world could not read. However, most Americans could read, thanks to the innovations of public education that we will examine in chapter 11, "Literacy and Public

Education." In this newly literate nation, where most people could read—and where most people had learned to read by reading the Bible—these arguments based on the Christian Bible resonated with the mainstream population.

The Liberator's publisher, Garrison, credited one book with influencing him more than any other: *Letters on Slavery* written by a Christian Presbyterian minister, John Rankin.

John Rankin

John Rankin, a Presbyterian minister, was among the sixty-two founders of the American Anti-Slavery Society. His writings and friendship shaped William Lloyd Garrison, Harriet Beecher Stowe, and dozens of other prominent abolitionists.

Rankin's personal journey with slavery started when he first became a pastor. He was assigned to a church in the pro-slavery state of Tennessee—a church where some worshipers owned slaves. From Scripture, Rankin had concluded that slavery was morally evil.

On a Sunday morning, Rankin stood in front of his church and declared (I am paraphrasing here), "If you really want to follow Jesus, you need to free your slaves."[35]

At this time in the South, that particular church replied (I am again paraphrasing), "Then we don't want to follow Jesus. We

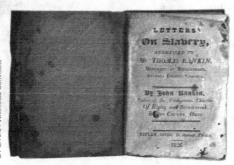

Figure 10.12. Presbyterian minister John Rankin wrote *Letters on Slavery*, a Bible-based argument against slavery that shaped many of the most influential abolitionists in the United States.

would rather get fat and use people and follow Christianity only if it's convenient for us." So that corrupt church fired Rankin. They actually ran him out of town.

Rankin escaped to the North and set up a new church on the north side of the Ohio River. The north riverbank was Ohio, a free state for slaves. The south riverbank was Kentucky, a slave

Figure 10.13. John Rankin's house.

state. Many slaves believed that if they could get across the Ohio River, they could be free.

Rankin intentionally bought a house on the north side of the Ohio River, and it became one of the first stops on the Underground Railroad, a network of safe places where anti-slavery activists would hide slaves on their journey out of the South to freedom in the North.

The house is still there today in a town called Ripley, Ohio (see fig. 10.13). In the front window of the house, Rankin would place a lamp (like the one shown in fig. 10.14). The slaves who were escaping from Kentucky would see the lamp blinking in Rankin's front window and based on the number of times it blinked would know if it was safe to cross the river.

You can visit Ripley, Ohio, today and see where Rankin hid escaping slaves in his house.

Figure 10.14. View from Rankin's window overlooking the Ohio River.

Multiple times pro-slavery mobs crossed the river and burned down Rankin's house and barn. Yet as an activist, motivated by his Christian beliefs, the pastor continued to rebuild his home, harbor escaping slaves, and help them journey to the North.

One winter day the river was mostly iced over, but the ice was starting to break. Rankin looked out his window and saw a slave woman holding a child as she ran across the river, barefoot on the breaking ice. Rankin was able to help her to safety. He then fed her and helped her escape to the North.

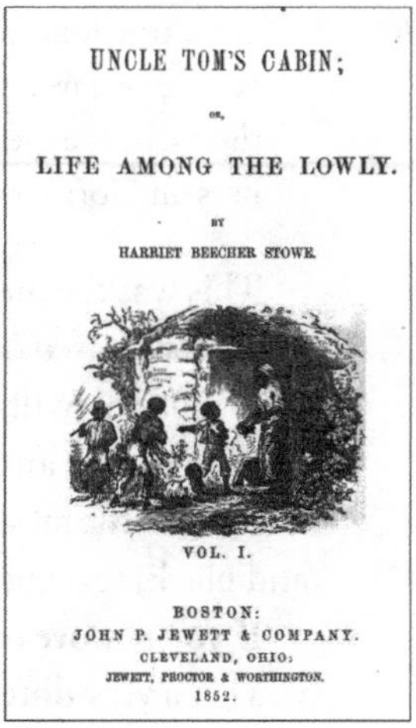

Later, Rankin told this true story to a friend of his, Harriet Beecher Stowe, and she took that true story and wrote it into

UNCLE TOM'S CABIN;

OR,

LIFE AMONG THE LOWLY.

BY

HARRIET BEECHER STOWE.

VOL. I.

BOSTON:
JOHN P. JEWETT & COMPANY.
CLEVELAND, OHIO:
JEWETT, PROCTOR & WORTHINGTON.
1852.

Figure 10.15. Book cover of *Uncle Tom's Cabin* by Harriet Beecher Stowe.

one of the most influential books of the abolitionist movement: *Uncle Tom's Cabin*.

Along with other writings by abolitionists, *Uncle Tom's Cabin* helped turn the national mood in the United States against slavery. In today's culture, these writings may seem foreign, but in their original time, they were bright lights in the dark—calling for the freedom of slaves. Like so many other anti-slavery writings, *Uncle Tom's Cabin* argues from Scripture.

What's the Point?

In my examination of the influential abolitionists who led the work to overthrow slavery, I did not find one who was *not* a Christian. Their consistent message, in my own modern paraphrase, was this:

> If you read your Bibles, you will see that slavery is declared evil by God. Anyone who claims to be a Christian while owning a slave is

not a true follower of Christ. And all those who sit by while others are enslaved also cannot claim to be loving their neighbor as themselves, as Jesus taught. Therefore, as Christians, we give our lives and fortunes to end this evil in our land.

This was the message that the Quaker Christians began spreading in 1688 based on the teachings of Jesus. It was the same message that William Wilberforce spread in England to turn that nation against slavery and to free millions of slaves in the British Empire. And it was the message of a coalition of American Christians, white and black, serving side by side to end slavery in the United States.

If you remove these sincere Christ followers from world history, you get a very different world than the one we were born into. Not just a few of the influential abolitionists were Christians; no, every single influential abolitionist I studied was a Christian.

Just as followers of Jesus today stand intellectually alongside Isaac Newton and the other founders of the Scientific Revolution, so followers of Jesus today can claim that they share the same beliefs as Harriet Tubman, William Wilberforce, and the other anti-slavery activists who overthrew slavery. This is both a privilege and a responsibility—to be the agents of Jesus's kingdom and justice for a new generation.

For Further Study

If you had never before heard that the leaders of the anti-slavery revolution were devout followers of Jesus, then I encourage you to examine more of the Primary Evidence. Learn for yourself what motivated them in their historic fight to end slavery. You will find quotations from Jesus and Christian ideas in the writings of these influential abolitionists:

Edward Beecher	Samuel Cornish
Thomas Clarkson	Frederick Douglass

John Fee	Samuel Sewall
Charles Grandison Finney	John Jay Shipperd
William Lloyd Garrison	Harriet Beecher Stowe
Joshua Giddings	Arthur Tappan
Julia Ward Howe	Charles T. Torrey
Elijah Parish Lovejoy	Sojourner Truth
Asa Mahan	Harriet Tubman
John Monteith	Theodore Dwight Weld
Franz Pastorius	William Wilberforce
John Rankin	John Woolman
Benjamin Rush	Theodore S. Wright

Christians Improving Society Today

The Story Continues:
The Fight to End Human Trafficking

Stephanie Garman Freed
Cofounder and Executive Director of Rapha House

I was surprised in my investigation to learn that slaves continued to be bought and sold in the 1900s in regions of Africa and Arabia long after the Civil War had ended in the United States. As one historian wrote:

> Many do not know that the tragedy of slavery continued in a number of countries for more than a hundred years after it was outlawed in the United States in 1865. Ethiopia had slavery until 1942, Saudi Arabia until 1962, Peru until 1964, and India until 1976. Moreover, it still exists to this day in Sudan, Africa's largest country.[36]

While slavery has now been officially outlawed in all modern

157

nations, human trafficking, a form of modern-day slavery, still happens unofficially, every day, around the world.

Some societies still encourage or allow slavery. In other places, the black market for slavery skirts the laws and operates out of sight.

The International Labour Organization reports that "at any given time . . . an estimated 40.3 million people are in modern slavery."[37]

Sadly, human trafficking continues in our world today. It is estimated to be a $150 billion per year industry worldwide. It thrives primarily in societies that have not had historical Christian influence.[38] The majority of persons sold into forced labor or sexual exploitation are women and children. Approximately 1.2 million children a year are sold into slavery.[39]

Thankfully, dozens of activist groups are fighting to end this slavery—both through law and through actual cultural engagement. In Cambodia and Thailand alone, dozens of Christian-founded groups are working today to prevent the selling of young children and to provide safe housing, education, and jobs for girls and boys who have been freed from modern slavery.

One of these ministries, Agape International, has rescued more than one thousand children, women, and men from slavery. The group has also prevented the enslaving of more than fifty-five hundred people and has restored more than eight hundred survivors of slavery.[40]

Stephanie Garman Freed is a Christian who has launched a similar ministry to end slavery in our day. What caused a self-proclaimed soccer mom from Joplin, Missouri, to join the fight against human trafficking by starting a global organization to love, rescue, and heal child victims of modern-day slavery and sexual exploitation?

In 2002, Stephanie was sitting at her dinner table listening to her father, Joe, talk about his recent trip to Cambodia for a church leadership conference. Joe described to Stephanie the young girls he saw on the streets—girls who were being sold to older men for sex. He also told her that his Cambodian colleagues relayed stories about staggering numbers of young girls who went missing from their villages each month. The pastors told him these girls were being enslaved for sex or labor in the city and that they felt powerless to do anything about it.

With tears in his eyes, Joe expressed his heartbreak over this then-hidden issue and asked Stephanie, "What are we going to do about this?"

Stephanie, who describes herself as highly analytical and skeptical, inwardly questioned whether this was truly an epidemic because she hadn't heard anything about it anywhere else. She didn't know that slavery still existed because it wasn't being reported in the news at that time.

While she was touched by her father's emotion, she recalls that the challenge made her angry initially. "I had two little girls at the time, and my whole world was wrapped up in them," she says. "I thought to myself, 'I'm probably not going to do anything because what can I do? Who am *I* to do anything?'"

Despite Stephanie's reluctance to get involved, Joe asked her to research the issue to determine whether it was happening as widely as they said and, if so, what could be done about it. Stephanie spent six months researching the pastors' claims of human trafficking each night after she put her kids to bed. She began to see that it was really happening, and her heart was tugged in sorrow for the children caught up in it.

One night as she was praying over her sleeping young daughters, she says that God spoke to her through the Holy Spirit and said that her girls were no different from the little girls being trafficked in karaoke bars, massage parlors, and other places. "I said, 'OK God, I'm completely unqualified, but if you open the doors, I'll walk through those doors,'" Stephanie says.

In early 2003, Stephanie embarked on a research trip to Cambodia and met with those same local church leaders who had told Joe about the problem. She was touched by their sincerity and passion. They took her to a local junkyard to help negotiate the release of a young girl who had been bought and sold twice, most recently to extended family members who owned the junkyard. They had forced the little girl into labor and had sexually abused her.

Stephanie says, "I will never forget the pain in my heart, meeting the eyes of that little girl and fully realizing the hopelessness she faced in her prison of slavery. During our visit, she begged me repeatedly, 'Please don't leave me here; please help me.' The Lord used that experience to change the trajectory of my life."

Stephanie says that all the statistics she had discovered became real to her in that little girl, and she felt compelled to do something. Months later, she started a US-based nonprofit organization called Rapha House to provide safe houses for girls who had been rescued from slavery and sexual exploitation. Rapha House currently operates safe houses in Haiti and southeast Asia, including Cambodia and Thailand. In 2017, these safe houses provided aftercare (food, medical care, counseling, life skills, and vocational training) for more than 135 girls rescued from slavery. In addition, through its Kids Club program, Rapha House and its partners sponsor more than 800 children in these countries to educate them and to provide social services to their families to help them identify and attack the root causes of exploitation.

"Rapha" is a Hebrew word meaning "healing." Stephanie says that her own freedom and healing in Christ drive her to do more, one child at a time. "In that moment [in the junkyard in Cambodia], it became real what Christ had done for me—we were slaves in a junkyard, and Christ walks us in to freedom, to live out his destiny and his calling."[41]

eleven

Literacy and Public Education

Go ye therefore, and teach all nations.

Jesus's final command to his followers, as quoted in the historically verified Gospel of Matthew[1]

Imagine your life if you and your neighbors could not read. Not only would you be unable to convey information, but you would also lack doctors, dentists, and engineers who know how to heal you, alleviate your pain, and design modern heating and cooling.

Why would we lack these anchors of modern society? Because all advanced trades depend on reading the written word. In this sense, education is not some boring thing to be endured; it is the difference between the Stone Age and the modern age.

A friend once told me, "Whether or not you believe in Jesus, you can thank him for fifty-two days off per year. You have Sundays off from work because of the Christians. You don't have to believe in Jesus to be thankful that he gave you Sundays off of work."

I looked it up and learned that my friend was correct. It was a defining moment for me—realizing how much Christianity has shaped the world I think of as normal. (Like I learned about the sea otters as a keystone species in the ocean ecosystem, it was a moment when I realized just how Christian-influenced the water I swim in is, whether I realized it or not.)

I began to realize that Jesus's life has impacted my world in practical and nonreligious ways I still do not fully understand. Take, for example, the fact that you are able to read these words on this page. Whether or not you believe in Jesus, you can be thankful that others did believe in him, because it was Christians who established schools for children, planting the seeds of public education and giving us the ability to read and write today.

In his book *Ancient Literacy*, Columbia professor William Harris concludes that only 10 to 15 percent of the most literate ancient populations could write a single sentence.[2] That figure is not controversial. For most of world history, only one out of ten people could read.

Earlier we imagined the sum total of 108 billion people who have ever lived. Consider now that more than 95 billion of those people never learned how to read or write. That puts you and me in the privileged minority of people throughout history who have been taught to read and write—fewer than 15 percent of the people who have ever lived.

So why were we born into a world in which nearly everyone we know is able to read and write?

The answer lies—much as it did with university education—in Christians who wanted others to learn to read so that they could study the Bible.

The Seeds of Literacy and Public Education

In chapter 7, we saw how Oxford University (with its motto "The Lord is my light") functioned as a seed university. The world's most influential universities today sprouted up from that seed and its offspring, planted by the founders of Oxford and other early Christian universities.

Another of those early Christian universities, founded in the 1200s, was Cambridge University. In the 1600s, a group of devout Christian graduates from Cambridge created the first school in the United States. Their aim was to teach all boys and girls how to read the Bible. Valuing the need for every Christian to be able to read the Bible personally, these Puritan Christians launched a world-changing law requiring towns to provide free education to all children.[3] That law is today considered a historic cornerstone of public education and social literacy (societies in which all people can read).

In Europe, nearly one hundred years earlier, a similar law had been set in place—by devout Christians named Martin Luther and John Calvin. Their aim was the same as that of the Puritans: they desired that all children in their society be able to read the Bible for themselves.[4]

These social policies were the seeds of public education. They were a turning point from a world in which most people could *not* read to a world in which most people *can* read. The literacy rate spiked shortly after these schools were implemented—but only in the Christian-saturated world. It would take another couple hundred years for Christians to send missionaries around the world, carrying literacy and public education with them.

As a result of those early laws and what they produced, you and I were educated as children. We are able to read the words on this page because early American Christians instituted the education of all children in their villages.

One of the laws that early American Christians put into place was called the "Ye Ole Deluder Satan Act" of 1647. It required that any village with more than fifty households had to start a school and begin teaching their children how to read. This was at a time in world history when no other major civilizations were requiring this.[5] (As an aside, the law was known as "Ye Ole Deluder Satan Act" because they believed that Satan kept humanity in the darkness by ignorance, and so if people were trained to read the Bible, they would make their way into the light.)

Teaching all children to read seems normal to us today, but this was a revolutionary innovation at that time. Never before had this happened in history, at least not in a lasting and meaningful way.

While this movement was taking place in the United States—driven by Christians who wanted their children to read the Bible—the same sort of movement was taking place in Germany, also driven by Christians who wanted their children to read the Bible. (This was all happening in the 1600s, a time when Protestant Christians were trying to purify the Christian faith. They believed that Christians being able to read the Bible for themselves was the key to this.)

Graduates of the early Christian schools and universities often used their education to start other schools. And so public schools began spreading from those first seeds, planted by sincere followers of Jesus. As generations built on their learning, many innovations and improvements followed. Many generations later, world-changers would emerge as products of these early seeds in public education, people such as Thomas Edison (the light bulb), the Wright brothers (the aircraft), and Henry Ford (the automobile assembly line).

The improvements led by students of these schools began to affect education as well—beginning a compounding improvement of education. Take, for example, the modern kindergarten, which was created by a graduate of a Christian school. The father of German student Friedrich Frobel was a minister in a Lutheran church. Frobel was himself trained in a Lutheran Christian school. Later, as an adult, he saw a need for children to begin their education at an even younger age, and so he started one of the world's first *Kinder* (child) *Garten*s (garden) in Germany. Frobel's concept and name stuck, and today we still use the German word *Kindergarten* to describe early childhood education before first grade. As with so many of our norms and staples in education, both the name and the institution were planted by a follower of Jesus.

Before the revolution of public education, only a minority of people in world history were ever taught to read, and girls were almost always banned from education. This Christian movement broke through those walls, and as a result, girls and boys alike and children of all social classes were educated.

Figure 11.1 shows a page from the *New England Primer*. This is one of the early books used by Christians to create the reading revolution. Notice how the first lesson begins with Adam and Eve from the Bible. Then the next line refers to the importance of reading "this Book," which refers to the Bible. In case any child was not clear about what "this Book" referred to, the authors carefully wrote BIBLE on the illustration of the book.

Figure 11.1. Page from the *New England Primer*, demonstrating the Christian influence in public education, which led to the world's first literate society and has forever changed global literacy and education.

The *New England Primer* became the on-ramp to literacy for an entire nation.

The Christians who launched this movement had a vision for a nation in which all kids would grow up reading, "Adam and Eve, their God did grieve," and, "Thy life to mend, this Book attend," in reference to the Bible.

Today it is difficult for us to imagine the world in which these Christians were giving their lives and their fortunes to create the first public schools—often one-room cabins. Let's remember that this was before electric heating or air-conditioning or lights. This was before automobiles. This was before hospitals. This was before modern chemistry, which makes our farming so productive. This was back in an era when people spent most of their days gathering, hunting, or planting food and finding firewood to keep them warm in the winter.

Like John Harvard, who died in his thirties, many of these early American Christians died from sicknesses and diseases because modern medicine and hospitals did not yet exist. Yet they planted the seeds of education that would someday produce the hospitals and the medicine that we now think of as normal.

In such a harsh and pioneering world, these early American Christians went out of their way—teaming up at great cost to themselves—to make certain that the next generations would be able to read the Bible for themselves. Their hope was that a Christian society would be created unlike any other—a society in which all people could choose or reject Christianity and those who chose it would be free to practice it as they read the Scriptures for themselves.

When the *New England Primer* was being taught to children in America, "public education" was not yet a thing. It was not considered a right. It did not exist as we know it today.

Social literacy—as instituted by followers of Jesus—changed the social fabric of the colonies that would later become the United States. As a result, the United States became the wealthiest country in the world, driven along by innovations such as Edison's light bulb and Ford's assembly line.

In time, America's model of education (and Europe's, which was also founded by Christians) changed the assumptions of the entire world. Free public education gave information, individual thought, individual liberty, and the power of knowledge to all people in a society—so that all people could act with freedom and liberty according to their own beliefs. In the course of history, this was revolutionary.

We cannot fully calculate the global impact of reading and writing in making the world a better place, but we can see some of their results. For example, in the fight to overthrow slavery in the United States and England, books and newspapers led the movement—spreading anti-slavery ideas. If the authors of those books and articles had not been taught to write, and if the people of the country had not been taught to read, then the books and newspapers that helped to end slavery would have been nothing more than paper and ink.

As public education spread across the United States, it laid the foundation for social progress and cultural change, led by generations who had been taught to read, to write, and to think by Christian-founded institutions. Then, during the 1900s, these social advances spread from the United States to other parts of the world.

We see this demonstrated in visual graphs, produced by objective historians, that show the rapid rise of literacy around the world. Figure 11.2 demonstrates that the explosion of people being taught to read in the 1600s happened in the United Kingdom, Germany, Sweden, the Netherlands, and the United States. What did those nations have in common at this time in history? If we look at the history of those nations, we see that they were all dominated by Christianity. At that time, Christianity's emphasis was on all people being able to read the Bible for themselves.

So it turns out to be true. You can thank Christians for your ability to read these words. You can also thank them for your

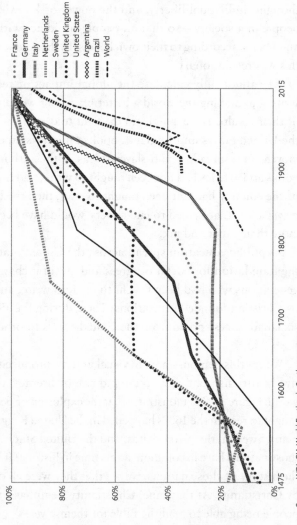

Literacy Rate

Estimates correspond to the share of the population older than fourteen years that is able to read and write. Specific definitions and measurement methodologies vary across countries and time.

France
Germany
Italy
Netherlands
Sweden
United Kingdom
United States
Argentina
Brazil
World

100%

80%

60%

40%

20%

0%

1475   1600   1700   1800   1900   2015

Source: WDI, CIA World Factbook, & other sources

Figure 11.2. Literacy rate graph.

ability to write your own thoughts and opinions, including those that disagree with Christianity. Just like having Sundays off from work traces back to Jesus, our ability to read and write traces back to Jesus's followers.

If you study the chart closely, you can see that as recently as the 1600s, only a handful of nations had populations in which more than one out of five people could read. Remove Christians from the last five hundred years, and the evidence suggests that we would be much closer to the illiterate average of world history. That is, without the Christian-founded norm of public education, the letters on this page would make no more sense to us than they do to a chipmunk.

The lower chart on figure 11.3 shows that as recently as one hundred years ago, the global average of people who could read was only 21 percent. In other words, just one hundred years ago, only one in five people around the world knew how to read. It also shows that Western Europe and Western offshoots led the world in public education in the 1800s and 1900s. "Western offshoots" refers to the United States, Canada, Australia, and other countries that embody the Western values of England, France, and others. Western Europe was once so associated with Christianity that it was referred to as "Christendom." (A simple survey of historical beliefs by country reveals that Christianity was prevalent in these nations during that time. For example, Gallup polls of the United States reveal that 91 percent of Americans identified as "Christian" as recently as 1948.)[6]

Public education as we have inherited it trickled down from the Christian-founded universities we learned about in chapter 7. As those universities began training more and more graduates, those graduates began going out into their communities, intent to teach their children, grandchildren, and neighbors how to read the Bible and think for themselves. Like the Puritan graduates of Cambridge, these early Christians began creating schools in their towns and villages.

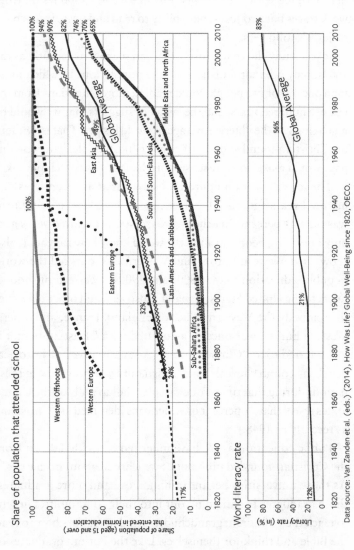

Figure 11.3. Chart of rising education around the world.

What Does All of This Mean for Us?

People who cannot read cannot be trained to do complex jobs—or train others. A society of people who cannot read will never have advanced engineers or medical doctors or computer programmers.

To state it more positively, the first societies to prioritize reading and education for their children became the societies that led the world in scientific and medical breakthroughs.

History reveals that societies heavily influenced by Christianity have led the world in science, medicine, and industry for the last two hundred years. This is a direct result of their populations being educated to read and write at a time when the populations of many other world cultures did not know how to read and write.

So many people who changed the world were able to do so because of social literacy. Students who learned to read and write in Christian-founded schools and universities would go on to do the following:

- launch the Industrial Revolution[7]
- create the first society in which girls were provided the same education as boys[8]
- create and spread Western democracy as we know and enjoy it today[9]
- invent eyeglasses and thousands of other life-changing innovations[10]
- create modern hospitals[11]
- create lifesaving vaccines, which have saved millions of lives[12]
- fight for women's rights[13]
- abolish slavery first in Christianized Europe,[14] then in Christian England, and then in the United States (only after slavery was abolished in Christianized Europe and

North America did the abolition of slavery spread as a norm to the rest of the world)[15]

- export these improvements around the world, thus improving humanity in ways we cannot fully grasp or measure[16]

Each of these claims can be measured as true or false. These achievements were not produced by any single nation or race but rather by various ethnicities and nationalities who had one thing in common: education from Christian-founded institutions.

The men and women who changed history in these ways were shaped by Christian-instituted norms such as public education. That fact alone would be a significant accomplishment for Christianity, but we can see from the evidence that Christianity was not an accidental or coincidental catalyst.

When I dug deeper into the writings of these innovators who ended slavery, created modern education, and so much more, I saw something undeniable. The people who emphasized reading and public education were motivated by their personal Christian faith.[17] These were men and women who truly believed that Jesus was God, that Jesus died on the cross for the sins of the world, and that faith in Jesus leads to an eternal life. These men and women sacrificed comforts and fortunes to build universities and schools. And what motivated them in their sacrifice was their Christian belief in a God who will judge and who has given a standard of justice.

Regardless of whether we personally agree with these people's Christian beliefs, it is a fact that their belief in God led them to establish social literacy, which in turn led to breakthroughs in hospital care, medicine, human rights, science, and the ending of slavery.

In this way, Christians have fulfilled one of Jesus's ancient predictions about them. Jesus once said of his followers, "You are the light of the world. A city set on a hill cannot be hidden."[18] This is an interesting prediction when considering that electric lights and the ability to read both originated in Christian cultures and both have spread globally. If you wish to study further the clear role of Jesus's followers in creating public education and social literacy, consider investigating the following:

- Justin Martyr established catechetical schools in the second century, which led to cathedral schools.
- Cathedral schools spread throughout Christendom in monasteries and churches.
- Martin Luther, in the 1500s, established the first equivalent of public education for all.
- John Sturm, in the 1500s, established "graded" education.
- Philip Melanchthon, in the 1500s, established tax-funded education.
- Puritan Christians established "Ye Ole Deluder Satan Act" in the American colonies in the 1600s.
- Louis Braille, in the 1830s, established education for the blind.

Each of the education innovators named above was a devout follower of Jesus according to their own Primary Evidence writings.

Christians Improving Society Today

The Story Continues:
Education

Katie Davis Majors
Founder and Chief Visionary of Amazima Ministries [19]

A passion to follow Jesus prompted eighteen-year-old senior class president and homecoming queen Katie Davis Majors to move halfway around the world to serve children and families in an impoverished village in Uganda. Ten years later, Katie has nurtured her passion into an international nonprofit that gives more than seven hundred children an education, food, and healthcare.

During her senior year in high school, Katie spent three weeks in Uganda on a short-term mission trip. The impact of that trip caused her to commit to a year of teaching kindergarten at an orphanage after she graduated from high school. That one year turned into her life's calling. Katie learned that many of the kids at the orphanage actually had families, but they had given up their parental or guardianship rights because they couldn't provide their children's basic needs. Katie also discovered that for a couple hundred dollars, a child could attend school for a year. She began raising money in the United States to send children to school and to meet their needs so that they could remain at home with their families.

Out of these initial efforts, Katie founded Amazima Ministries in 2008 to live out the love of Jesus by educating and empowering the people of Uganda. By the time Katie was twenty-three years old, she had adopted thirteen Ugandan girls.

"I never intended to start an organization and grow it into this big thing," Katie says, "but God continued to bless it."

The word *amazima*, which means "truth" in the Luganda language, reflects Katie's desire to see lives transformed, relationships restored, and communities changed through the truth of Jesus Christ.

In addition to administering a scholarship program to enroll and retain children in school, Amazima provides its own secondary boarding and day school (high school) and vocational school for older students. Through both programs, the organization feeds and provides basic healthcare to children and families. The organization also provides a beading circle for women in the community where they are taught jewelry-making skills to support their families.

Katie doesn't consider herself a world-changer. Instead, she focuses on serving a living, loving Jesus, who she says gives her the grace to continue serving others.

Katie says that God continues to use "flawed human beings" like herself to change the world one person at a time. Her chief advice to others (and herself) is, "Keep seeking to love Him and the next person He places in front of you, and He'll take care of the rest."[20]

twelve

Summary Thoughts on Christian Influence

In the previous chapters, we saw a wealth of Primary Evidence, including images, names, writings, and irrefutable facts, that revealed a mega-pattern: sincere Jesus followers—motivated by the ideas of Jesus—have led world-changing innovations that have benefited humanity and bettered education, health, freedom, and society. Jesus's followers have done this on a scale that is unrivaled by any other single movement or group in history.

The Primary Evidence showed what Jesus's ideas and his followers created:

- the Scientific Revolution and its resulting improvements for billions of people
- the modern university and college system, which has lifted civilization from ignorance to intelligence, and specific seed institutions that have changed the world for the better, including Oxford, Cambridge, Harvard, Yale, Princeton, and Johns Hopkins
- modern medicine, including vaccines and nursing, and many of the world's most significant hospitals
- the end of open slavery, which previously had been a global norm
- social literacy, which led to unrivaled progress in science, medicine, technology, and human well-being; education for women as well as for men; and free public education

It is not a leap to conclude that if these advances were removed from history, then you and I would be living in a vastly different world more comparable to that of the Dark Ages, a barbaric, brutal world that held humanity captive for so many thousands of years.

In the profiles at the end of select chapters, we also saw that Jesus's followers today continue to advance human health, rights, and education around the world.

To me, these findings—taken as a whole—are notable in measuring whether Christianity is a force for good or not. The evidence led me to a bold but undeniable conclusion: whether I like Jesus's followers or not, whether I believe in Jesus's spiritual claims or not, Jesus bears studying, for his movement has been—by multiple measures—among the most powerful movements for social good in all of human history.

This conclusion about the impact of Jesus's followers led me to study Jesus himself. I needed to answer some important questions:

Can we know if Jesus existed?

Can the movement called Christianity actually be traced back to him?

How does Jesus continue to impact so much of the world?

What is it about Jesus that draws one out of three people alive today to follow him?

I address Jesus and these questions in part 3 of this book.

Christians Improving Society Today

The Story Continues:
Women's Rights

John Keshe
Founder of Maasai Community Education and Support Program and Principal Partner with Kenya Community Education and Action

The fight to end slavery overlapped with the Christian idea that all people are made in the image of God. An examination of the Americans who fought to abolish slavery in the United States reveals that many of these same heroes also fought to establish women's rights in the United States.

While the Christian record is far from perfect on the issues of slavery and women's rights, the reality remains that many of the people who led the fight to end slavery and establish women's rights were Christians.

Many Christians continue the fight for women's rights today.

One native African was changed by the message of Christianity and is now giving his life to fight for women's rights in his indigenous culture. Without a formal education, women are deprived of basic rights. They are stymied in their earning potential, trapped in a generational cycle of poverty, constrained by poor health, and robbed of equality in their families and communities. Moreover, uneducated women are less likely to send their own children to school, perpetuating these issues into future generations.

Giving girls access to education significantly empowers women, families, communities, and nations. A woman's earnings may increase by as much as 12 percent with each year of school she completes. A child born to a mother who can read is 50 percent more likely to survive past the age of five. Educated mothers are twice as likely to send their children to school. Access to education positively affects women's health, nutrition, well-being, and ability to contribute to society.

Approximately sixty-four million girls between the ages of six and fourteen worldwide currently are not in school. Sub-Saharan Africa has the highest out-of-school rates and the highest rates of gender disparity, with 123 girls denied the right to education for every 100 boys of primary school age.[1]

For more than a decade, John Keshe has been working in his home country of Kenya to increase opportunities for girls to complete their education. John is a community leader in the Maasai Tribe, one of the most impoverished tribes in East Africa. Traditionally, Maasai girls learn from an early age that their only role is to complete household chores, care for their siblings, and later bear children. Providing a formal education to girls is not a priority in the culture. Instead, most Maasai girls are circumcised (a form of genital mutilation for females) and married between the ages of twelve and fourteen. Given these cultural traditions and the fact that high school is not free in Kenya, only one out of ten Maasai girls who go to school continue their education beyond the sixth grade.

John says that in 2004, God opened his eyes to the enormous need for education among Maasai girls. After sharing this vision with his wife, Paris, the couple invited tribal leaders, pastors, and other community members to their home to discuss providing a high school education to more Maasai girls. John says that while many supported his vision, others questioned whether families would accept this initiative, given the costs both financially and culturally due to breaking away from the non-Christian tradition of child marriage.

After this meeting, John and Paris started teaching workshops during school holidays to educate youth about the importance of staying in school and the harmful effects of female circumcision and early marriage. These workshops built trust, and the youth began viewing John as their guidance counselor for placement in high school.

John says that a pivotal moment came when one of their youth, Josphine, was forced by her father to drop out of high school after two years in order to get married. Josphine was the only girl from her village to attend high school. Because of a severe drought that killed most of their cattle, Josphine's father was desperate to receive the dowry (bride price) from the intended husband's family to support his own family. John visited Josphine's father and convinced him that Josphine should stay in school. John agreed to pay her school fees himself, and the next day John and Paris returned Josphine to school.

Josphine's situation caused John to see even more clearly the need to educate community members about the value of education for their children. He founded the Maasai Community Education and Support Program (MCESP)[2] to educate parents and provide financial scholarships to Maasai girls so that they can complete their education. These scholarships cover school fees and supplies, the cost of transportation to and from school (because most people live in remote areas), medical expenses, and life skills conferences for the sponsored students. MCESP partners with a US-based nonprofit organization, Kenya Community Education and Action (KCEA), to raise funds for scholarships and to promote awareness about education for Maasai girls. Currently, KCEA supports seventeen girls in high school and ten girls in primary school.

John says that his own background fueled his passion to educate Maasai girls. He was the only boy in his village to complete high school, and no girls in his village went to high school until much more recently. "I have a strong belief that educational opportunities for women make a significant difference in the lives of women and in the well-being of the whole society," John says. "I am so passionate about supporting girls' education because traditionally in our Maasai community, education for girls is not given the proper value."

John's long-term vision is to build a high school in his own village so that even more girls can access secondary education.

"The most significant message I tell girls in our program is 'Education is power!'" John says. This message is being embraced by current KCEA-supported students, who aspire to be doctors, lawyers, teachers, and other professionals. In addition, alumni of KCEA programs are now IT managers, medical professionals, teachers, and social workers.

After completing high school, Josphine pursued higher education to became an elementary school teacher. She is happily married with a family of her own.

John is living proof of a story that has played out on every populated continent, among hundreds of tribes, societies, and civilizations. Sincere Christians—motivated by their faith and beliefs—are making a positive difference in the world. Christians created modern education and the university as we know them. And today sincere Christians continue taking education to parts of the world where it is not prevalent.

To learn more and to support KCEA through program or student sponsorship, please visit https://www.educationfor maasai.org.

PART 3

The Most Influential Person

thirteen

Did Jesus Actually Exist?

If Christ has not been raised . . . we are of all people most to be pitied.

Paul the Apostle, writing about twenty years after Jesus's crucifixion[1]

One of my early suspicions, when I first considered Christianity, was that maybe Jesus never existed at all. That may sound odd to you, but as I have said, I am a skeptic by nature.

I remember thinking, *Could it be possible that all these Christians have been duped into believing in someone who never even existed?*

I wanted to see Primary Evidence with my own eyes so I could know for certain whether Jesus actually lived as a historic figure. I wanted to discover whether there was strong evidence—outside the Bible—for Jesus's life.

A careful examination revealed far more evidence than I expected. In fact, the evidence for Jesus's literal and physical existence astonished me. As you will see below, my suspicion that Jesus might not have existed was dead wrong. Like so many people's opinions about Jesus and Christianity, my doubt was based on ignorance and imagination—rather than on facts and history.

In this chapter, I will show you physical artifacts and writings. Within the evidence, I was surprised to learn that the specific cities, rulers, and people Jesus interacted with were real. They are documented in history, and you can still visit many of the cities and locations today (such as Jerusalem, Bethlehem, and the Jordan River, among others). I learned in my investigation that, outside the Bible, more than a dozen non-Christian writers from Jesus's era described Jesus and his movement in ancient documents.

I also learned that the consensus of respected historians (including non-Christian historians) is that Jesus clearly existed. The reason for this agreement among respected scholars is that the ancient evidence is clear and compelling. We have far more evidence for Jesus's existence than we have for most other figures of history from two thousand years ago.

But since we are not in the habit of trusting experts to define reality for us, let me share with you some of the Primary Evidence that led me to conclude that Jesus definitely lived. These ancient authors and writings described Jesus's existence. And again, these sources are all from *outside* the Bible.

Each of the following ancient sources, from the era of Jesus, confirmed the existence of Jesus or his followers:

Cornelius Tacitus, Roman historian[2]
Suetonius, secretary to Roman emperor Hadrian[3]

Flavius Josephus, Jewish historian (whom I previewed in
    chap. 1)[4]

Thallus, as cited by Julius Africanus[5]

Pliny the Younger, a Roman author and government official[6]

Emperor Trajan[7]

Emperor Hadrian[8]

Jewish Rabbinic Talmud[9]

Toledot Yeshu, Jewish biography of Jesus[10]

Lucian of Samosata, Greek[11]

Mara bar Serapion, Syrian[12]

Gospel of Truth by Valentinus, Gnostic[13]

Apocryphon of John, Gnostic[14]

Gospel of Thomas, Gnostic[15]

Treatise on the Resurrection, Gnostic[16]

Clement of Rome[17]

Ignatius[18]

Quadratus[19]

Barnabas[20]

Justin Martyr[21]

Each one of these represents a real person who undeniably
existed or a writing that undeniably existed, and all of them tell
us about another real person—a guy named Jesus or the Christ
(also referred to as Christus), who lived in the same era of history and who initiated a movement of followers, today known
as Christians.

These authors and writings are acknowledged by legitimate
historians, including non-Christian historians. (You can examine
each one of them by visiting JesusSkeptic.com or through the
sources in this endnote.)[22]

What mattered for my investigation was the simple reality that each of these historically documented figures and writings validated Jesus or his movement during the era of Jesus's lifetime. And we still possess historically valid manuscripts of these writings today. Taken together, they verified the following:

- Jesus lived in Judea, an actual geographic location that still exists.
- Jesus lived around AD 0–33.
- Jesus was born Jewish.
- Jesus was an esteemed teacher.
- Jesus's teachings were considered honorable.
- Jesus had a reputation for displaying Godlike abilities or performing miracles.
- Jesus's followers worshiped him as God.
- Jesus interacted with another well-documented historical figure: Pontius Pilate.
- Jesus was crucified near Jerusalem.
- There was an earthquake and a period of darkness (possible solar eclipse or volcanic eruption darkening the sky with ash) about the time of Jesus's crucifixion.
- Jesus's followers claimed he rose from the dead.
- The disappearance of Jesus's body, following his very public crucifixion, caused an uproar in the ancient world.
- Jesus's followers then began spreading his teaching, and the movement multiplied.

These facts were all stated by ancient writers who were not themselves Christians. (I will quote some of them below.) As such, these specific statements about Jesus are matters of established world history. These facts exist in human reality regardless of personal belief. Below I will show Primary Evidence, including ancient coins and writings, that verify the legitimacy of these reports.

Non-Christian Sources of Jesus's Life and Followers

The record of Jesus's life and impact is substantial and is diversely documented among ancient Greek, Roman, Jewish, and other authors—to such an extent that the ancient evidence for Jesus's existence could not possibly have been fabricated. Below I've listed just a few historical figures who wrote of Jesus's existence even though they were not among his followers.

Tacitus

Tacitus, a respected Roman writer from the time of Jesus, described how this mysterious new group of Christians began.[23] In the process, he referred to Jesus as Christus, or Christ. He explained that Jesus was a real person who was crucified by Pontius Pilate, a specific historical figure. And he explained that Jesus's followers spread rapidly from Judea to Rome, a specific, measurable geographic area. Here's what he wrote:

Figure 13.1. Tacitus, a Roman historian, described Jesus during the first century, citing where Jesus lived, stating that he was crucified by Pontius Pilate, and describing Jesus's followers.

Nero fastened guilt and inflicted the most exquisite tortures on a class hated for their abominations, called Christians by the populace. Christus [an ancient way of saying Christ], from whom the name had its origin, suffered the extreme penalty [crucifixion] during the reign of Tiberius at the hands of one of our procurators, Pontius Pilate, and a most mischievous superstition [referring to the belief that Jesus was God], thus checked for a moment [with Jesus's death], again broke out not only in Judea . . . but even in Rome.[24]

Like every piece of evidence presented in this chapter, this was not taken from the Scriptures but was in accordance with ancient writings and witnesses entirely separate from and independent of the Bible.

Josephus

Josephus, a Jewish historian who lived around the time of Jesus, was also not a Christian. He described Jesus as a dynamic teacher who was crucified by Pilate, followed by disciples, reportedly raised from the dead, and then proclaimed to be the Messiah.[25]
Josephus wrote:

At this time there was a wise man who was called Jesus. His conduct was good and [he] was known to be virtuous. And many people from among the Jews and the other nations became his disciples. Pilate condemned him to be crucified and to die. But those who

Figure 13.2. Josephus, a Jewish historian.

Figure 13.3. Cover page of Josephus's works.

had become his disciples did not abandon his discipleship. They reported that he had appeared to them three days after his crucifixion, and that he was alive; accordingly he was perhaps the Messiah, concerning who the prophets have recounted wonders.[26]

Figure 13.4. Today we have copies of Flavius Josephus's manuscript in the original language. The portions referring to Jesus are outlined.

Before my investigation of Christianity, I had read and heard a common myth about Christianity. It goes like this: "Sure, Jesus was a good teacher, but he never claimed to be God. Even his early followers never thought that. It was all made up hundreds of years later so that the church could gain political control."

That common myth, however, does not align with the Primary Evidence. Non-Christian writings from the time of Jesus (including those of Tacitus and Josephus) state that Jesus's followers viewed him as God or Christus (Messiah, who is God in human form).

Pliny the Younger

Pliny the Younger, a Roman author and administrator, wrote during the era in which Jesus lived. He confirmed not only that Jesus lived but also that Jesus's followers worshiped him as God from the very beginning of his movement. Pliny the Younger wrote:

Figure 13.5. Pliny the Younger, a Roman contemporary of Jesus, confirmed that Jesus lived, that the early Christians worshiped Jesus as God, and that early Christians were unusually moral people.[27]

They [the Christians] were in the habit of meeting on a certain fixed day before it was light, when they sang in alternate verses a hymn to Christ, as to a god, and bound themselves by solemn oath, not to any wicked deeds, but never to commit any fraud, theft or adultery, never to falsify their word, nor deny a trust when they should be called upon to deliver it up; after which it was their custom to separate, and then reassemble to partake of food—but food of an ordinary and innocent kind.[28]

Lucian of Samosata

Lucian of Samosata actually despised the early Christians. He was a skeptic and critic of the movement. Yet Lucian never doubted that this man Jesus was a real person. As a critic of the early Christian movement, he wrote, "The Christians, you know, worship a man to this day—the distinguished personage who introduced their novel rites, and was crucified on that account."[29]

As much as Lucian despised the early Christian movement, he never argued that Jesus never existed. Nor did he ever argue that Jesus was not worshiped as God. Lucian assumed that Jesus and his bizarre followers would soon be forgotten in the circles of important people like himself. Ironically, some two thousand years later, few people in the world know who Lucian of Samosata was, but most people in the world know about Jesus.

These ancients, who were closest in time to Jesus's actual life, knew that the Jesus movement had originated with a real person named Jesus or referred to as Christus (Christ), and they knew that Jesus was revered as God by his devoted followers.

Figure 13.6. Lucian of Samosata, a Greek author who wrote about the famous and powerful people of his day, wrote that Jesus was "a man," that he lived, that he was crucified, and that he was worshiped as God by the first Christians.[30]

When I learned that even the skeptics of Jesus's day freely acknowledged his existence and the basic tenets of Christianity, I realized just how irrefutable Jesus's existence is. If I wanted to write off Christianity, then I would have to look for a better reason than a lack of evidence for Jesus's existence.

Historical Artifacts That Point to Jesus's Existence

Figures 13.7 and 13.8 show ancient artifacts that verify the existence of some of the authors listed above who gave testimony of Jesus's existence in the ancient world. Each of the Primary Evidence pieces here is non-Christian in origin.

Chuy1530, CC BY-SA 4.0 / Wikimedia Commons

Figure 13.7. Coin with image of Roman emperor Trajan.

Incidentally, the Christian Gospel accounts of Jesus's life also described Pilate as the ruler who approved the public killing of Jesus on a wooden cross. Of note here is that Tacitus and Josephus—both of whom were not Christians—described Jesus's life and death in a manner that aligns precisely with the Christian Gospel accounts of Jesus's life and death. Both described the same historical figure, Pontius Pilate, as the one who had Jesus crucified. (Those quotations from Tacitus and Josephus were included above.)

This is significant because, within ancient literature, made-up or mythical characters were not written about by multiple historical figures—of multiple beliefs and nationalities. They were also not written about as actually existing and having specific physical interactions with actual historic contemporaries, such as Pontius Pilate. This is

Irton33, CC BY-SA 3.0 / Wikimedia Commons

Figure 13.8. "Hadrianus" is inscribed on this surviving coin from the reign of Emperor Hadrian,[31] whose secretary Suetonius[32] described Jesus and his followers.

known as the corroboration of multiple witnesses.

Ancient accounts such as those of Josephus and Tacitus confirm that Jesus lived in a manner consistent with the description in the Gospels. These writers would have had no thinkable motivation to write about an invented person as if he actually existed, nor is it likely that multiple writers would have made up identical interactions between Jesus and a real person named Pontius Pilate. In fact, they could have faced death for making up such stories about a ruler like Pilate.

Figure 13.9. Pontius Pilate is well documented as the ruler over the region where Jesus was crucified. Tacitus, the Roman writer, and Josephus, the Jewish historian, both described that Pontius Pilate interacted with Jesus and had Jesus crucified.

Ancient Believers Who Witnessed Jesus's Life

The non-Christian sources described above validated that Jesus lived, was crucified, and was worshiped as God. They confirmed a number of other details too. Of the twenty ancient witnesses I listed at the beginning of this chapter, fifteen were not Christians.

As a skeptic, the non-Christian witnesses spoke loudest to me. However, there were also Christians from that era who wrote about what was happening, not in the Bible but in their personal letters.

Some of my fellow skeptics argue that ancient Christians cannot be trusted, but on further reflection, I concluded this to be an unfair argument. Here's why. As a reporter, I learned in real-life reporting that the people closest to the action are often the best sources.

For example, when I wanted to report on heroin drug use in Arizona, my best sources were heroin addicts and dealers living in drug houses. When I wanted to report on drug trafficking across the Arizona border, my best sources were those involved with either moving or stopping drugs from moving across the border. When I wanted to report on the lifestyle of an NFL athlete, my best sources were NFL athletes and the family members who lived in their homes with them.

In every other domain or investigation, we view the people who have inside knowledge and experience as the *best* sources—not as unqualified sources. Here I witnessed a double standard when it comes to Christianity. If a national news reporter wants to know about Islam, they ask an academic who is a Muslim. But I have seen some national news reporters, when they want to know about Christianity, refuse to ask an academic who is a Christian because in the case of Christianity, they consider insider knowledge biased. As a reporter, I believe this is a double standard.

With that said, we do have ancient insider sources—Christians— who lived around the time of Jesus and who wrote about him. I am referring here to Christians whose writings did not make the cut to be included in the Bible, yet their writings are valuable for documenting Jesus's existence and the early beliefs of Jesus's followers.

There are at least five of these ancient insider witnesses to Jesus's life. Each stated that Jesus was a literal man, and as believers, they also believed this man was God and was raised from the dead. We will examine two here.

Clement of Rome

Clement of Rome[33] was an ancient Christian who lived alongside Paul the Apostle and Jesus's disciples Peter and John. Clement wrote nonbiblical accounts of the early Christian movement. In one historically verified document, Clement confirmed that Jesus lived, that Jesus claimed to be God, and that Christians worshiped him as God from the very beginning of the movement.

Even if we do not share Clement's belief that Jesus was God, we have to acknowledge how unlikely it would be for people to risk their lives to follow someone—in their lifetimes—if that person did not actually exist. Also bear in mind that early Christians were hated, hunted, and burned alive by Nero as a punishment for their belief that Jesus was God. Christians were publicly killed, and their homes and possessions were seized by the government, so there was no motivation for people to commit their lives to an imaginary conspiracy when the consequence for that belief was death or imprisonment.

Clement wrote, "Having been fully assured through the resurrection of our Lord Jesus Christ and confirmed in the word of God . . . they [the first Christians] went forth with the glad tidings that the kingdom of God should come."[34]

Note that this same Clement, while not an author of the Bible, may be referred to in a Bible passage in the book of Philippians: "Yes, and I ask you, my true companion, help these women since they have contended at my side in the cause of the gospel, along with Clement and the rest of my co-workers, whose names are in the book of life."[35]

Ignatius

Writings from Ignatius,[36] also from the era of Jesus, confirmed Jesus's existence and documented other details from his life.

Jesus Christ who was of the race of David, who was the Son of Mary, who was truly born and ate and drank, was truly persecuted under Pontius Pilate, was truly crucified and died in the sight of those in heaven and on earth and those under the earth;

who moreover was truly raised from the dead, His Father having raised Him, who in the like fashion will so raise us also who
believe on Him.[37]

I will not drag you through the details of each of the rest of the
twenty ancient witnesses. Instead, I will summarize that, in my
review, all twenty are historically valid individuals. Their writings
about Jesus have stood up under hundreds of years of critique
from academics, critics, and skeptics.

Fact-Based Conclusions

In summary, when I began looking for evidence of Jesus's existence, I was astonished to learn how much ancient evidence still
exists—considering that Jesus lived two thousand years ago and
that numerous wars, fires, and natural disasters have destroyed so
much of the ancient world and its writings.

Dozens of historians have given their lives to the study of the
ancient Jesus. These historians have written thousands of pages on
Jesus's historic existence. The consensus of this work, according
to the Primary Evidence and also to the experts who have most ex-
amined it, is that Jesus of Nazareth was a real, historic figure who
did indeed launch the movement known today as Christianity.

**Multiple ancient witnesses—including those who had no mo-
tivation to make up a mythical story—documented the century in
which Jesus lived, who his peers were, who had him crucified, the
geography and politics in which he lived, his specific interactions
with other historical figures, and so much more.**

Based on the number of these ancient non-Christian witnesses
and based on the reality that their diverse accounts all agree on
a host of factors central to Jesus's life, geography, death, claims,
and movement, it is clear to me as an investigator that Jesus's
existence can be proven with as much certainty as exists for any

other individual from the ancient world. In fact, Jesus's existence has been proven with far more evidence than is available for most people from the ancient world. (If you want to examine this matter further, I recommend five books listed in this endnote.[38] Each book will point you toward legitimate historians and legitimate ancient documents.)

So do we know for certain that Jesus lived?

As an investigative reporter who sides with facts, the evidence convinced me that Jesus clearly lived. Spiritual claims and beliefs aside, the existence of Jesus as a historical figure and a spiritual teacher is as clear as the existence of any other ancient figure.

Indeed, if a person will not admit the existence of Jesus based on this evidence, then the same person would need to refute the existence of Socrates, Genghis Kahn, Muhammad, and most other historic figures.

What does all of this mean?

To me, it means that the widespread global impact of Christianity (as documented in part 2) ties back to a real person. This real person—Jesus—spoke words and lived in such a way that he motivated real people toward deep belief and radical action. He ignited a movement that has spread for two thousand years. This Jesus movement motivated many of the key figures who ushered in our modern world, and this Jesus movement now includes one out of three people alive today.

Jesus, a Leader of Skeptics

Paul the Apostle is a historically documented first-century figure who was among the first skeptics of Jesus. Paul knew without a doubt that Jesus existed, but he refused to believe that Jesus could be God. Paul actually hated the early followers of Jesus.

Then one day—according to Paul's own writings (written around AD 55)—the risen Jesus appeared to Paul and convinced him that he was both alive and God. Whether you believe Paul's report or not, the fact of history is that Paul the Apostle had a dramatic conversion and became a devoted believer in Jesus. He went on to write some of the most-read books in the world. Today those books are included in what Christians call the New Testament of the Bible.

Paul interacted with thousands of people who had seen Jesus publicly crucified near Jerusalem. More than five hundred of those people who had watched Jesus die later claimed to have seen Jesus raised from the dead. After attacking and assaulting this group, Paul eventually joined them, following his conversion.

Paul gave himself to the radical message that Jesus is God and can provide eternal life to all who believe in him. That enthusiasm cost Paul his career, his comfort (he was often beaten by anti-Christian mobs), and eventually his life (he was killed for his belief in Jesus). Like many early followers of Jesus, Paul continued to declare that Jesus was risen, even after being arrested, jailed, and threatened with death.

One time when Paul was arguing that Jesus is God, he made this statement to a group of first-century skeptics: "If Christ has not been raised . . . we are of all people most to be pitied."[39] In other words, if Jesus did not actually rise from the dead, then the hope of Jesus's followers is a sad thing.

Whatever Paul saw with his own eyes—when he claimed to see the resurrected Jesus—so convinced him that he was willing to be killed while proclaiming Jesus. Paul was *that* confident that he too would rise from the dead someday, just as Jesus had. This is all well documented in first-century history and in Paul's own ancient writings.

It is interesting to me that one of the most influential Jesus followers in history started out as a skeptic. Some who had seen Jesus in person struggled to believe that he had risen from the dead. That makes me feel a bit less "pagan" for questioning whether Jesus had lived at all.

Now that I have seen the evidence, I know with confidence that Jesus lived, claimed to be God, and launched Christianity. These are not religious beliefs but facts. I conclude these things because I have seen the Primary Evidence with my own eyes.

We live at a time when most people and ideas appear on our screens as videos. So it can seem as if things we cannot see with our own eyes may be fake. In this sense, I suppose it was normal for me to wonder if Jesus actually lived. After all, I couldn't see him with my eyes. I have since come to realize, however, that I cannot see many important things with my eyes, including the wind, atoms, and the force of gravity, yet I am convinced that those things exist because I see their impact.

Now that I have seen the evidence with my eyes, Jesus's existence is clear. His impact is also clear.

By the way, Jesus predicted that it would be hard for people in our time to believe. Talking to followers who saw him in person, Jesus once said, "You believe because you have seen me. Blessed are those who [will] believe without seeing me."[40] Here the word "believe" referred to believing that Jesus is God in a human body, that he arrived on earth to rescue us from death and from suffering.

Believing that Jesus is God is a step of faith that requires believing in what we cannot see. Yes, it takes faith to believe that Jesus rose from the dead and can provide eternal life. But it turns out that it does not take faith to believe that Jesus existed. Nor does it require any faith to acknowledge that this real person launched a global movement. Jesus's existence is an established fact of history, proven by ancient artifacts and writings. And this conclusion has stood up to frequent critique and investigation for two thousand years.

We must each decide for ourselves what we will do with Jesus's claims about peace, rest, and eternal life. But knowing that Jesus lived and launched a positive movement is a matter of fact rather than a matter of faith.

As for my personal journey, I reached a point when the mountain of evidence convinced me of a few facts:

- Jesus clearly lived, as documented by ancient artifacts and verified non-Christian accounts.
- This same Jesus launched a global movement of social good.
- Jesus's followers have made the world I live in a better place (see part 2).
- This same Jesus claimed to be God and to offer peace and forgiveness from sins.
- This same Jesus claimed to be the only way to eternal life or immortality beyond this world.

All of this left me at a crossroads. My investigation of facts— not religion or opinion but facts—had led me to the conclusions above. Together, the findings forced me to ask myself two questions:

What will I make of Jesus's radical claims? and *Who do I believe this Jesus is?*

fourteen

What Is the Actual Impact of Jesus's Life?

> "But what about you?" [Jesus] asked. "Who do you say I am?"
>
> Simon Peter answered, "You are the Messiah, the Son of the living God."
>
> Jesus and Peter, as recorded in the historically verified Gospel of Matthew[1]

As a journalist, I have interviewed all sorts of people, from celebrities and professional athletes to drug addicts and murderers on death row. None of these people ever claimed to be God.

But it turns out that Jesus did. That's right. Jesus claimed to be God.

So should we take Jesus's claim seriously?

My answer would typically be no. Most people who claim to be God belong in mental facilities or on strong medication. But Jesus, we have seen, is not most people.

For one, we have seen that his teachings inspired specific people who have led humanity forward in education, healthcare, and human rights. Thanks to the work done by Jesus's followers, most of us know how to read today, and we will live about twice as long as average people in history.

There is another reason to consider Jesus's radical claim of being God. It turns out that Jesus may be the most influential person in history, and not by a small margin. That is, he has impacted other people more than any other person who has ever lived.

Apart from religion or church or Christianity, I find myself curious about the words of the most influential person in history—all the more notable because that person claimed to be God.

In this chapter, I will show you the evidence indicating that Jesus is likely the most influential person who has ever lived. When the most influential person of all time—and I mean the most influential person in *all* of human existence—claims to be God, well, I'm more inclined to hear what this person has to say.

Yes, the claim is crazy (though if there is a Creator, maybe it's not a big leap for that Creator to join the creation in some manifestation, as Jesus claimed he did). Lots of crazies have claimed to be God, but Jesus is fundamentally different.

Here is what I mean.

- Person claims to be God and claims his movement will spread to the ends of the earth.[2]
- Person claims his movement will improve humanity around the world.[3]

- Person claims his movement will continue growing unstopped, forever.[4]
- Person's movement then *does* spread to the ends of the earth.[5]
- Person's movement *does* measurably improve humanity around the world.
- Person's movement grows rapidly, every year, for two thousand years and continues to grow.
- Person becomes the most-followed person of all people in all of history, ever.
- After two thousand years, person is followed by one out of three people in the world—far more than any other person in history.

As a reporter of facts, I found myself wondering, *What are the chances of just one of these outrageous claims actually happening for any person in history?*

Alexander the Great and others predicted that their empires would cover the entire earth, but none of them came close to accomplishing that prediction.

In our day, social media influencers and celebrities work tirelessly to gain as many "followers" as they possibly can. In every generation, millions of people have played "king of the hill," climbing over each other in the pursuit of bigger platforms and more influence.

No other figure in history has accomplished even *one* of the bullet points listed above on the scale Jesus did—let alone *all* those things. Jesus, it turns out, has done all those crazy things. His is a crazy amount of impact.

So as skeptical as I was about any person claiming to be God, the evidence compelled me to continue investigating. Here are the next questions I needed to answer in my own journey:

*Is Jesus actually—by objective measurements—among the
most influential people in history?*

*And if so, can I measure Jesus's impact in a nonreligious
way?*

For me, the answers to these questions would inform whether
I would keep considering Jesus's radical claim to be the Creator
God come to earth to help humanity.

As with all the research in this book, I determined to measure
Jesus with non-Christian and nonreligious measures. I set out
to determine Jesus's impact with numbers and facts that could
be applied to Shakespeare, Muhammad, Gandhi, Alexander the
Great, or any other person.

My goal was to apply the same standard to Jesus as I would
apply to any other historical figure and to see how this man who
claimed to be God stacked up. Here is what I found.

Fame and Influence

We admire people who have great influence and many followers.
Famous athletes such as LeBron James and Stephen Curry. Famous
actors or musicians such as Denzel Washington, Taylor Swift,
Beyoncé, or U2's Bono.

Below I have noted today's most famous celebrities and their
number of followers on Instagram.[6] At the bottom, I list the number of followers Jesus has today in our world, as measured by the
non-Christian Pew Research Center.[7]

Jesus versus Modern Celebrities

Celebrity	Followers
Stephen Curry	21.6 million
LeBron James	41.6 million
Taylor Swift	111 million

Celebrity	Followers
Kylie Jenner	114 million
Kim Kardashian	116 million
Beyoncé	117 million
Jesus	2.3 billion (or 230 million times 10)

The biggest celebrities of our day top out at about 100 million followers. Today Jesus has 100 million followers times 23. That is 2 billion, 300 million people.

Visually, we could look at it like this:

100 million (the round estimate of followers for today's biggest celebrities)

x 23

2,300,000,000 (2.3 billion) followers of Jesus today

Put another way, compared with the most famous celebrities of our time, Jesus has twenty-three followers for every one of their followers—even though Jesus lived two thousand years ago. But Jesus's followers aren't merely watching on Instagram as he shops or vacations. Jesus's followers are worshiping him as God. While today's celebrities are admired and even stalked by some fans, none are worshiped as God or claim to be God. In contrast, Jesus both claimed to be God and is worshiped as God. In fact, many of these celebrities themselves worship Jesus as God.

Many additional people who do not worship Jesus as God admire him and try to follow his teachings. If we added that group, the number of Jesus's casual followers (the kind of followers LeBron James or Kylie Jenner has) likely tops 4 billion, or more than half of the world's population.

Let's play it safe though and say that Jesus has *only* 2.3 billion followers today. If we count only the people who worship Jesus as God, then with about 7 billion people alive in the world today,

Jesus's worshiping followers account for one out of three people on earth.

The first time I stared this math in the face, I had a realization. Making fun of Christians is the same as making fun of one out of three people alive today. Saying that Christianity is just for small-minded people is saying that I am smarter than one out of every three people alive today—many of whom are PhD researchers, leading scientists, medical doctors, and effective leaders of governments, schools, and universities.

My study of fame also confirmed the old cliché about fifteen minutes of fame—that is, fame quickly evaporates in history. Most of the celebrities listed above will be forgotten in one hundred years (I demonstrate this below). In contrast, Jesus's following—as demonstrated by the evidence we have considered in this book—has continued to grow with every new century since his birth twenty centuries ago. It is not uncommon to see special-edition magazines about Jesus on sale at the grocery store or to see crosses and Christian fish symbols as tattoos, jewelry, and bumper stickers two thousand years after Jesus's birth. Next to those special editions about Jesus, we see magazines featuring today's celebrities, but we don't typically see magazine covers featuring celebrities from two hundred years ago.

One hundred years from now, in the 2120s, most people will not recognize the name Kim Kardashian. Sure, her biography will exist as history on sites such as Wikipedia, but hers and other celebrities' faces and names will no longer be on the cover of *People* magazine or the latest celebrity gossip websites. Most people one hundred years from now will not know who LeBron James or Taylor Swift was.

I do not say this as an opinion but as a general rule of how fame fades in history. Here is an example of why I make this assertion.

Can you name either of the two people in figures 14.1 and 14.2?

Figure 14.1. American composer and playwright.   Figure 14.2. Canadian actress.

Neither could I when I first saw them.

If you and I lived one hundred years ago, we would know these two people as world-famous celebrities. George M. Cohan and Mary Pickford were Taylor Swift–like celebrities in the early 1900s. They were among the most famous people in the world—just like the celebrities from our time listed above. Yet a mere one hundred years later, most of us don't recognize these "famous people," let alone know what they did.

Below are twenty of the most famous people in the world from between the years 1900 and 1918 as compiled by a historian. See how many names you recognize.

Roald Amundsen	Albert Einstein
Theda Bara	Henry Ford
Louis Bleroit	Sigmund Freud
Francis X. Bushman	Mata Hari
Enrico Caruso	William S. Hart
Charlie Chaplin	Harry Houdini
Marie Curie	Henry James

Jack Johnson	Paul von Hindenburg
Florence Lawrence	Wilhelm II
Robert Falcon Scott	Wilbur and Orville Wright[8]

How many names did you recognize?

I would be surprised if many of us under age thirty-five know more than half the names on the list. Keep in mind that these people lived not three hundred years ago but just one hundred years ago.

Even the people we do recognize, such as Albert Einstein and Henry Ford, are not necessarily people we would follow enthusiastically. We know of them, and we are familiar with maybe one or two of their accomplishments, but we do not model our lives after Albert Einstein or Henry Ford.

The reality is that the majority of famous people are forgotten after about one hundred years. And then, with each additional century that passes, the number who are still remembered decreases more and more. If we were to go back two hundred years, we would recognize even fewer of the top celebrities—people such as Beau Brummell, Lola Montez, and Honinbo Shusaku. Sure, a few historians or enthusiasts may remember these people, but for most celebrities from two hundred years ago, their followings no longer number in the hundreds of millions. They number in the thousands.

This is the normal trajectory of famous and influential people in history. Like sandcastles slowly being eroded on the beach, the fame and influence of even the most famous people in history erode after one hundred years. The sands of time and the crashing waves of new generations have a way of burying even the most famous figures from every generation.

Take, for example, Robert Redford, Bob Geldof, and Cliff Richard. These were three of the world's most famous celebrities just within the last fifty years. Yet many Americans under the age of thirty-five do not know their names—though all three are still alive as I write this.

A few years ago, hip-hop artist Kanye West collaborated on a song with Beatles founder Paul McCartney. McCartney is without a doubt one of the most famous people of the 1900s. After Kanye released his song with McCartney, a young generation of Americans started tweeting things like this: "I don't know who Paul McCartney is, but Kanye is going to give this man a career with this new song!!"

That is a real tweet.

Paul McCartney is one of the most famous people of the last fifty years. He is still alive, and already a new generation of young adults does not know who he is.

This is just the way history works. The sands of time bury everyone.

Very few historic figures have any dramatic cultural impact or fame one hundred years after their lifetimes. Then, with every added century, the impact of a typical famous person continues to decrease.

Only a small percent of influential people remain famous for more than one hundred years after their deaths—people such as George Washington, Leonardo da Vinci, Shakespeare, and Napoleon. (Note that even these lived within the last five hundred years.) But even among those few who stand the test of time, very few have a devoted following of hundreds of millions of people who remember them daily.

Jesus of Nazareth is the only historic figure I could find who continues adding millions of new followers every year, even two thousand years after his life. Not only that, but we will see below that every year thousands of babies and buildings are named after him and his followers. We will also see that some entire nations have centered their constitutions and governments around Jesus. (That is probably never going to happen for the celebrities we follow on Instagram.)

Is Jesus Really the Most Influential Person in History?

Once Jesus's existence was confirmed and I realized that Jesus has more followers today than any other person has had in history, I became curious. *Is it possible*, I wondered, *that Jesus is the most influential person in history?*

If Jesus turned out to be the most influential person in history, then I wanted to know what he said, I wanted to know what he did, and I wanted to know how he came to be so influential.

So I determined to find out.

As with many of my news investigations, I began by listing logical questions that could be answered with hard evidence. When taken together, the answers to those questions would create a pattern indicating a person's influence in history.

Here are some of the questions I used to measure impact. We could apply these same questions to Barack Obama, Abraham Lincoln, or any other person in history to measure their impact.

What is this person's documented number of followers today?

What is this person's documented impact on nations?

What is this person's documented impact on civilizations?

Is this person's impact on humanity increasing or decreasing over time?

What is this person's documented impact on the human calendar?

What is this person's documented impact on globally recognized holidays?

What is this person's documented impact on worldwide cultural norms?

What is this person's documented geographic reach of influence? Is this person's impact limited to one region/continent, or is it global?

How many cities and structures are named after this person?
What is the documented amount of real estate and buildings
dedicated to this person?

Each of these questions can lead to hard data, measurable facts, statistics, and realities that we can compare among historic figures. With this approach, I was saying, "Let's apply to Jesus the same standard we apply to every other historic figure." Let's not give Jesus special treatment, and let's not give him unfair treatment. Let's just measure Jesus's influence by the same measure we use to consider the influence of Socrates, Plato, Muhammad, Leonardo da Vinci, or Genghis Khan. Let's push all these historically influential figures through the same filter. Let's put them all on the same examination table and determine who has really influenced humanity the most.

What is this person's documented number of followers today?

As mentioned above, Jesus wins the number of followers category by a long shot. With about 2.3 billion followers today, Jesus has more followers than any other person in the history of the world. The next most influential person by this measure is Muhammad, the prophet of Islam.[9] He has about 1.8 billion followers (though they do not worship him as God). It is difficult to say who is in third place. I could not find any other person—past or present—who has more than 1 billion followers.

To demonstrate how vastly Jesus outstrips any competition in this area, consider that even the world's biggest dictators never had close to 1 billion followers (and many of those "followers" were forced, not voluntary). Joseph Stalin, at the peak of the Soviet Union (USSR), had about 170 million followers. Mao Zedong had about 600 million in China. Neither reached even one-fourth of what Jesus has today. And both fail the test of duration—that is, they have far fewer followers now than when they were alive.

What is this person's documented impact on nations?

Not many people in history have impacted entire nations in a way that continues shaping history long after they lived.

We are speaking here of the scenario in which a government formally says, "We as a nation believe that the best way to alleviate poverty, the best way to deal with crime and injustice, the best way to have a fair society with human rights is to follow this one person's teachings."

Not many people rise to that level of influence. But there are a few. Karl Marx is one of those people.

More than two dozen nations have said, "We believe that Marxism (the teachings of Karl Marx) is the best way to run a nation." As of this writing, four countries in the world still reference Marxism in their constitutions: China, Cuba, Laos, and Vietnam.

Marx lived within the last two hundred years, so the test of time (duration of impact) will be to see how many nations are following Marx's framework in another eighteen hundred years.

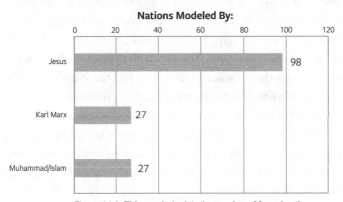

Figure 14.3. This graph depicts the number of formal nation-states, past and present combined, that cite each individual (Jesus, Muhammad, Karl Marx) as their model for society.

In Jesus's case, throughout history, ninety-eight nations or empires have overtly stated that they are a "Christian state." Not many people in history can claim that an entire nation has modeled itself after them, let alone dozens of nations and over the duration of two thousand years.

Figure 14.3 shows the number of formal nation-states, past and present combined, that cite significant individuals as their model for society.

Note that figure 14.3 represents only those formal nation-states that overtly declared themselves a Marxist, Christian, or Muslim nation. Many nations have large Christian or Muslim populations but are not formally Christian or Muslim.

What is this person's documented impact on civilizations?

Impacting a civilization is much broader than just impacting one nation. By "civilization," we are talking about broad values that reach across national boundaries and often across centuries, things such as "Eastern thinking" and "Western thinking." Impacting a civilization means affecting dozens of nations over the course of eras. We can measure such impact broadly to determine who has impacted Western civilization and other civilizations.

As documented in part 2 of this book, Jesus's life and teachings have impacted Europe, America, and the rest of the Western world through the presence of churches and the founding of the modern university, which grew out of cathedral schools. These cathedral schools began in various countries such as France, England, Spain, and others, but they all contributed to what historians long referred to as "Western civilization." Western civilization was so intertwined with Christianity that it was referred to for hundreds of years as "Christendom."

In the last one hundred years, Christendom or Western civilization has shaped the global world order and global civilization in ways so vast that they cannot be fully measured. For example, the advent of electricity, modern medicine, NATO, the United Nations, the globalized workweek, the global model for the stock market, and many other global norms originated in Christian-influenced Western civilization. We saw in part 2 how Christian-educated people launched the modern hospital, the Scientific Revolution, and other advances that have now spread around the world.

Here again Jesus of Nazareth is in a very small crowd. Of all the billions of people throughout human history, his weight of impact on an entire civilization and now on the global order is greater than any other. Again, second place likely goes to Muhammad, the prophet of Islam. Chinese and many other influential *cultures* have had massive global impact too, but those cultures do not trace back to one person as do Christianity (Jesus) and Islam (Muhammad).

Is this person's impact on humanity increasing or decreasing over time?

The trend of impact for nearly all figures in world history is an eventual peak and then a decline. Some are remembered for a few centuries, but most people are forgotten within a few decades of their deaths.

Yes, we have all heard of Joan of Arc and Socrates, but very few of us are influenced by them on a daily basis. On the other hand, one out of three people in the world today claims to be influenced by Jesus—many of them on a daily basis and nearly all of them when they gather yearly for Christmas (Jesus's birth) and Easter (Jesus's crucifixion and resurrection from the dead) or weekly for Sunday worship (the day Christians claim Jesus rose from the dead).

Musicians use the term "crescendo" to describe when a sound is getting louder. So we are here asking, *Is this person's impact crescendoing? Or is it decreasing?*

Let's consider the impact of French ruler Napoleon Bonaparte. His impact increased dramatically about two hundred years ago. But ever since his death, it has decreased. Other examples of this peaking and then declining influence include Abraham Lincoln, Joseph Stalin, Adolf Hitler, and many others who had dramatic impact (both for good and for evil) during their lives. As with most figures in history, their impact began waning the day they died.

Figure 14.4. Napoleon Bonaparte.

Shakespeare is another good example of this principle. Shakespeare had incredible influence in human language for hundreds of years, but his influence peaked somewhere in the 1800s. Today his influence is clearly declining. Also, Shakespeare's influence never pierced Asia, Africa, or South America.

This is the normal trajectory of history. Even the most influential people are limited by region, and then their influence diminishes after a few hundred years.

Figure 14.5. William Shakespeare.

Here again Jesus's increasing influence, expanding on every continent, stands alone. Jesus's profound impact on individual lives, the combined number of people he has impacted, and his global reach all continue to crescendo, getting bigger and bigger with every passing year. This is exceptional in world history. This is notable.

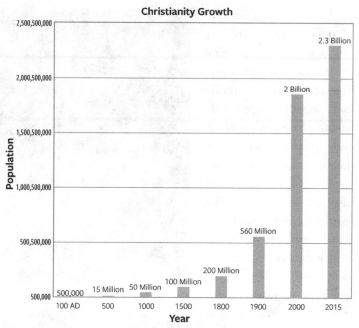

Figure 14.6. Estimated number of Christians since the time of Jesus.

What is this person's documented impact on the human calendar?

How about the impact on the human calendar? Throughout history, different empires have tried to control the calendar. During the French Revolution, the revolutionaries decided to create a new calendar, with the Revolution as year zero. But that calendar did not stand the test of time. Nobody uses it today.

The Soviet Union (USSR) did the same thing just within the last one hundred years. In 1929, leaders declared, "For the new Soviet Union, this is a new calendar. No one in the USSR will use the old global calendar anymore." That claim and calendar did not last even one hundred years. Nobody uses that calendar today.

There is one calendar that is accepted around the world today in every major global society, and it is a fact of history that this one globally accepted calendar is based on the life of one real person in human history—Jesus, the Christ.

The calendar that we use today—and that the world uses—is based on a Latin term, *anno Domini*, which means "the year of our Lord," referring to the year of Jesus's birth and abbreviated AD, and another phrase, "before Christ," abbreviated BC. The "zero" of this calendar is the estimated birth of Jesus. Years after his birth are labeled AD, and years before his birth are labeled BC. Some scholars have recently attempted to change BC and AD to BCE

Figure 14.7. Rejected French calendar.

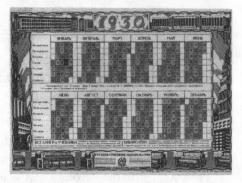

Figure 14.8. Rejected Soviet calendar.

and ACE. They want to substitute "Common Era," or CE, for any reference to Jesus. However, changing the letters does not change two thousand years of history and the fact that the calendar is based on the birth of Jesus.

And so as I write this, the year is 2019, or 2,019 years after the birth of "our Lord." This is why Primary Evidence writings from history frequently include the historic phrase "in the year of our Lord, 1942 [or another year]."

Now, whether you believe Jesus is God or not, whether you believe in the spiritual realm or not, it is a fact of history that the year of your birth is based on the year of Jesus's birth. The entire globe today uses a calendar that is based on the estimated birth year of Jesus of Nazareth. No other figure in history can make that kind of claim about the global calendar.

None.

It is ironic to me that when an atheist dates a check or when a follower of Muhammad celebrates a birthday, they cannot do so without acknowledging Jesus, on whose birth date the entire global calendar is based.

In some of the areas of measurement above, the number of influencers at Jesus's level was narrowed down to two or three. In this area, Jesus has no competitor.

What is this person's documented impact on globally recognized holidays?

Can you think of any figures from history who have been so influential that once per year hundreds of millions of people pause to remember them?

Often, after a celebrity passes away, millions of people will watch a TV special or post on social media about that person. But I have noticed that after just a few years, even cultural influencers such as Michael Jackson, Robin Williams, and John F. Kennedy are forgotten by many on the day of their birth. They are remembered by some but not by most. And the number who pause to remember them will keep dwindling down toward an eventual handful.

There is no national holiday—or cultural holiday across nations—to honor most influential people in history. In this category, a few people have holidays named after them. But no person in history has as many holidays dedicated to them—celebrated by as many people—as Jesus does.

Let's consider this: two of the most celebrated holidays around the globe today are Christmas (the remembrance of Jesus's birth) and Easter (the remembrance of Jesus's resurrection). Whether you believe Jesus is God or not, you can thank him for giving you multiple days off from work or school.

It turns out that several other holidays are named after Jesus's followers from history, people whose faith in Christ motivated their lives and who are known as "saints." These include:

- St. Patrick's Day
- St. Valentine's Day
- All Saints' Eve (or All Hallows' Eve), today known as Halloween

Even when we observe Martin Luther King Jr. Day, we honor a man who, as documented in part 2 of this book, wrote that Jesus's life and teachings shaped him as a leader.

As I studied global figures who have holidays named after them, I was shocked to learn the following: even the word "holiday" actually comes from Jesus and his followers. The early church called days of remembrance about Jesus and his followers "holy days." Over time, the term "holy days" was shortened to become "holidays." So even when people use the word "holiday" to avoid saying Christmas or other Christian terms, they are still—often ignorantly and unawares—using a Christian term. The fact that the word "holiday" would not exist if not for Jesus is symbolic of how, like fish unaware of the water in which they swim, we live in a Christian-influenced world far more than we even realize.

Jesus's influence can be measured factually against that of other figures in history, and when it comes to holidays, Jesus is again unrivaled by anyone else in history in his influence on humanity, both past and present.

What is this person's documented impact on worldwide cultural norms?

Here is an interesting question: *How many people in history have influenced the very days of your week?*

You can thank Jesus that you most likely get Sundays off from work.

Did you know that pausing from work on Sundays was not the norm for most cultures before Jesus lived? The early Christians gathered to meet every Sunday morning because that is when Christians believe Jesus rose from the dead. (You may recall that one of the ancient witnesses we studied above, Pliny the Younger, wrote about Jesus's followers gathering in this way soon after his crucifixion.)

Culture in Europe and America was so influenced by Christianity that for a few hundred years, nearly everyone went to church on Sundays. Christianity has now so impacted the globe that billions of people in the world still get Sunday off from work, whether they use the day to attend church or not.

The global stock market for every major country in the world is closed on Sunday. This traces back to Jesus's followers refusing to work on Sundays. Here again Jesus is unrivaled in his influence on how people live their lives, literally every week of their lives.

What is this person's documented geographic reach of influence? Is this person's impact limited to one region, or is it global?

When we consider geographic reach, we are taking the entire globe into account to determine whether a person's influence is focused in just one area or whether it transcends the boundaries of continents and countries.

221

Here is what I mean. We know that in Europe the game Americans call "soccer" is referred to as "football." And if you go to any European country, the European footballers there are as famous and well known as any other celebrity, even as famous as royalty. Yet most Americans don't know the names of Europe's biggest footballers. The same is true about most NFL athletes in America, who are largely unknown in Europe.

In this sense, football is an example of influence that is geographically focused in one region. Some people are famous in Europe, but they are not known in the United States. Other people are famous in the United States, but they are not known in Europe.

And so when we measure the influence of people in history, this is another way we can determine a person's influence. For example, Muhammad, the prophet of Islam, is incredibly followed throughout the Middle East and Northern Africa, but he is less followed in most of China, Russia, North America, and South America.[10]

More recent figures, such as Michael Jordan and Michael Jackson, demonstrate what it is to be universally known around almost the entire globe. In the same way, when we look at how recognized Jesus is on every continent and in every country and civilization, we see that Jesus's influence has invaded every corner of the globe. Religious figures usually see their impact focused on a specific geographical region, but Jesus's impact is a global phenomenon.

How many cities and structures are named after this person?

Could you imagine being so influential that someday people name an entire city after you? Alexander the Great left such a mark on history. There is a city to this day in Egypt called Alexandria. That is a big deal. That is an influential person.

I don't know about you, but I don't expect to have any cities named after me in my lifetime and especially not long after I am gone.

Now here is the thing about Jesus. Jesus's followers, out of reverence, rarely name their cities or children "Jesus" (some do in South America and Mexico), but many Jesus followers name their kids or their cities after Jesus's disciples and followers or saints.

For about three years, I lived in one of the wealthiest cities in the United States, San Jose, California. This city was named after a Christian saint, St. Joseph. And this city is just down the road from another city called St. Francisco (San Francisco). The capital of California is named after the Christian sacraments (Communion and baptism) and is called Sacramento.

Today thousands of cities around the world and even some countries have been named after Jesus and his followers. These cities and countries span the entire globe. Here are just a few examples.

Christchurch, New Zealand
Christmas Island in the South Pacific
El Salvador (Spanish for "the Savior")
Holy Island in England
Port St. John's, South Africa
Saint-Louis, Senegal
San Fernando, Philippines
San Isidro, Costa Rica
San Jose, Costa Rica
San Juan, Puerto Rico
San Salvador, Argentina
Santa Cruz, Bolivia
Santiago, Chile

Santo Domingo, Dominican Republic

Sao Paulo, Brazil (named after St. Paul, an author of the
New Testament)

St. John's, Newfoundland (named after St. John, one of Jesus's disciples)

St. Petersburg, Russia (named after St. Peter, one of Jesus's
disciples)

Here is just a sampling of the many cities within the United
States alone that have been named after Jesus, his followers, or
key locations in Jesus's life and story.

Bethlehem, Pennsylvania (one of three Bethlehems in the
United States; Bethlehem is the name of the town where
Jesus was born)

Christian County, Missouri

Corpus Christi, Texas (literally "the body of Christ" in
Latin, a reference to Christ's crucifixion and also to the
Christian sacrament of Communion)

Las Cruces, New Mexico (Spanish for "the crosses")

Los Angeles, California (Spanish for "the angels")

Philadelphia, Pennsylvania (from the New Testament Bible
words for "brotherly love")

Providence, Rhode Island ("providence" being a Christian
word for the idea that God is a benevolent provider of
good things)

San Antonio, Texas (named after St. Anthony, a Christ
follower)

San Bernardino, California (named after St. Bernard, a Christ
follower who also had a dog breed named after him)

San Diego, California (named after St. Diego, a Christ follower)

San Francisco, California (named after St. Francisco, a Christ follower)

Sangre de Cristo Mountains (Spanish for "blood of Christ" mountains)

San Jose, California (named after St. Joseph, Jesus's stepfather)

Santa Ana, California (named after St. Ana, a Christ follower)

Santa Barbara, California (named after St. Barbara, a Christ follower)

Santa Clara, California (named after St. Clara, a Christ follower)

Santa Fe, New Mexico (Spanish for "holy faith")

St. Augustine, Florida (named after St. Augustine, a Christ follower)

St. Paul, Minnesota (named after St. Paul, an author of the New Testament)

St. Petersburg, Florida (named after St. Peter, one of Jesus's disciples)

	Country	
1	France	8,963
2	Spain	4,444
3	Italy	2,683
4	Portugal	797
5	Austria	694
6	Greece	664
7	Belgium	464
8	Hungary	464
9	United Kingdom	327
10	Germany	244
11	Albania	175
12	Croatia	152
13	Russia	118
14	Switzerland	97
15	Slovenia	91
16	Czech Republic	70
17	Slovakia	63
18	Netherlands	58
19	Poland	55
20	Lithuania	48
21	Bulgaria	44
22	Ukraine	35
23	Ireland	34
24	Belarus	28
25	Serbia	23
26	Romania	21
27	Estonia	13
28	Macedonia	13
29	Latvia	8
30	Bosnia-Herzegovina	5
31	Kosovo	5
32	Montenegro	3
33	Liechtenstein	2
34	Norway	2
35	Sweden	2

U.S. National Geospatial-Intelligence Agency / Polish Infographic

Figure 14.9. Number of "Saint" city names in Europe, ranked by country.

I have not been able to find a definitive count of the number of cities and countries named after Christ and his followers. But I did find one astonishing statistic that represents a fraction of the total. Figure 14.9 provides a list of the number of cities—only within

Europe—that begin with "Saint" and are named in honor of a representative of Jesus. By one researcher's count, just this category alone contains 20,864 cities.[11]

Remember that this is only in Europe, and these are only the cities that begin with the word "Saint." Cities such as Christchurch are not included in this list. The thousands of additional "Saint" cities in South America, North America, and beyond are also not included in this list. Taking this into consideration, it may be possible that there are as many as thirty thousand or forty thousand cities named in honor of Jesus around the world today.

I found more than one hundred such Christ-themed city names within the United States.[12] Thousands more exist in Asia, Australia, Africa, and South America. They are found on every populated continent.

Here again Jesus of Nazareth has no comparison, no peers, in his measurable global influence.

What is the documented amount of real estate and buildings dedicated to this person?

We have talked about cities, and we discovered that literally tens of thousands of cities have been dedicated to Christ. Now let's talk about real estate.

Perhaps at your college or high school, a science lab or a lecture hall is named after a wealthy donor. As we learned in our study of universities, Harvard is named after a Christian pastor named John Harvard, who donated his library of Christian books and Bibles to the school. Johns Hopkins University is similarly named after its Christian founder and financier.

How cool would it be to someday have a building or even a few buildings named after you?

Put your name in the blank below:

The _____ Research Center

Real estate—or buildings—is another physical and tangible way that we can calculate how much influence a person has had on the world.

Today some sphinxes and pyramids in Egypt are still standing. They still proclaim the influence of Egyptian pharaohs who are long dead.

To have one piece of real estate dedicated to a person is significant. Even among famous people, most have fewer than three structures named after them.[13] If you start to count up above fifty or five hundred structures, the company gets pretty sparse.

In my research, one of the people with the most structures named after him is Andrew Carnegie. In the early 1900s, Carnegie built more than two thousand libraries around the world, and most of them still bear his name, as does the famous Carnegie Hall in New York City. That is a great deal of influence.

Here is what is interesting about Jesus. In many parts of the world, it is impossible to drive more than a few miles without seeing a building dedicated to Jesus, also known as a church. Next time you drive through a populated area, count the number of churches.

I remember living in San Jose, California. Today it ranks among the least Christian cities in the United States. Yet even in the least Christian part of the United States, I could not drive for more than about four minutes without seeing a church building. Some were big. Some were small. But they seemed even more prevalent than Starbucks.

When I began to zoom out and study this globally, I learned that when we talk about Jesus, we are not simply talking about a person with billions of followers. We are talking about a person with millions of monuments and buildings built in his honor and more buildings continuing to be built in his honor two thousand years after his life. This is significant.

We can travel to distant countries and island nations and still find churches there. Even when there is not a Starbucks or a McDonald's, we will often find churches and monuments built to honor Jesus. Compare the numbers in the following table.

Starbucks versus McDonald's versus Allah versus Jesus

Building	Person Dedicated To	Number in United States	Number in World
Starbucks	none	13,000	27,000[14]
McDonald's	Ray Krock	14,146	37,000[15]
Mosque	Allah	2,106	3.6 million[16]
Church	Jesus	320,000	37 million[17]

Mammoth, historic, stone Christian cathedrals (such as those in figs. 14.10 and 14.11) exist in more than 120 countries, and many of these countries have more than one hundred of this type of church.[18] Within Christianity, cathedrals represent just a small percentage of actual church buildings, with many church buildings being much smaller and humbler.

Figure 14.10. St. Peter's Basilica, Rome.

Figure 14.11. Cologne Cathedral, Germany.

A Logical Conclusion

There are many other measurements we could add to this list. We could create more questions to gauge Jesus's influence on humanity. But in the end, the Primary Evidence about Jesus's impact on humanity is clear, convincing—and different from my initial hunch. What became clear to me in my research was not only that Jesus lived but also that he is without a doubt the most influential human ever to live, period.

It could be said—not tongue in cheek—that the influence of this one man is nearly Godlike.

So I was left with the question: *If Jesus's impact on world history is nearly Godlike, what does this mean as I weigh his radical claim to be God?*

fifteen

The Surprising Influence of Jesus

I am the light of the world. If you
follow me, you won't have to walk
in darkness, because you will have
the light that leads to life.

Jesus, as quoted in the historically
verified Gospel of John[1]

We have seen evidence that Jesus
is among the most influential
people in history, if not *the*
most influential.

As I grasped the one-of-a-kind impact
that Jesus has had on human history, I
came across historians who have reached
the same conclusion.

Historian H. G. Wells was not a Christian. He is often quoted as saying, "I'm a historian. I'm not a believer. But I must confess as a historian, this penniless preacher from Nazareth is irrevocably the very center of history." Then he added, "Jesus Christ is easily the most dominant figure in all of history."[2]

Jaroslav Pelikan, a historian from Yale, once summarized Jesus's impact this way: "Regardless of what anyone may personally think or believe about him, Jesus of Nazareth has been the dominant figure in the history of Western culture for almost twenty centuries."[3] He added, "If it were possible, with some sort of super magnet, to pull up out of that history every scrap of metal bearing at least a trace of his [Jesus's] name, how much would be left?"[4]

That is a fascinating quotation from an expert who was the Sterling Professor of History Emeritus at Yale University and who authored more than thirty books.[5]

As he studied history, Pelikan became so amazed at Jesus's influence that he began to consider Jesus's claim to be God. In time, Pelikan became convinced that Jesus's outsized influence was the result of his being more than human.

To separate our thinking from church and religion, the idea of Jesus being God is similar to our concept of Superman and other superheroes—a godlike figure who comes into our world to rescue us from evil. As Pelikan studied the life of Jesus, he became convinced that Jesus is such a superhero—the God who created our world and returned to it to rescue us from evil.

Pelikan was not the only brilliant expert on the ancient world to become a believer in Jesus as God based on the evidence. In the early 1900s, British author and medieval professor C. S. Lewis was a living legend at both Cambridge and Oxford Universities. Lewis's fellow professors and his students recognized that he possessed a once-in-a-generation intellect. An expert in ancient literature and original languages, Lewis was an atheist when he began his study of Jesus.

Then as Lewis read the historical accounts of Jesus's life, he concluded—as an expert in ancient literature—that the accounts of Jesus were not mythical. They were historically valid writings.

Once Lewis became convinced that Jesus was an actual historic figure, he then began reading Jesus's words. In Jesus's teachings, Lewis found something that was otherworldly and on a different level than anything else he had encountered in his expansive studies of ancient literature—and modern.

By his own account, Lewis found not only that the words of Jesus were historically valid but also that they seemed to speak to the realities and tensions of the universe as well as the struggles in his own inner person. At one point in his intellectual journey, Lewis reached the conclusion that Jesus was either a liar (because he claimed to be God) or a lunatic (because he claimed to be God) or actually the Lord of the universe (as he claimed). Responding to the common argument that Jesus was merely a good moral teacher (but not God), Lewis wrote:

> That is the one thing we must not say. A man who was merely a man and said the sort of things Jesus said would not be a great moral teacher. He would either be a lunatic—on the level with the man who says he is a poached egg—or else he would be the Devil of Hell. . . . You must make your choice. Either this man was, and is, the Son of God, or else a madman or something worse. You can shut him up for a fool, you can spit at him and kill him as a demon or you can fall at his feet and call him Lord and God, but let us not come with any patronising nonsense about his being [merely] a great human teacher. He has not left that open to us. He did not intend to.[6]

Lewis ultimately answered this question for his own life, deciding that Jesus was indeed the Son of God. Like the early Christians who were killed for that belief, and like the billions of people since, Lewis began to experience internal peace, hope, and joy that he had never before experienced. He became convinced of Jesus's reality as a spiritual being and sought Jesus's help for both this life and the next.

Lewis's book *Mere Christianity* remains a global bestseller and timeless proof that many highly intelligent individuals have read Jesus's words and as a result have come to believe in Jesus as God and Lord. This continues to happen in every generation.

We saw one example in the world-renowned scientist Francis S. Collins (see the profile at the end of chap. 4), who recently became a believer in Jesus as a result of studying human DNA. Like Collins, like Lewis at Oxford, and like Pelikan at Yale, you and I must each decide for ourselves what we will make of Jesus. Will we conclude that he was a liar or that he was a lunatic? Or will we conclude that he is the Lord of the universe as he claimed?

Your answer to this question—*What will you make of Jesus?*—may be the most important decision you make in your life.

If Jesus was wrong and there is no heaven and hell, then there is no risk in believing in him as the Creator during your short life. But if Jesus is correct about being God, if he is correct in his claim to be the only way into a better dimension, an eternal life, well, the implications for you and me are eternal.

sixteen

What Does Jesus's Influence Mean for Me?

> Come to me, all you who are weary and burdened, and I will give you rest. Take my yoke upon you and learn from me, for I am gentle and humble in heart, and you will find rest for your souls.
>
> Jesus, as quoted in the historically verified Gospel of Matthew[1]

I had to see this one with my own eyes. A Grammy-winning rock star was quitting his band, walking away from millions of dollars, and claiming that faith in Jesus had cured him of a ten-year drug addiction to meth. As a reporter, I was skeptical.

I wanted to meet this "born-again" man for myself. I wanted to learn why he was *really* walking away from the fame and fortune. I wanted to dig into his life to learn what was actually fueling his dramatic public claims.

Could belief in Jesus actually cure a ten-year drug addiction? Having seen meth and heroin addictions firsthand in my work as a reporter, the skeptic in me doubted it.

Could Jesus's words give fulfillment to a man who had tasted every pleasure in this life—and was still suicidal?

So I pitched the story to my newspaper editor. I would profile this rock-star-turned-Jesus-follower, and I would get to the bottom of his dramatic claims of new life.

My editor approved the story, and I reached out to the publicist of Brian Welch, who had recently quit the band Korn—a death metal band known for suicidal lyrics and slasher songs. I scheduled to spend a number of days with Welch, then I would spend additional weeks researching his background and interviewing his family, friends, and ex-wife. I aimed to find the truth beneath these hysterical religious claims.

As a journalist, I had met some unique people—NFL athletes, celebrities, lawmakers, lawbreakers, millionaires, billionaires, cosmetic surgeons, and homeless heroin addicts. But I had never heard of or met someone with such a radical Jesus story as Brian Welch.

When Welch walked away from his fame and fortune as a rock star, his music videos were still playing on MTV. He left a band known for its dark lyrics and traveled to the Jordan River to be baptized in the waters where Jesus had been baptized. TV cameras from CNN and MTV followed Welch to the Jordan River. As a skeptical journalist, I suspected this was all a publicity stunt. I kept waiting for the reveal.

After two months investigating Welch's life, and after days interacting with him and his daughter in their home, in his recording studio, at his favorite restaurants, and even in his car, I concluded that this man's life transformation was genuine.

Faith in Jesus, Welch said, had transformed him. During our interviews, Welch described a time—before he trusted in Jesus—when he and his wife were both high on meth and he punched her in the face. With her blood on his knuckles, he passed out, leaving their toddler alone on a pool chair next to an open pool, where she could have drowned. That is one small glimpse into the broken life of drugs and insanity that Welch had lived.

In his own words, Welch's transformation began on an Easter weekend. He was, at that time, suicidal and addicted to meth. He was globally famous and worth millions of dollars. He had been featured on a *South Park* TV episode, had won a Grammy, owned millions of dollars' worth of property in California, and had had his face splashed across MTV. But he spent most of his time locked in the back of his personal tour bus, doing drugs and trying to escape from reality. He had tried every earthly pleasure, and he was completely unfulfilled.

That is when he walked into an Easter church service and heard these simple words from Jesus: "Come to me, all you who are weary and burdened, and I will give you rest."

Welch heard a preacher explain that faith is needed to believe that Jesus can actually forgive our mistakes, free us from shame, and lift the heavy burdens we feel in our emotions, spirits, and souls. Welch chose to believe this. And that is when his transformation began.

It has now been several years since I interviewed Brian Welch, and he remains a changed man—free from his drug addiction and a devoted father to his daughter.

Welch's story is unique because of the fame and money involved. But the dramatic change and lifelong hope he found in

Jesus are not so unique. Welch is just one of the millions of people who claim to find peace, forgiveness, and new life in Jesus every year.

One Example among Millions

On our journey, we have seen that Jesus's followers have played an undeniable role in five of humanity's biggest leaps forward. We have also seen from Primary Evidence that Jesus clearly lived. We have seen that Jesus made the crazy claim of being God, and we have seen that his impact on the world has been Godlike, far eclipsing that of other influential people in history.

Now, in this chapter, we will examine why Jesus's fame continues growing and expanding. One reason is that stories of transformation, like Brian Welch's, continue to be told every day.

Whether we believe in the supernatural realm or not, these stories of transformation continue happening, and they are very real for the people who experience them—from rock stars such as Alice Cooper and Brian Welch (who each experienced a radical life transformation after believing in Jesus) to schoolteachers, accountants, plumbers, and natives in undeveloped jungles. Millions of new people claim to experience radical peace and life transformation through Jesus every year. These people and their experiences are a form of Primary Evidence.

We cannot scientifically document exactly *why* the lives of these believers in Jesus changed. But when I asked people who experienced radical change what happened, they reported that they encountered the supernatural power of Jesus, whom they fully believe to be Creator God. That was their conclusion. Whether we agree with them or not, we cannot deny the evidence that millions of people claim this transformation every year.

For lack of a better term, I will refer to this living, breathing Primary Evidence as "a parade of changed lives."

In my investigation of Christianity throughout history, I discovered individuals in every era who were dramatically changed after they believed in Jesus. We met some of these people through their writings, people such as Frederick Douglass, William Wilberforce, Blaise Pascal, Martin Luther King Jr., Harriet Tubman, Florence Nightingale, Francis Collins, and many others. Brian Welch, a transformed rock star who is now free from addiction and filled with hope, is just one more person in this parade of changed lives—a parade that continues marching along through every century, in every significant culture, and on every populated continent. This parade of changed lives traces back two thousand years, all the way to the time when Jesus lived and spoke the words that continue changing human history.

What is most remarkable about this parade, what defies explanation at the merely human level, is that it continues growing two thousand years after Jesus was born. Every day a new generation of Brian Welches, William Wilberforces, and Frederick Douglasses believes in Jesus as God and experiences the same transformation and motivation to help others in self-sacrificing ways that make the world a better place to live.

If this parade stopped for just one generation, then Jesus's following would decrease, decline, and cease to exist—just as has been the case for every other historical figure. But somehow Jesus's parade continues growing larger and larger, louder and louder.

The Radical Claims of Jesus

By their own account, Christians say that the words of Jesus were paramount in their transformation. The power is in Jesus's ideas and claims. According to these believers, when they *believed* the words of Jesus, when they considered Jesus as God offering to help them, something transformative happened within them.

Let's consider two of Jesus's radical claims. Both are predictions that we can measure as true or false, and both are predictions that would be impossible for any normal person to achieve on the scale of billions of people and across thousands of years.

Unbelievable Claim #1: Jesus predicted that he would become known "to the ends of the earth."

Specifically, Jesus said this to his followers: "But you will receive power when the Holy Spirit comes upon you. And you will be my witnesses, telling people about me everywhere—in Jerusalem, throughout Judea, in Samaria, and to the ends of the earth."[2]

This was not figurative language, as Jesus cited specific geography. This is a measurable prediction, and we can trace it back through ancient documents to the era of Jesus. It was not made up after the fact.

When Jesus made this prediction, he had fewer than five hundred followers. Those followers had no land, no army, and no political power, and they were geographically limited to one city.

The idea that Jesus's followers would spread to the ends of the earth was an impossible prediction at the time, given the tiny footprint and resources of Christianity. Also, at that time, no movement in world history had ever spread to the ends of the earth. The prediction looked even more impossible because two ancient civilizations were arresting and killing Christians.

This is an interesting prediction for another reason too. According to accounts of Jesus's life, he was a gentle person who embraced social outcasts and who had women followers at a time when other leaders did not. This was a man who touched "untouchable" lepers and who welcomed children. Jesus was not a ruler and never had an army. This matters because nearly all other powerful people in history spread their messages using armies or governments. Jesus instead said that his disciples would be empowered by the Holy Spirit and would spread word of him around the globe.

Jesus's outrageous claim is documented in history. It involves real geography that existed two thousand years ago and can be measured today. Jerusalem is still there today. We know precisely where Judea is. We know where Samaria is.

As a researcher, this matters to me. Jesus did not make a vague pie-in-the-sky, fortune-cookie, horoscope prediction. He made a specific, measurable prediction that his followers would spread to Judea, then to Samaria, and then to the ends of the earth.

As investigators, we can measure this claim. We can look at a map to see where Christians are in the world today, and we can conclude whether or not that prediction from Jesus came true.

Today an organization called the Pew Research Center spends millions of dollars per year measuring the global spread of world religions. According to Pew Research findings, Christianity has indeed spread to the ends of the earth, around the entire globe (see fig. 16.1).[3] And a detailed examination of history reveals the pathway through which Christianity spread. It started in Jerusalem, then spread to a region known as Judea, then to Samaria, and then throughout the last two thousand years to the ends of the earth. The spread of Christianity throughout the world is not controversial. Historians and researchers like the Pew Research Center have documented it. The prevalence of Christianity is also obvious to anyone who travels the world. There are churches in every major society, and global Christian impact is well documented both in history and in our present reality. The outcome is also physically verifiable in the 2.3 billion living, breathing Christians who are spread around the globe today.

So here's the thing. Whether we believe that Jesus is God or not, his outrageous prediction has come true. Impossible as it was, Jesus's followers have spread his name to the ends of the earth.

Jesus's movement is Godlike in its massive size and historic influence. It is unrivaled. And it turns out that Jesus's movement is also unique in that its growth was predicted—not only in size but also in geography, time, and trajectory.

% of population Christian

90–100
80–90
65–80
50–65
30–50
15–30
7–15
1–7

Figure 16.1. Pew Research map of Christianity worldwide.

Unbelievable Claim #2: Jesus predicted that he would give rest to restless souls who seek him.

This is what Jesus predicted for people who seek him as God: "Come to me, all you who are weary and burdened, and I will give you rest. Take my yoke upon you and learn from me, for I am gentle and humble in heart, and you will find rest for your souls. For my yoke is easy and my burden is light."[4]

At first glance, this prediction may appear less empirical, less measurable. But people and their experiences can be measured. We can interview people who have "come to Jesus" and ask if they have found his claim to be true.

This claim sounds insane. Any lunatic can *claim* to give peace to people's souls, but who can actually *do* this—and do it consistently for millions of people? And do it in such a manner that the people are so convinced of this "rest for their souls" that they then go and convince others to also believe?

Jesus said, more or less, "You have an inner spiritual part that no one else knows about, and that part of you is restless, so come to me and I will give peace to that part of you. As your Creator, I am the only one who can give this rest to your internal self, your eternal self."

It sounds crazy. It sounds unbelievable. Yet every year millions of new people claim to experience this peace and rest as a result of believing in Jesus.

Having witnessed dozens of transformations like Brian Welch's and having seen the mountain of evidence in this book, I found myself wondering, *If Jesus was right about his claim that his movement would reach the ends of the earth, then what if he was also right about his claim to provide peace and rest to his believers?*

What is it that we need peace and rest from? Jesus taught that we all carry shame, guilt, pain, and regret around with us. We carry these broken parts of our past like backpacks full of rocks. We have painful memories, broken identities, regrets, and failures.

Jesus explained that all this brokenness results from a rupture in the foundation of the universe—that all humanity has been ripped away from the Creator by a force of evil. That evil is a thing we both inherit and perpetrate. Essentially, Jesus taught that our souls are worn out from being separated from their Creator, who is the life source.

Jesus's radical claim is that when humanity was broken in this way, the Creator chose to step into humanity to repair the rupture. Jesus claimed to be this God, walking in a fully human body. He claimed to be on earth on a mission that culminated at the cross, where he died for the sins of all people. The end goal was to create a door that anyone can walk through to be reconnected to their Creator. Jesus described himself as this door, and he described faith as the footsteps that walk a person through it.

This is the significance of one of the most famous quotations in all of world history, taken from the Gospel of John: "For God so loved the world [humanity] that he gave his one and only Son [Jesus], that whoever believes in him shall not perish but have eternal life."[5]

Jesus claimed to see through our facades, our reputations, and our job titles. He claimed to look right into our souls, and he said, more or less, "You have an inner part, and nobody else knows it, but I know your inner part is weary. I can give it rest." What an incredible claim.

From Rock Stars to Auto Mechanics

I have witnessed this rest and transformation in the lives of many people. I would like to tell you the story of another man who is not famous but who is as real as people can be. This man, who has never been on TV or won a Grammy, represents the kind of experience that is happening every day as people around the world believe in Jesus.

This man is named Bruce. Bruce stands about six feet, five inches tall. He is a big, towering hulk of a guy. Sadly, when he was a boy, Bruce was sexually molested by his older brother. Bruce grew up carrying the shame, guilt, and brokenness that resulted from being sexually abused at a young age. He was weary and burdened.

As Bruce went through life, he became an alcoholic. He didn't know it at the time, but looking back, he used alcohol as a way to escape from the shame and pain of what had happened to him. That trauma had marred the deepest parts of his identity and dignity.

As Bruce's issues with alcoholism grew, he became an angry, bar-brawling hulk of a person. He ran an auto repair shop in a little town in Montana, and he drove around during the snowy and icy winters in his pickup truck, sliding from bar to bar. Everywhere Bruce went, people knew to stay away from him. Violent, powerful, and abusive, he was not a person you wanted to cross.

Then one day Bruce gave Jesus's claims a try. Like Brian Welch, Bruce decided—having tried everything else—that he would take Jesus up on the same simple promise: "Come to me, all you who are weary and burdened, and I will give you rest."

I have seen Bruce radically transformed with my own eyes.

He is no longer an alcoholic.

His disposition has transformed.

His habits have changed.

His thoughts and deeds have changed.

If you don't believe me, you can ask Bruce's wife or kids.

Bruce is the most convincing Primary Evidence I have encountered—revealing that these words of Jesus do bring about measurable life change for people who believe, as Bruce did. A man who was once feared by an entire town is now a mentor and a tender grandfather-like figure to dozens of people who feel safe and comforted in his presence. Bruce is now among the most loving, gentle people I have ever met. I can take my kids over to his house, and they can play there in safety.

By all human measures, Bruce is a different person. Ask the people who were closest to the old Bruce, and they will all tell you that the difference in the new Bruce has come as a result of his belief in Jesus and his attempts to follow and live out the words of Jesus. Although Bruce's faith enters into the immeasurable and the spiritual, the outcomes and life change are measurable to even a nonreligious observer.

Every weekend around the world, people like Bruce gather in buildings called churches. At their purest and simplest, these gatherings are simple social movements of people who have experienced what Bruce experienced.

Yes, it is true that many churches have been corrupted by evil or by selfish people who no longer represent what Jesus taught. But there are still many pure movements of Jesus's followers.

When you see a church building or hear about a church that is out helping people, you will probably find some people like Bruce there. The parade of changed lives continues growing.

Experiences like Bruce's have been happening for two thousand years now. And so far, the movement of Jesus's followers has not been stopped by the failure of its imperfect people. Nor has the movement been stopped by tanks or swords or dictators. When the Soviet Union outlawed Christianity, Christians kept meeting, even when many were killed or sentenced to freeze in the icy Gulag camps. The movement still kept growing.

When Nero and other ancient Roman emperors began feeding Christians to the lions in coliseums and when Nero lit them on fire to illuminate his garden parties at night, the movement kept growing.

When members of opposing religions used swords to slaughter villages of Jesus's followers and to kill the devout who lived in mountain monasteries, the movement still continued to advance around the world.

The crescendo of Jesus's influence hasn't been stopped by fashion trends or language barriers. It hasn't been stopped by continental divides, cultural divides, or the implosion of civilizations.

Ever since Jesus lived and claimed to be God, his movement has been growing, and no power on earth or in hell has been able to silence, stifle, or stop it. To me, that is notable.

What does all of this mean?

The radical transformation of a drug-addicted rock star. The radical transformation of an alcoholic auto mechanic. The parade of transformed lives, stretching back two thousand years and defying all odds. We cannot deny the reality of these stories.

But as a researcher, I had to ask, *Is there any way to empirically measure if this faith in Jesus is actually what produces the life change these people are experiencing?*

seventeen

Empirically Measuring Jesus's Claims

I believe; help my unbelief!

father of a sick child,
begging Jesus for a miracle[1]

I was twenty-one years old when I graduated with my bachelor's degree in journalism. I started writing for a small Arizona newspaper. About four months in, my editor gave me an unusual assignment.

"John, I want you to write an in-depth report on skydiving in Arizona. I want it to include the number of people who die per year, how much it costs, what people's odds of dying are if they skydive, who these people are who go skydiving, and what motivates them."

I replied that the story sounded fun and I'd be happy to do it.

"One more thing, John," he replied. "To do this story right, you'll need to go skydiving yourself. That way you can describe the experience."

At the time, I was willing to do anything to advance my career, and so I agreed. My editor sent me out with a little joke. "Just be careful out there, John. You know the ones who die actually bounce off the ground at impact."

Very funny, Mr. Editor, I thought as I returned to my office.

My editor was teaching me one of the truths of serious reporting. For some investigations, the only way to discover the whole truth is to experience it.

I certainly experienced that during my skydiving adventure—when my parachute failed to open during our first jump. Thankfully, the backup chute *did* open. But it opened late, and the instructor and I hit the ground hard and about a mile away from where we were supposed to land.

When I called my editor to describe the crash landing, he sounded genuinely worried. Then he told me to go back up so I could describe the difference between a jump that goes right and a jump that goes wrong. (Talk about messing with the newbie reporter, though that editor remains a good friend to this day.)

The second jump went as planned. The main parachute opened as designed, and the experience really was a lot of fun. My editor was right that some things have to be experienced to be understood.

This was further validated when I got into more serious stories. Every year dozens of immigrants die from dehydration in the Arizona desert as they illegally cross the border. To understand these deaths and fully explain the truth of the situation, I spent two days walking the same border trails with Border Patrol agents and a humanitarian group who provides water to dying immigrants. I also flew over the border in the airplane of a vigilante who volunteers to patrol the border for the US government.

I felt the dirt, the heat, and the expanse of the open desert for myself. I saw the trails of trash and clothes. I watched groups move across the border on foot. Back on the ground, I saw the exact places where dead bodies had been found. I learned the tragic stories of immigrants who were abused by "coyote" traffickers simply because nobody else was around to stop it from happening.

I could have read about these things, sure. But there is a big difference between reading and seeing. There is an even bigger difference between seeing and experiencing. Knowledge can only take an investigation so far.

This became true in my investigation of Jesus and his movement. At a time when I didn't yet believe in God, I began praying a simple prayer like this: "God, if you're there, I want to know you. Jesus, if you are God, then I want to know you and be friends with you. If you're there, help me believe."

It was a skeptic's prayer really, but it was honest.

The only way for you or me to actually measure Jesus's claim to offer peace is to take him up on the offer, crazy as it may seem. If we go to him with our burdens and our needs, then we can experience for ourselves whether these radical transformations are mere fiction or if they are something more.

My thinking went something like this: *If all of this is made up, I risk nothing by praying to the ceiling. But if some of this is real, then I risk too much to turn away just because I have a skeptical personality.*

As we have seen on our journey, to consider Jesus as God does not mean that you are weak-minded or dumb. Some of the smartest people in history—thinkers such as Isaac Newton, who gave us Newtonian physics, intellectual giants such as C. S. Lewis, and people such as Francis Collins, who is one of the leading scientists in the world today—have believed that Jesus is God and that he died on the cross to rescue all people.

Should you choose to believe that Jesus is God, you will be joining the ranks of Martin Luther King Jr., Abraham Lincoln, John Harvard, Johns Hopkins, Harriet Tubman, and the dozens of other world-changers documented in this book. It is not bad company.

Of course, you have to decide for yourself.

Jesus taught that all humans have an internal "will." Only you can choose what you believe. No person can force you. Based on ten years of research, and now based on the peace and joy I experience because of my faith in Jesus, my advice is this: choose wisely.

In my case, with my skeptical nature, I did not start with a lot of faith. But I took Jesus up on a story from his life. There was a time when a guy came to Jesus, asking for a miracle for his son. The man told Jesus, "I believe; help my unbelief!"[2] Jesus honored that prayer. The man had a tiny bit of faith, and Jesus met him there.

That is how my personal life journey has been. My investigation of Jesus slowly moved from merely intellectual to something spiritual. Something started changing when I prayed, "I believe. Help my unbelief." Something metaphysical began happening in my spirit and my soul—even as I offered awkward prayers. Some days I whispered those prayers with no faith, and other days I did so with wavering, weak, doubting faith.

Jesus once said that we don't need a lot of faith to believe in him. He likened the amount of faith we need to the tiniest seed his audience knew—a mustard seed. I have handled mustard seeds. They are about the size of the salt flecks that fall out of a salt shaker.

Jesus's point was that the amount of our faith is not what connects us to God. Instead, the object of our faith—Jesus—is the point.

If we are honest with ourselves, we all have some faith in something. Many of us—in our youth and with good health—place faith in our own ability to meet our needs. Or maybe we believe in someone we trust. Jesus talks about trusting others and about having healthy self-confidence. But Jesus teaches that our greatest needs can be met only by him as God.

What are those needs?

- a secure identity and sense of self-worth here in this life
- forgiveness for even our worst mistakes
- rest and freedom from our shame or regrets
- reconnection to our Creator
- freedom from addictions and negative behaviors
- the ability to give and receive genuine love consistently
- an internal peace that no people or circumstances can take away
- a community of spiritual siblings who will care for us unconditionally
- protection from negative, unseen forces
- access into God's dimension for eternal life, once this life ends

Jesus claims to give these things as free gifts when we choose to trust in him—even if it is only a mustard seed of faith that we bring.

What a rush of emotion I felt when I climbed out onto the wing of a flying airplane for that first skydiving story. To experience the truth about skydiving, I had to climb out of a perfectly good airplane, thousands of feet above the ground. It was windy on that airplane wing. It was crazy. And it was scary. And then, moment of truth, I had to let go of that wing and free-fall down toward earth.

I didn't have a ton of faith in my parachute when I let go of that wing, but I guess I had enough faith, because ultimately I did let go.

My journey with Jesus has been about the same (rough landings and all).

Yours doesn't have to be any fancier.

Conclusion

I will never forget that night. It was the worst food poisoning I have ever had. My wife and I had eaten a nice dinner at a fancy Chinese restaurant. I felt great until about 1 a.m. Then I spent the rest of the night throwing up. It was some of the most violent vomiting of my life.

Why do I tell you this?

Because most of us have had experiences with so-called Christians or Jesus followers that caused the same reaction as I had to that contaminated Chinese food. Sadly, history is freckled with evil people who falsely claimed to be Christians.

And not just history. If you are like me, you have met some angry, hateful people today who claim to be Christians. These hypocrites are full of hate and self-interest, even as they claim to follow the Jesus who said, "By this everyone will know you are my disciples, if you love one another."[1]

Jesus actually predicted that there would be imposter Christians in every generation. These imposters hide their evil behind a Christian title. They leverage Jesus's fame and reputation for their own benefit, but in their hearts, they don't genuinely believe—as their actions demonstrate. (Incidentally, Jesus said we can know true believers in him by their actions—if they model his way of grace and love while they share God's unchanging truth.)[2]

Why do I mention this?

Because one of the biggest obstacles to believing in Jesus can be the people who claim to be his followers. Maybe you can relate.

And that is why I told you my disgusting food poisoning story. Here is my point. After that night of throwing up, I have never again eaten at that particular Chinese restaurant. It is a national chain, and if I am anywhere in the country and someone suggests that restaurant, I politely decline.

But there is something else you should know. I have not stopped eating at all restaurants everywhere. That's right. I still eat at pizza parlors, burger joints, and lots of other restaurants. I avoid the restaurant chain that made me sick, but I have not boycotted eating altogether (thankfully). I have enjoyed hundreds of other restaurants since that night of terrible food poisoning.

The analogy I am making is this: If you know some people who claim to be Christians or Jesus followers but their lives are defined by hatred and self-interest, then feel free to avoid those people. But please don't let some phonies stand between you and the "Bread of Life."[3]

Yes, there are terrible people who claim to be Christians. Jesus predicted it would be this way until his return. Jesus also had words for these phony Christians; he said he spits them out of his mouth.[4]

Since the food-poisoning incident, I have found that many more restaurants serve good food than the small percent of restaurants that serve contaminated food. It is the same with sincere followers of Jesus. Today there are millions of sincere followers of Jesus who want to feed the poor, care for the outcasts, and improve humanity. Don't let a few bigots define Jesus for you. The stakes are too high and the food is too good to let that happen.

My relationship with Jesus as God has brought me consistent identity, security, purpose, fulfillment, peace, and joy that I never experienced anywhere else in this world. I am tasting and experiencing things I never tasted apart from Jesus.

My hope for you is that you experience the same.

As we have seen, believing that Jesus is God is not anti-intellectual. And, as we have seen, believing that Jesus is God has the potential to motivate you and strengthen you to live a life that benefits others (as well as yourself).

Whatever you choose to believe, know that I will respect you and will work for your best in this world. That is what sincere followers of Jesus do.

My only nudge is that you remain someone who genuinely pursues the truth and who remains open to unexpected findings. They are the most exciting kind of findings in my experience.

We have seen Primary Evidence about Jesus's life, global influence, and positive impact on humanity.

We have learned that we do not need faith to accept that Jesus lived.

We have learned that no faith is required to accept the fact that Jesus's movement is the biggest in history.

We also do not need faith to accept that specific followers of Jesus have made our world a better place, as demonstrated by the Primary Evidence we surveyed in part 2.

Where faith gets involved is in believing that this same Jesus is God, believing that he died on the cross and rose again in a mission to rescue all people. And that tiny mustard seed of faith is all you need to call out to Jesus for rescue wherever your life has gotten broken.

So if I now believe that Jesus is God, am I still a skeptic? In my case, yes, I am. I take the position that you can be a skeptic by nature—as I am—and still conclude that Jesus is God. Here's why. Genuine skeptics are after the truth. We skeptics are not people who refuse to believe anything. We just refuse to believe lies. We skeptics want to believe the truth—and reject what is false.

Skeptics are welcome in Jesus's movement—as Paul the Apostle demonstrated in the first century and as I demonstrate (much less gracefully) in our time.

Fellow skeptic, if you are still after the truth, I applaud you.

I have yet to find any evidence that disproves Jesus's claim to be God. On the other hand, I have found plenty of evidence suggesting that Jesus just might be God—or at least that Jesus is more likely to be God than any other expression of "God" I have found.

I want to encourage you to keep pursuing Jesus for yourself. For my life and family, I am so glad I didn't stop seeking him. Today Jesus's words and power have improved my life in every domain. My thoughts are healthier and more positive. My habits are healthier. My relationships are far more stable and deep and rewarding. I wake up every day with purpose and belonging.

And as crazy as this sounds, I have developed a genuine confidence that sickness, old age, and death will not be the end for my soul. Like Isaac Newton, Frederick Douglass, and Martin Luther King Jr., I am confident that my final breath on earth will be separated by a mere blink before I will awake in the presence of my Creator—all thanks to a real-life superhero who descended to earth and left a Godlike mark on the human story.

You can experience these same things if you desire and choose. Jesus once said, "I am the way and the truth and the life. No one comes to the Father [our idea of heaven] except through me."[5] That first skeptic, Paul the Apostle, put it this way:

> If you openly declare that Jesus is Lord and believe in your heart that God raised him from the dead, you will be saved. For it is by believing in your heart that you are made right with God, and it is by openly declaring your faith that you are saved. . . . Anyone who trusts in him will never be disgraced.[6]

You don't have to agree with the politics of so-called Christians to believe in Jesus in this way. Nor do you have to do things exactly like any church you have experienced. The freedom and the power are found in the words of Jesus, his person, his promises, and his pattern for life. The power is not in Christian denominations, buildings, or religious rituals. Those things come and go, but the movement of Jesus across humankind and across history continues advancing.

Jesus was a revolutionary. His teachings still bring peace, joy, fulfillment, purpose, and passion to those who believe.

I invite you to continue seeking. Here are three specific ways:

- Get information and updates about my upcoming book by sending a blank email to Friend@IAmStrong.com.
- Connect with me on any social media platform: @JohnSDickerson
- Explore videos and sharable evidence at JesusSkeptic.com.

I am honored that you took the time to read about my journey, and I would be delighted to keep in touch with you on your journey. As you seek your own answers to the universal questions of who we are, why we exist, and where we belong, I want to encourage you. No matter what you have been through in life, there is a Creator who loves you. He is reaching out to you today in the person of Jesus.

My own turning point came as I read Jesus's words for myself. You can read his words at JesusSkeptic.com/JohnsGospel.

Lastly, even if there has been food poisoning in your life, my hope for you is that you don't stop eating. Don't stop seeking and don't stop believing.

Appendix A

For Further Reading

To explore hundreds of additional pieces of evidence and find images and videos to share on social media, visit JesusSkeptic.com.

To receive new evidence of Jesus's impact and significance every week:

Email: Curious@JesusSkeptic.com

Follow: @JesusSkeptic on Instagram, Twitter, Facebook, Snapchat, and YouTube.

To explore if faith in Jesus is anti-intellectual, see:

Lewis, C. S. *Mere Christianity*. Rev. ed. New York: HarperCollins, 2009.

To explore another journalist's investigation into Jesus, see:

Strobel, Lee. *The Case for Christ: A Journalist's Personal Investigation of the Evidence for Jesus*. Grand Rapids: Zondervan, 2016.

To explore Christianity compared to other major worldviews, see:

Murray, Abdu. *Grand Central Question: Answering the Critical Concerns of the Major Worldviews*. Downers Grove, IL: InterVarsity, 2014.

To explore more evidence about the ancient Jesus and the Bible, see:

McDowell, Josh. *The New Evidence That Demands a Verdict*. Nashville: Thomas Nelson, 1999.

To explore more about God and science, see:

Collins, Francis S. *The Language of God: A Scientist Presents Evidence for Belief*. New York: Free Press, 2006.

Lennox, John C. *God's Undertaker: Has Science Buried God?* Oxford, UK: Lion Books, 2009.

To explore additional journalistic research, see:

Strobel, Lee. *The Case for a Creator: A Journalist Investigates Scientific Evidence That Points Toward God*. Grand Rapids: Zondervan, 2004.

————. *The Case for Faith*. Grand Rapids: Zondervan, 2006.

————. *The Case for the Real Jesus*. Grand Rapids: Zondervan, 2007.

To explore a homicide detective's investigation of Jesus, see:

Wallace, Warner. *Cold Case Christianity: A Homicide Detective Investigates the Claims of the Gospels*. Colorado Springs: David C. Cook, 2013.

To explore the existence of God, see:

McDowell, Sean. *Is God Just a Human Invention?* Grand Rapids: Kregel, 2010.

To explore the social ends of atheism versus Christianity, see:

Geisler, Norman L., and Frank Turek. *I Don't Have Enough Faith to Be an Atheist*. Wheaton: Crossway, 2004.

Zacharias, Ravi. *The Real Face of Atheism*. Grand Rapids: Baker Books, 2004.

To explore reason and Christianity, see:

Moreland, J. P. *Love God with All Your Mind: The Role of Reason in the Life of the Soul*. Colorado Springs: NavPress, 2012.

To explore more about the historical Jesus, see:

Habermas, Gary R. *The Historical Jesus: Ancient Evidence for the Life of Christ*. Joplin, MO: College Press, 1996.

Van Voorst, Robert E. *Jesus Outside the New Testament: An Introduction to the Evidence*. Grand Rapids: Eerdmans, 2000.

To explore the intellectual rigor of Christianity, see:

Craig, William Lane. *Reasonable Faith: Christian Truth and Apologetics*. Wheaton: Crossway, 2008.

To compare the second largest religion in the world, Islam, with Christianity, see:

Qureshi, Nabeel. *Seeking Allah, Finding Jesus: A Devout Muslim Encounters Christianity*. Grand Rapids: Zondervan, 2018.

Appendix B

Baselining in Investigations

An Example of Baselining

In chapter 1, I described the jailhouse beating and subsequent death of Juan Farias. After I wrote Farias's story, I began a broader series of newspaper investigations into the horrific and deadly conditions in that specific Arizona jail system.[1]

As my newspaper stories were published, phone messages and emails flooded in. Dozens of people provided additional accounts, claiming that their relatives, friends, or clients had also been abused or killed in this jail. (By the way, "jail" is where you sit while you await your courtroom trial if you are accused of a crime. Under US law, an accused person is innocent until proven guilty. Most of these people died before they ever had their day in court to be found innocent or guilty of their charges.)

Soon I had documented more than fourteen inmates who had died in this jail under circumstances of abuse or neglect. I also found that thousands of people were suing this jail every year, claiming that they had also been beaten by guards or denied basic medications such as insulin, among other things.

So was this jail (the Maricopa County Jail in Phoenix, Arizona) worse than other jails? Was an inmate in this jail more likely to die than an inmate in another jail of similar size in a different part of the country?

As a serious journalist, I could not jump to the conclusion that these tragic deaths proved this jail was worse than others in America. To discover that truth—to know if there was a pattern of abuse and deadly neglect in this jail—I needed to answer an important question: *Compared to other jails of this size, did this jail have an average number of deaths and lawsuits per year, or did this jail see dramatically more deaths and lawsuits?*

To answer that question with Primary Evidence, I needed to establish a baseline so that I could objectively measure this jail by comparing it to other jails of similar size. In complex investigations, I often need to establish a baseline from which I can make sense of the information I uncover. I call this step in my reporting process "baselining."

In the case of this jail, I needed to establish a baseline number of deaths and lawsuits that are normal for a jail of this size. Then I could compare the baseline to this jail to see if it had more deaths and lawsuits.

Baselining allows me as a researcher to know if the instances I know of (jail deaths in this case) are isolated, tragic incidences, or if they may be part of a much larger pattern.

Here is how I determined the baseline for this investigation. Because this jail was one of the four largest in the nation, I began gathering statistics and reports from the other three largest jails in the United States. (If you are curious, the other three largest jails in the nation are in Chicago, Los Angeles, and Houston.)

Since all four jails were of similar size, I was able to use data from each to build my baseline. That baseline showed me the conditions, number of deaths, and number of lawsuits that were normal in the other three jails.

I spent about a month gathering information and building a small galaxy of statistics on all four of these large institutions.

To find and organize this information, I interviewed national experts, dug through court records, and studied statistics and inspections.

To create an accurate baseline, I needed to learn the following:

- how many inmates each jail had per year?
- how many inmates died per year in each?
- what the national standards and expectations were for a jail of that size?
- what national jail inspectors (there is such a thing) expected from a jail of this size, and which of the four jails were complying with national standards and expectations?
- how much money each jail spent per inmate per year?
- how many times per year each jail was sued for abuse or wrongful death?
- how much money each jail spent on legal costs for lawsuits?

Once I compiled this information (from multiple sources and for all four jails), I had a clear baseline. Such a baseline brought simplicity to the complicated investigation (complicated in the sense that there were thousands of jail inmates, hundreds of employees, and dozens of other factors).

Why did I need such a baseline? Very simple. The baseline enabled me to see how the jail I was investigating measured up compared to other jails of its same size.

What did I learn from the baseline information? I learned the following:

- The jail I was investigating was far more deadly than any of the others.
- The jail I was investigating was in violation of basic national standards that the other three were meeting.

- The jail I was investigating was getting sued thousands of times, while the other jails were getting sued only dozens or hundreds of times.

The baseline told me there was indeed a story that needed to be reported about this jail in Arizona. While none of these large jails were heaven on earth (they were jails after all), the baseline gave me a clear understanding that the jail in Arizona was far out of line with the national standards and averages. It had far more deaths and lawsuits.

By creating a fact-based baseline, I was able to determine that the tragic deaths I first reported on were not random or coincidental. Those deaths were indeed part of a pattern of abuse, neglect, and mismanagement that was costing dozens of human lives and hundreds of millions of dollars. I was able to conclude that the jail in Arizona was possibly the most deadly and poorly managed jail in the country. This gave my investigation serious weight and drew attention to the situation.

Baselining Christianity

In my jail investigation, the baseline allowed me to move from a few tragic stories to a much larger trend. As I began investigating Christianity, the stories of Christians improving the world began to pile up. But ten thousand stories of Christians doing good wasn't enough to prove that Christianity has been a global force for human good at a historic level. No, to determine that I needed to create a baseline just as I did in my news investigations.

The global influence of Christians such as Martin Luther King Jr., Abraham Lincoln, and Isaac Newton led me to consider whether there was a broader pattern of Christianity improving the world. I began to wonder, *Could these Christian innovators be part of a larger pattern at work—a pattern in which Christian beliefs inspire people to improve human health, freedom, rights, and education?*

Can a question like that be answered definitively? As an investigative reporter, I believe it can be.

So just like with my jail investigation, I set out to create a baseline. In the case of Christianity, baselining required me to answer the question, *What was life like for average people before Jesus influenced the world?*

To measure whether Christianity has been a force for good or for evil, I needed to create a baseline understanding of what the world was like before Christianity existed. Only then could I know if Christianity has improved the societies where it has been embraced.

Chapter 5 discusses the Primary Evidence I uncovered to baseline what human life was like before Jesus's birth and before his followers began spreading his ideas throughout the world. With a baseline understanding of human conditions before Christianity, I could begin to chart innovations such as modern medicine to see if they just "happened" to sprout up in Christian-saturated areas or if these innovations were part of a pattern of life improving where Christianity took root in a culture.

Appendix C

Anchor-Point Research Methodology

Our biggest challenge in measuring the impact of Jesus's movement is the movement's sprawling scope—not only in number of followers today but also in time. It has been two thousand years from the time of Jesus until now, and the global movement of Christianity today claims one out of three people on earth. That's a lot of ground to cover.

An Example of Anchor-Points

As a research journalist, I often investigated topics that seemed impossible to measure at first glance. I once investigated the monitoring of every medical doctor in Arizona. To measure such a massive subject, I began with specific "anchor-points" of study. Each anchor-point led me to information, patterns of data, and specific findings. When I gathered Primary Evidence around those anchor-points, larger patterns began to emerge, and my investigation inched into the territory of fact rather than opinion.

Here are three anchor-points I used to gain a factual understanding of the twenty thousand doctors in Arizona.

1. I investigated doctors who were drug or alcohol addicts. I was able to identify hundreds of known drug and alcohol

addicts who were still practicing medicine as doctors in Arizona, and then I identified specific patients who likely had died as a result of those doctors practicing while intoxicated or impaired.

This anchor-point began with a logical question: *How does Arizona monitor doctors who are known alcoholics or addicts?*

2. I investigated doctors who were banned from other states. I identified specific doctors who had been banned from practicing medicine in other states but were practicing legally in Arizona.

   This anchor-point began with a logical question: *How does Arizona handle doctors accused of harming or killing patients in other states?*

3. I investigated alternative medicine doctors. I found specific alternative medicine doctors whose treatments had led to suspicious deaths among their patients, yet those doctors were allowed to continue practicing medicine in Arizona.

   This anchor-point began with a logical question: *How does Arizona handle doctors who practice alternative medicine?*

By choosing three specific anchor-points, I was able to take a broad question about twenty thousand doctors and move toward some specific facts, stories, and conclusions. In the end, I did not know everything about every one of Arizona's twenty thousand doctors, but I had found a clear pattern of dangerous doctors being allowed to practice openly in the state.

The result of this investigation was a series of news stories, each filled with Primary Evidence and each of which gained the attention of state lawmakers and national news media leaders.

In a similar way, I did not need to know every detail of Christian history to begin discerning whether the movement has had a record of helping or harming humanity. But I did need to know the role that Christianity has played in key anchor-point advances of social progress.

Anchor-Points for Measuring Christianity's Impact

As with my news investigations, when I considered Jesus and his movement, I needed to identify anchor-points: areas of inquiry around which I could begin compiling Primary Evidence. I decided to choose nonreligious anchor-points—improvements that have clearly changed the world for the better, such as modern medicine, the harnessing of electricity, college education, and so forth. Regardless of religious belief, we can all agree that advances such as these have helped humanity worldwide.

In simple terms, my process went like this:

1. Identify five universal improvements that have benefited humanity in world-changing ways, regardless of religion.
2. Find Primary Evidence to reveal the specific people who initiated these advances.
3. Discover and read the direct writings of these world-changers to learn if Christianity was a nonfactor, a positive factor, or a negative factor in their work.
4. After completing this process for multiple advances, zoom out and look at the whole—to see the larger pattern (or mega-pattern).

Did Jesus's ideas or followers birth a number of these global human advances? Or were Jesus's ideas and followers a nonfactor? Was Christianity merely a bystander while humanity improved itself? Was Christianity a barrier to these advances?

Our modern society and rights are linked to and enmeshed with these advances. Each has fundamentally improved human

271

existence for billions of people. And each advance continues helping humanity and producing more improvements. Below I have listed the five human breakthroughs I set out to investigate on my journey to find out who Jesus is.

1. *The launch of the Scientific Revolution.* Without the Scientific Revolution, we would still be using candles for light and coal or wood to heat our homes. We would not have electric appliances, lights, phones, or medical technology such as pacemakers. The Scientific Revolution led to modern farming, which has eliminated the famines that haunted most of human existence. It also brought about the Industrial Revolution, the Information Age, and eventually even the internet.

   So my questions were: *Who were the specific people who started the Scientific Revolution, and did Jesus's followers or ideas play a key role in producing this human advance?*

   Primary Evidence to answer these questions appears in chapter 4.

2. *The birth of the modern university.* Without college education, we would not have engineers, doctors, lawmakers, and most of the human infrastructure that enables modern society. Things as basic as sewer sanitation for human waste and as complex as surgical tools and internet devices would not exist without the modern university. The modern university has produced graduates who launched the Scientific Revolution, invented modern appliances and medicines, pioneered Western democracy, created the concept of human rights as we inherited it, and so much more. The university as we know it began about one thousand years ago. While it has spread globally, we can trace today's universities back to specific origins, institutions, and motives.

So my questions were: *Who were the specific people who founded the modern university, and did Jesus's followers or ideas play a key role in producing this human advance?*

Primary Evidence to answer these questions appears in chapter 7.

3. *The founding of modern medicine and modern hospitals.* Not long ago, people died from basic infections that today are cured with simple antibiotics. The human life span has more than doubled since the time of Jesus. These gains in length of life and quality of life can be traced to specific advances in medical science, including the founding of the modern hospital.

So my questions were: *Who were the specific people who created modern medicine and modern hospitals, and did Jesus's followers or ideas play a key role in producing this human advance?*

Primary Evidence to answer these questions appears in chapter 8.

4. *The end of open slavery.* As I studied slavery, I was surprised to learn that slavery was a global norm long before the United States existed and that slavery was documented among most major world civilizations. One expert estimates that, in the history of the world, two out of five people have been slaves.

So my questions were: *Who were the specific people who ended open slavery, and did Jesus's followers or ideas play a key role in producing this human advance?*

Primary Evidence to answer these questions appears in chapters 9 and 10.

5. *The creation of social literacy.* The vast majority of people in human history never learned how to read.

Within the last four hundred years, that has changed. Wherever social literacy goes, it changes the population for the better. People who can read are able to write universal laws and claim their own rights. Social literacy produces more equal wealth distribution, racial equality, gender equality, individual ownership, and human rights.

So my questions were: *Who were the specific people who founded societies in which all people were taught to read, and did Jesus's followers or ideas play a key role in producing this human advance?*

Primary Evidence to answer these questions appears in chapter 11.

I investigated these specific human advances and allowed the Primary Evidence to speak for itself—leading me to a fact-based conclusion about Jesus's impact on social justice and human progress.

Primary Evidence, if honestly assembled, can lead us to a pattern. I allowed the facts to testify about the specific people who so dramatically improved human society and life. I discovered photos and quotations that revealed the motivation and the thinking that produced world-changing benefits.

The evidence was clear, convincing, and consistent, so the mega-pattern from all five of these advances together led me out of the realm of opinion and into the realm of fact regarding the role of Christianity in advancing social progress and improving humanity.

Acknowledgments

So many people have walked with me in the journey of my life and the journey of this book. A special thank you to David and Julie for the months, years ago, when you let a young freelance journalist live in your house. The same goes for you too, Paul and Stacy.

A special thanks to news editors who believed in a young reporter, specifically Steve Strickbine, Amy Silverman, and Rick Barrs. And to my writing coaches Deb Solomon and John McCandlish Philips, please forgive my passive verbs, clichés, and lazy syntax. Life has gotten busy.

Specific friends encouraged me to write this book. Thank you, Tom Steipp, Chi-Hua, Russ Pulliam, and Wes Yoder for pushing me to do so.

Every day I get to "work" with a team that brings purpose, fulfillment, and joy to my life. Thank you, Greg, Craig, Denise, Mike, Brooke, Dan, Neil, Aaron, and everyone on my staff. Each of you make "going to work" something I look forward to and enjoy.

This book benefited from the excellent editorial guidance provided by Robin Turici, Lois Stuck, and Brian Thomasson. Thank you, friends, for your professionalism and diligent work improving the manuscript.

Giles and Alison, you both know I couldn't have done this project without you. Thank you for being living, breathing answers to my prayers.

The most important team to thank is my home team: Melanie, Jack, Zoey, and Evie. You each know how much I cherish you.

Notes

Introduction

1. The Livingston Award for Young Journalists, year 2009.
2. Frederick Douglass, *The Life and Times of Frederick Douglass: From 1817–1882* (London: Christian Age Office, 1882), 63. Available at https://books.google.com/books?id=X8ILAAAAIAAJ.

Chapter 1 A Dead Body

1. John Dickerson, "Sheriff Joe Arpaio's Own Records Raise Serious Questions about Inmate Juan Mendoza Farias's Violet Death," *Phoenix New Times*, November 20, 2008, http://www.phoenixnewtimes.com/news/sheriff-joe-arpaios-own-records-raise-serious-questions-about-inmate-juan-mendoza-farias-violent-death-6432543.
2. Here are five stories that developed as I investigated the facts surrounding Juan Farias's death in the Maricopa County Jail:

- John Dickerson, "Was Juan Mendoza Farias Beaten to Death by Sheriff Joe Arpaio's Guards?" *Phoenix New Times*, September 11, 2008, http://www.phoenixnewtimes.com/news/was-juan-mendoza-farias-beaten-to-death-by-sheriff-joe-arpaios-guards-6393724.
- John Dickerson, "Mugshot Reveals Inmate in Joe Arpaio's Jail Had No Facial Bruises before His Death," *Phoenix New Times*, September 22, 2008, http://www.phoenixnewtimes.com/news/mugshot-reveals-inmate-in-joe-arpaios-jail-had-no-facial-bruises-before-his-death-6647091.
- John Dickerson, "Video Footage Finally Released from Joe Arpaio's Jail Stops Abruptly before the Suspicious Death of an Inmate at the Hands of Guards," *Phoenix New Times*, November 13, 2008, http://www.phoenixnewtimes.com/news/video-footage-finally-released-from-joe-arpaios-jail-stops-abruptly-before-the-suspicious-death-of-an-inmate-at-the-hands-of-guards-6636305.

- John Dickerson, "Sheriff Joe Arpaio's Own Records Raise Serious Questions about Inmate Juan Mendoza Farias's Violet Death," *Phoenix New Times*, November 20, 2008, http://www.phoenixnewtimes .com/news/sheriff-joe-arpaios-own-records-raise-serious-questions -about-inmate-juan-mendoza-farias-violent-death-6432543.
- John Dickerson, "Inhumanity Has a Price," *Phoenix New Times*, December 20, 2007, https://www.phoenixnewtimes.com/news/in humanity-has-a-price-6432212.

3. For additional information about Flavius Josephus, see Robert E. Van Voorst, *Jesus Outside the New Testament: An Introduction to the Ancient Evidence* (Grand Rapids: Eerdmans, 2000), 12, 15–16, 21, 32, 47, 48, 51, 70, 81–104, 129–34; Gary R. Habermas, *The Historical Jesus: Ancient Evidence for the Life of Christ* (Joplin, MO: College Press, 1996), 193; Bart D. Ehrman, *Did Jesus Exist?* (New York: HarperOne, 2012), 45, 57; and Lee Strobel, *The Case for the Real Jesus* (Grand Rapids: Zondervan, 2007), 80, 116–20, 127, 131.

4. This translation of Josephus from the Arabic is by Professor Schlomo Pines of the Hebrew University in Jerusalem, as quoted by James H. Charlesworth in *Jesus within Judaism: New Light from Exciting Archaeological Discoveries* (New York: Doubleday, 1988), 95. See also Flavius Josephus, *The Works of Flavius Josephus*, trans. William Whiston, 4 vols. (Grand Rapids: Baker, 1974).

5. For additional information about Emperor Hadrian and Suetonius, see Van Voorst, *Jesus Outside the New Testament*, 29–38; Habermas, *Historical Jesus*, 190; and Ehrman, *Did Jesus Exist?*, 53.

6. Cited in Martin Luther King Jr., *Stride toward Freedom* (New York: Ballantine Books, 1958), 128.

7. King, *Stride toward Freedom*, 117.

8. Mark 12:31 KJV.

9. See Luke 4:18.

Chapter 2 Suspicions about Christianity

1. For the *New York Times* report about the arrest of my editors and those same black Crown Victorias that occasionally tailed us reporters around town, see David Carr, "The Knock in the Night in Phoenix," *New York Times*, May 12, 2008, http://www.nytimes.com/2008/05/12/business/media/12carr.html; and David Carr, "Media Executives Arrested in Phoenix," *New York Times*, October 19, 2007, http://www.nytimes.com/2007/10/19/business/media/19cnd-arrest .html?_r=0. The wrongful-arrest lawsuit my editor later won as a result of the corrupt arrest is reported in Matthew Hendley, "Joe Arpaio Loses: New Times Co-Founders Win $3.75 Million Settlement for 2007 False Arrests," *Phoenix New Times*, December 20, 2013, http://www.phoenixnewtimes.com/news/joe-arpaio -loses-new-times-co-founders-win-375-million-settlement-for-2007-false-arrests -6651491.

2. Conrad Hackett and David McClendon, "Christians Remain World's Largest Religious Group, but They Are Declining in Europe," Pew Research Center,

April 5, 2017, https://www.pewresearch.org/fact-tank/2017/04/05/christians-rem
ain-worlds-largest-religious-group-but-they-are-declining-in-europe/.

3. "Shameless Self-Promotion," *Tucson Weekly*, September 27, 2007, accessed
June 23, 2019, http://www.tucsonweekly.com/tucson/shameless-self-promotion
/Content?oid=1089126.

Chapter 3 Keystone Species

1. Thank you to my friend Rob Watler for helping me understand this better.
For more on keystone species, visit http://nationalgeographic.org/encyclopedia
/keystone-species/.

2. "Giant Kelp," Monterey Bay Aquarium, 2019, https://www.montereybay
aquarium.org/animal-guide/plants-and-algae/giant-kelp.

3. Avery Comarow and Ben Harder, "2018–19 Best Hospitals Honor Roll and
Medical Specialties Rankings," *U.S. News & World Report*, August 14, 2018,
https://health.usnews.com/health-care/best-hospitals/articles/best-hospitals
-honor-roll-and-overview.

4. See note 23 in chapter 8 for information about the founding of the Mayo
Clinic.

5. Founder George Washington Crile was educated at Wooster Medical College, which was founded by the Presbyterian Church. "On December 18, 1866,
the Presbyterian Church authorized the creation of the Wooster University." See
"College of Wooster," Ohio History Connection, accessed June 23, 2019, http://
ohiohistorycentral.org/w/College_of_Wooster.

6. Johns Hopkins was a devout Quaker Christian.

7. Massachusetts General Hospital grew out of Harvard University, an overtly
Christian university at its founding and at the time it birthed the hospital. The
hospital was the vision of the Christian pastor John Bartlett.

8. Father Gabriel Richard and Rev. John Monteith founded the University
of Michigan.

9. UCSF Medical Center founder Hugh Toland was educated at Transylvania
Medical School, which was started by the Christian Church (Disciples of Christ).
Later, Toland's medical school merged with the University of California, which
was founded by Congregationalist Christian minister Henry Durant. Eventually,
the system merged with another Christian hospital, Mount Zion (a phrase used
throughout the Old Testament signifying the city of David). The University of
California motto, "Let there be light," is a quotation from the Bible (Genesis 1:3)
and a metaphor for the "light" of Christian learning.

10. The UCLA Medical Centers are offshoots of the University of California
School of Medicine. See note 9 for information about the UCSF Medical Center.

11. Cedars-Sinai Medical Center is a Jewish nonprofit hospital. Many of its
early superintendents and leaders were educated at Christian-founded or Christian-offspring institutions, such as the University of Iowa, where Sarah Vasen, a
female pioneer in medicine, was trained.

12. Founders Jane and Leland Stanford were devout Christians, as evidenced
by the Stanford Memorial Chapel, which Jane Stanford had built at the center of

the university campus. See "Stanford Memorial Information," Stanford: Office for Religious Life, accessed May 29, 2019, https://religiouslife.stanford.edu/me morial-church/stanford-memorial-church-information.

13. This hospital is the result of the merging of two hospitals, both with Christian roots. One was founded by Presbyterian Christians, and the other was founded by multiple parties, including a Christian-educated physician named Samuel Bard, who was also the personal physician to George Washington.

14. Rankings for this and the following tables are from "Gender Gap Report 2015," World Economic Forum, accessed May 29, 2019, http://reports.weforum .org/global-gender-gap-report-2015/rankings/. By clicking on the name of any of the countries listed, you can access detailed information about the equality or inequality between genders in economic, educational, health, and political areas.

15. "Populations by Religious and Life Stance Organizations 1998–2019," Statistics Iceland, 2019, https://px.hagstofa.is/pxen/pxweb/en/Samfelag/Samfelag __menning__5_trufelog/MAN10001.px/table/tableViewLayout1/?rxid=e9b676 06-d567-44f2-a62d-92903ddcca5d.

16. "Church of Norway, 2013," Statistics Norway, 2019, http://www.ssb.no /en/kultur-og-fritid/statistikker/kirke_kostra/aar/2014-05-06?fane=tabell&sort =nummer&tabell=171798#tab-tabell.

17. "Population Structure on 31 December," Statistics Finland, last updated January 4, 2019, http://tilastokeskus.fi/tup/suoluk/suoluk_vaesto_en.html#str ucture.

18. "Sweden," Pew-Templeton Global Religious Futures Project, 2016, http:// www.globalreligiousfutures.org/countries/sweden#/?affiliations_religion_id=0 &affiliations_year=2010&region_name=All%20Countries&restrictions_year =2016.

19. "Irish Census (2016)," Faith Survey, accessed May 29, 2019, http://faith survey.co.uk/irish-census.html.

20. "Rwanda: Percent Christian," GlobalEconomy.com, 2019, https://www .theglobaleconomy.com/Rwanda/christians/.

21. "Philippines Still Top Christian Country in Asia, 5th in World," Inquirer .net, December 21, 2011, https://globalnation.inquirer.net/21233/philippines-sti ll-top-christian-country-in-asia-5th-in-world.

22. "Switzerland," Pew-Templeton Global Religious Futures Project, 2016, http://www.globalreligiousfutures.org/countries/switzerland#/?affiliations_reli gion_id=0&affiliations_year=2010&region_name=All%20Countries&restrict ions_year=2016.

23. "Slovenia," Pew-Templeton Global Religious Futures Project, 2016, http:// www.globalreligiousfutures.org/countries/slovenia#/?affiliations_religion_id=0 &affiliations_year=2010&region_name=All%20Countries&restrictions_year =2016.

24. Table 28, 2013 Census Data, QuickStats about Culture and Identity, December 10, 2013, http://www.stats.govt.nz/Census/2013-census/data-tables /total-by-topic.aspx.

25. "Yemen: International Religious Freedom Report 2008," United States Department of State Bureau of Democracy, Human Rights, and Labor, 2008, http://www.state.gov/j/drl/rls/irf/2008/108496.htm.

26. "Approximately 1.6 percent of the Population Is Hindu, 1.6 percent Is Christian, and 0.3 Percent Belongs to Other Religions, such as Bahaism and Sikhism," "Country Profile: Pakistan," Library of Congress Federal Research Division, February 2005, https://www.loc.gov/rr/frd/cs/profiles/Pakistan.pdf.

27. Christians made up 5.2 percent of the population before the ISIS genocide on Christian communities. It is impossible to accurately correct the figure downward until the country stabilizes, but there are reports that many thousands of Christians have been intentionally killed by the Islamic State. "Religious Composition by Country, 2010–2050," Pew Research Center, April 2, 2015, http://www.pewforum.org/2015/04/02/religious-projection-table/2010/percent/all/.

28. "The World Factbook: Chad," Central Intelligence Agency, accessed June 23, 2019, https://www.cia.gov/library/publications/the-world-factbook/geos/cd.html.

29. "The World Factbook: Iran," Central Intelligence Agency, accessed June 23, 2019, https://www.cia.gov/library/publications/the-world-factbook/geos/ir.html

30. "The World Factbook: Jordan," Central Intelligence Agency, accessed June 23, 2019, https://www.cia.gov/library/publications/the-world-factbook/geos/jo.html

31. "The World Factbook: Morocco," Central Intelligence Agency, accessed June 23, 2019, https://www.cia.gov/library/publications/the-world-factbook/geos/mo.html

32. "Lebanon," Pew-Templeton Global Religious Futures Project, 2016, http://www.globalreligiousfutures.org/countries/lebanon#/?affiliations_religion_id=0&affiliations_year=2010&region_name=All%20Countries&restrictions_year=2016.

33. "The World Factbook: Mali," Central Intelligence Agency, last updated May 16, 2019, https://www.cia.gov/library/publications/the-world-factbook/geos/ml.html.

34. Egypt's population was 5.1 percent Christian before the Arab Spring, which indirectly resulted in the genocide of many Christians in Egypt. The percentage is most likely less now. "Religious Composition by Country, 2010–2050."

Chapter 4 The Scientific Revolution

1. John 14:6.

2. Albert Einstein, *Autobiographical Notes* (1946), 19, quoted in Alice Calaprice, ed., *The Ultimate Quotable Einstein* (Princeton: Princeton University Press, 2011), 397.

3. Elizabeth T. Knuth, "Pascal's Memorial," revised August 2, 1999, http://www.users.csbsju.edu/~eknuth/pascal.html.

4. Isaac Newton, "Theological Notebook (Part 1)," The Newton Project, published online September 2003, http://www.newtonproject.sussex.ac.uk/view/texts/normalized/THEM00180. Source: Keynes Ms. 2, King's College, Cambridge,

UK, Blondel against the Sibylls, purchased at Sotheby's, July 15, 1936, lot 235, Fr. Massam at Oats Highlaver Parish near Harlow, September 25, 1727.

5. For more information on Christians and the Scientific Revolution, see Rodney Stark, *For the Glory of God: How Monotheism Led to Reformations, Science, Witch-Hunts, and the End of Slavery* (Princeton: Princeton University Press, 2003), 121–201; Toby E. Huff, *The Rise of Early Modern Science: Islam, China and the West* (Cambridge: Cambridge University Press, 2017); and Isaac Newton's theological writings found at the Newton Project, http://www.newtonproject.sussex .ac.uk/prism.php?id=44.

6. Francis Bacon, Essay 16, "Of Atheism," accessed June 14, 2019, http://knarf .english.upenn.edu/EtAlia/bacon16.html.

7. Isaac Newton, *Philosophiae Naturalis Principia Mathematica* (*Mathematical Principles of Natural Philosophy*) (1687).

8. The National Library of Israel, http://web.nli.org.il/sites/NLI/English /collections/Humanities/newton/Pages/default.aspx.

9. The Newton Project, http://www.newtonproject.sussex.ac.uk/prism.php ?id=1.

10. For more about Newton and his theology, see Stephen D. Snobelen, "Statement on the Date 2060," Isaac Newton: Theology, Prophecy, Science and Religion, last updated June 2003, http://isaac-newton.org/statement-on-the-date-2060.

11. These quotations from Isaac Newton can be found in "Theological Notebook (Part 1)."

12. These quotations from Isaac Newton can be found in "Theological Notebook (Part 1)."

13. In part 2 of his theological writings, Newton writes, "that ancient MS. of Lincoln College in Oxford & those in Magdalen & New College have it not That of Magdalen Coll in Oxford [& in their publick library. Quære.] The Syriack Arabick & Æthiopick versions, which are very ancient. All the latine versions in Hieromes time as Hierome himself mentions." Isaac Newton, "Theological Notebook (Part 2)," The Newton Project, published online September 2003, http:// www.newtonproject.sussex.ac.uk/view/texts/normalized/THEM00181.

14. Wikipedia summary statement: "In his treatise *Ad Vitellionem paralipomena* [Emendations (or Supplement) to Witelo] (1604), Kepler explained how eyeglass lenses compensate for the distortions that are caused by presbyopia or myopia, so that the image is once again properly focused on the retina." Cited in Vincent Ilardi, *Renaissance Vision from Spectacles to Telescopes* (Philadelphia: American Philosophical Society, 2007), 244. See also Vasco Ronchi and Edward Rosen, *Optics: The Science of Vision* (Mineola, NY: Dover Publications, 1991), 45–46.

15. Johannes Kepler, *Mysterium Cosmographicum* (Tubingen, Germany: 1621).

16. John 8:12.

17. Blaise Pascal, *Pascal's Memorial* (1654). Available in French, Latin, and English at http://www.users.csbsju.edu/~eknuth/pascal.html.

18. Find links to recent Boyle Lectures at https://www.gresham.ac.uk/series /the-boyle-lectures/ or https://www.issr.org.uk/the-boyle-lectures/.

19. "John Ray (1628–1705)," accessed May 29, 2019, http://www.ucmp.berkeley .edu/history/ray.html.

20. Stark, *For the Glory of God*, 121–201.

21. Newton, "Theological Notebook (Part 1)."

22. Knuth, "Pascal's Memorial," emphasis added.

23. "Francis Collins, MD, PhD," *National Human Genome Research Institute*, accessed June 23, 2019, https://www.genome.gov/staff/Francis-S-Collins -MD-PhD.

24. "Biographical Sketch of Francis S. Collins, M.D., Ph.D.," National Institutes of Health, last reviewed June 27, 2017, https://www.nih.gov/about-nih /who-we-are/nih-director/biographical-sketch-francis-s-collins-md-phd.

25. "Collins: Why This Scientist Believes in God," CNN.com, April 6, 2007, http://www.cnn.com/2007/US/04/03/collins.commentary/index.html.

26. "Francis Collins," WGBH Educational Foundation, 2004, http://www .pbs.org/wgbh/questionofgod/voices/collins.html.

27. "Francis Collins."

28. "Collins: Why This Scientist Believes in God."

29. "Francis Collins."

30. "Collins: Why This Scientist Believes in God."

31. "Collins: Why This Scientist Believes in God."

Chapter 5 Life before Jesus's Influence

1. Toshiko Kaneda and Carl Haub, "How Many People Have Ever Lived on Earth?" Population Reference Bureau, March 9, 2018, https://www.prb.org /howmanypeoplehaveeverlivedonearth/.

2. For information supporting these claims, see Rodney Stark, *How the West Won* (Wilmington, DE: Intercollegiate Studies Institute, 2014), 1–32; Marvin Harris, *Cannibals and Kings: Origins of Cultures* (1977; repr., New York: Vintage, 1991), 234–35; Joseph Vogt, *Ancient Slavery and the Ideal of Man* (Oxford: Oxford University Press, 1974), 25; William V. Harris, *Ancient Literacy* (Cambridge: Harvard University Press, 1989), 272; Kirstin Olsen, *Chronology of Women's History* (Westport, CT: Greenwood Press, 1994), 1; and Cormac Ó Gráda, *Famine: A Short History* (Princeton: Princeton University Press, 2010).

3. On the horror of slavery as a global norm in pre-Christian civilizations, and present-day Sudan and Mauritania, see Harris, *Cannibals and Kings*, 234–35; Toby Wilkinson, *The Rise and Fall of Ancient Egypt* (London: Bloomsbury, 2010); Ronald Segal, *Islam's Black Slaves: The Other Black Diaspora* (New York: Farrar, Straus & Giroux, 2001); James Walvin, *Atlas of Slavery* (New York: Routledge, 2014); W. M. S. Russell, *Man, Nature, and History: Controlling the Environment* (New York: Doubleday, 1969), 99; Raymond Dawson, *Imperial China: The History of Human Society* (London: Hutchinson, 1972), 62; Seymour Drescher and Stanley L. Engerman, eds., *A Historical Guide to World Slavery* (Oxford: Oxford University Press, 1998); Milton Meltzer, *Slavery: A World History* (Boston: Da Capo Press, 1993); Page Du Bois, *Slavery: Antiquity and Its Legacy* (Oxford: Oxford University Press, 2010); and Christina Snyder, "Indian Slavery," American History,

Oxford Research Encyclopedias, December 2014, https://doi.org10.1093/acre
fore/9780199329175.013.5.

4. A. R. Bridbury, "The Dark Ages," *Economic History Review* 22 (1969): 533.

5. Blake De Pastino, "Victims of Human Sacrifice at Cahokia Were Locals,
Not 'Foreign' Captives, Study Finds," Western Digs: Dispatches from the Ancient
American West, updated December 31, 2019, http://westerndigs.org/victims-of
-human-sacrifice-at-cahokia-were-locals-not-captives-study-finds/.

6. Image rights description and availability for download or further study at
https://en.wikipedia.org/wiki/File:Sacrifice_Polyxena_BM_GR1897.7-27.2.jpg.

7. "What Made This Ancient Society Sacrifice Its Own Children?" *National
Geographic*, January 2019, https://www.nationalgeographic.com/magazine/2019
/02/chimu-people-sacrificed-children-llamas-peru-mystery/.

8. "Mexico Finds Flayed God Temple; Priests Wore Skins of Dead," Associated
Press News, January 3, 2019, https://apnews.com/e4e92bc35ead46309f632ec12
df8ddf8.

9. Dallas Museum of Art, Dallas, TX, General Acquisitions Fund, Otis and
Velma Davis Dozier Fund, and Roberta Coke Camp Fund, object number 2005.26.
Image rights description and availability for download or further study at https://
en.wikipedia.org/wiki/File:Maya_vessel_with_sacrificial_scene_DMA_2005
-26.jpg.

10. This 1989 book by investigative journalist Patrick Tierney describes a re-
cent human sacrifice in Chile, by a non-Western-influenced tribe: Patrick Tierney,
The Highest Altar: Unveiling the Mystery of Human Sacrifice (London: Penguin
Books, 1990).

Chapter 6 Seeds, Trees and Fruit

1. Ian Cowe, "Would You Put Your Pension on a Politician's Promise?" *Tele-
graph*, October 9, 2009, http://www.telegraph.co.uk/finance/personalfinance
/comment/iancowie/6274049/Would-you-put-your-pension-on-a-politicians
-promise.html.

Chapter 7 Universities

1. John 8:32.

2. John 8:12.

3. Remarkably, some of these fourteen-hundred-year-old Christian cathedral
schools have operated continuously to our present day. They include the King's
School, Canterbury (founded in AD 597), the King's School, Rochester (founded
in AD 604), and St. Peter's School, York (founded in AD 627), among others.

4. "A 21st Century Education at the UK's Most Historic School," the King's
School, Canterbury, accessed May 29, 2019, http://www.kings-school.co.uk.

5. In this era, Christianity became intertwined and polluted with political
power. As a result, there were some self-described "Christians" who professed
belief in Jesus merely to attain power or possessions—even as there were other
sincere followers of Jesus who professed to be Christian because they actually

admired Jesus and strived to live out his teachings. Interestingly, this polluting of the term "Christian" is something that Jesus predicted in a story he told about weeds growing up in a field of wheat (Matthew 13:24–29).

Despite the nonspiritual "Christians" who were not true to Jesus's teachings, there appears to have always been a remnant of genuinely motivated followers of Jesus, and it seems to be these followers who gave their lives to continue teaching the next generation rather than pursuing wealth or political power under the banner of Christianity.

6. See 1 Corinthians 15:45–50.

7. Toby E. Huff, *The Rise of Early Modern Science: Islam, China and the West* (Cambridge: Cambridge University Press, 2017), 179–89.

8. Rodney Stark, *How the West Won* (Wilmington, DE: Intercollegiate Studies Institute, 2014), 160–63.

9. Edward Grant, *The Foundations of Modern Science in the Middle Ages* (Cambridge: Cambridge University Press, 1996).

10. John 8:12.

11. Psalm 27:1.

12. John 8:12.

13. "New England's First Fruits Plaque, Harvard University," last edited September 1, 2013, https://commons.wikimedia.org/wiki/File:New_England%27s_First_Fruits_plaque,_Harvard_University_-_IMG_8969.JPG, emphasis added.

14. "The Nation's Largest Libraries: A Listing by Volumes Held," American Library Association, 2011, http://www.ala.org/tools/libfactsheets/alalibraryfactsheet22.

15. Anna K. Kendrick, "Harvard's Secularization," *Crimson*, March 8, 2006, https://www.thecrimson.com/article/2006/3/8/harvards-secularization-harvard-has-never-been/.

16. Matthew 16:18 KJV.

17. "Shield and 'Veritas' History," Harvard GSAS Christian Community, accessed May 29, 2019, http://www.hcs.harvard.edu/~gsascf/shield-and-veritas-history/.

18. "On the Progresse of Learning in the College at Cambridge [Harvard] in Massachusetts Bay," in *New England's First Fruits* (London: n.p., 1643), 26. Available at https://archive.org/stream/NewEnglandsFirstFruitsInRespectFirstOfTheCounversionOfSome/New_Englands_First_Fruits#page/n25/mode/2up. Available in person at Ohio State University Library, Americana Collection.

19. Kendrick, "Harvard's Secularization."

20. "Harvard: The Memorial Church," Harvard University, accessed May 29, 2019, http://memorialchurch.harvard.edu/history-0.

21. "The Yale Corporation Charter and Legislation" (New Haven: Yale University Press, 1976), http://www.yale.edu/sites/default/files/files/University-Charter.pdf.

22. "The Founding of Princeton," quoted in Alexander Leitch, *A Princeton Companion* (1854), https://etcweb.princeton.edu/CampusWWW/Companion/founding_princeton.html.

23. 1 Peter 5:4 KJV.

24. "The Charter of Incorporation of the Trustees of the College of New Jersey," http://pudl.princeton.edu/viewer.php?obj=7w62f826z&vol=phys1&log =log1#page/12/mode/2up.

25. Donald Tewksbury, *The Founding of American Colleges and Universities before the Civil War* (1932), cited in Alvin J. Schmidt, *How Christianity Changed the World* (Grand Rapids: Zondervan, 2001), 190.

26. George M. Marsden, *The Soul of the American University: From Protestant Establishment to Established Nonbelief* (Oxford: Oxford University Press, 1994).

27. Isaiah 26:2 KJV.

28. Center for World University Rankings, 2016, http://cwur.org/2016.php.

29. Christian minister John Harvard and his Puritan Christian colleagues were all devout followers of Jesus, as described in their own primary writings. See Tewksbury, *Founding of American Colleges and Universities*, cited in Schmidt, *How Christianity Changed the World*, 190; and Marsden, *Soul of the American University*.

30. Founders Leland and Jane Stanford were Christians. In addition, the influential early faculty were graduates of overtly Christian universities such as Yale.

31. MIT founder William Barton Rogers was himself a graduate of one of the first Christian universities—the College of William & Mary—which was overtly Christian, requiring students to be members of the Anglican Church and professors to adhere to the thirty-nine doctrines of Anglican Christianity. For more information, see Homer J. Webster, "Schools and Colleges in Colonial Times," *New England Magazine: An Illustrated Monthly* 27 (1902): 374.

32. Christian faculty from Oxford founded Cambridge.

33. Oxford has an overwhelmingly Christian heritage and foundation, having grown from a Christian cathedral.

34. Founded by the Church of England. See Fredrick Paul Keppel, *Columbia* (Oxford: Oxford University Press, 1914), 26.

35. Founder Henry Durant, a Yale graduate, was an ordained Christian minister. Early leadership was a mix of Christian Congregationalists and Christian Presbyterians. See Marsden, *Soul of the American University*, 134–40.

36. The University of Chicago was incorporated, funded, and founded by the American Baptist Education Society (Baptist being a Protestant Christian denomination). "Founded in 1888 for 'the promotion of Christian education, under Baptist auspices, in North America,' it was under the Society's supervision that the University of Chicago was founded in 1890." "Guide to the American Baptist Education Society Records 1887–1902," the University of Chicago Library, Special Collections Research Center, https://www.lib.uchicago.edu/e/scrc/finding aids/view.php?eadid=ICU.SPCL.BAPTISTEDU.

37. Princeton was founded by four devout, spiritually devoted pastors who longed to train another generation in reading and understanding the Christian Scriptures. "The Founding of Princeton," from Alexander Leitch, *A Princeton Companion* (Princeton: Princeton University Press, 1978), https://etcweb.prince ton.edu/CampusWWW/Companion/founding_princeton.html.

38. "Yale Corporation Charter and Legislation."

39. "New England's First Fruits Plaque, Harvard University."

40. "Yale Corporation Charter and Legislation."

41. Finding Aids, "Guide to the American Baptist Education Society Records 1887–1902."

42. Huff, *Rise of Early Modern Science*, 179–89.

43. Jonathan authored a book about their experiences in Papua New Guinea titled *Canopy of Darkness* (n.p.: Entrust Source, 2011), available through Amazon in paperback and Kindle versions. Sources and further information are available at https://youtu.be/W8f3L-R3OgM (Jonathan's testimony); "Missionaries Jonathan and Susan Kopf," Ethnos 360, https://ethnos360.org/missionaries/jonathan -and-susan-kopf; and Kopf's blog, https://blogs.ethnos360.org/jonathan-kopf/.

Chapter 8 Hospitals and Modern Medicine

1. Matthew 11:5.

2. John 10:10.

3. Seneca, *De ira*, *The Third Book of the Dialogues of L. Annaeus Seneca*, book 1, section 15, trans. Aubrey Stewart, https://en.wikisource.org/wiki/Of _Anger/Book_I#I.

4. Seneca, *De ira*.

5. Matthew 11:5.

6. See John 10:10 and Matthew 25:40.

7. James 1:27 RSV.

8. George of Diospolis, Afra of Augsburg, Alban of Verlamium, Nicholas of Myra, Fabiola Fabii, Telemachus of Laddia, and Barlaam of Antioch. Note: It is impossible to know with certainty the actual details of the lives of these Christian martyrs because so many legends were created and spread throughout the centuries following their deaths. What is sure is that the theme of Christians sacrificing their own lives to protect children, refugees, and others is what ties the legends and stories of these martyrs (and many more) together in Christian lore. In other words, what Christians chose to most remember these heroes for was their willingness to sacrifice themselves in caring for, hiding, and rescuing the sick, the poor, the unwanted, and the outcasts of society.

9. Guenter B. Risse, *Mending Bodies, Saving Souls: A History of Hospitals* (Oxford: Oxford University Press, 1999), 73.

10. Risse, *Mending Bodies, Saving Souls*, 73.

11. Matthew 25:40.

12. John 13:14 KJV.

13. Risse, *Mending Bodies, Saving Souls*, 73.

14. "About Edward Jenner," Jenner Institute, 2019, https://www.jenner.ac.uk /edward-jenner.

15. "Vaccines Bring 7 Diseases under Control," UNICEF, accessed May 29, 2019, https://www.unicef.org/pon96/hevaccin.htm.

16. Jessica Firger, "Smallpox Vaccine Saved Billions of Lives," *Newsweek*, October 11, 2017, https://www.newsweek.com/genome-sequencing-smallpox -vaccine-shows-not-cowpox-682793.

17. John Baron, *The Life of Edward Jenner: With Illustrations of His Doctrines, and Selections from His Correspondence* (London: Henry Colburn, 1838), 2:295.

18. "The Christ Follower Who Saved a Billion People," Christian Diarist, December 13, 2015, https://christiandiarist.com/2015/12/13/the-christ-follower-who-saved-a-billion-people/.

19. Lynn McDonald, ed., *Florence Nightingale's Suggestions for Thought* (Waterloo, ON: Wilfrid Laurier University Press, 2008), 11:96.

20. *U.S. News & World Report* ranking of top hospitals as reported in "Top 10 Hospitals in the World," Global Healthcare, July 8, 2011, https://www.health careglobal.com/top-10/top-10-hospitals-world.

21. "Johns Hopkins," Wikipedia, last edited May 7, 2019, https://en.wikipedia .org/wiki/Johns_Hopkins.

22. John 8:32.

23. For additional information on Mary Moes and the founding of the Mayo Clinic, see the PBS documentary *The Mayo Clinic: Faith—Hope—Science*, exec. prod. Ken Burns, aired September 25, 2018.

24. Philippians 4:8 KJV.

25. A reference to Jesus from John 1:14.

26. Avery Comarow and Ben Harder, "2018–19 Best Hospitals Honor Roll and Medical Specialties Rankings," *U.S. News & World Report*, August 14, 2018, https:// health.usnews.com/health-care/best-hospitals/articles/best-hospitals-honor -roll-and-overview.

27. See note 23 for information about the founding of the Mayo Clinic.

28. Founder George Washington Crile was educated at Wooster Medical College, which was founded by the Presbyterian Church. "On December 18, 1866, the Presbyterian Church authorized the creation of the Wooster University." See "College of Wooster," Ohio History Connection, accessed June 23, 2019, http:// ohiohistorycentral.org/w/College_of_Wooster.

29. Johns Hopkins was a devout Quaker Christian.

30. Massachusetts General Hospital grew out of Harvard University, an overtly Christian university at its founding and at the time it birthed the hospital. The hospital was the vision of the Christian pastor John Bartlett.

31. Father Gabriel Richard and Rev. John Monteith founded the University of Michigan.

32. UCSF Medical Center founder Hugh Toland was educated at Transylvania Medical School, which was started by the Christian Church (Disciples of Christ). Later, Toland's medical school merged with the University of California, which was founded by Congregationalist Christian minister Henry Durant. Eventually, the system merged with another Christian hospital, Mount Zion (a phrase used throughout the Old Testament signifying the city of David). The University of California motto, "Let there be light," is a quotation from the Bible (Genesis 1:3) and a metaphor for the "light" of Christian learning.

33. The UCLA Medical Centers are offshoots of the University of California School of Medicine. See UCSF Medical Center founding in the previous note.

34. Cedars-Sinai Medical Center is a Jewish nonprofit hospital. Many of its early superintendents and leaders were educated at Christian-founded or Christian-offspring institutions, such as the University of Iowa, where Sarah Vasen, a female pioneer in medicine, was trained.

35. Founders Jane and Leland Stanford were devout Christians, as evidenced by the Stanford Memorial Chapel, which Jane Stanford had built at the center of the university campus. See "Stanford Memorial Information," Stanford: Office for Religious Life, accessed May 29, 2019, https://religiouslife.stanford.edu/mem orial-church/stanford-memorial-church-information.

36. This hospital is the result of the merging of two hospitals, both with Christian roots. One was founded by Presbyterian Christians, and the other was founded by multiple parties, including a Christian-educated physician named Samuel Bard, who was also the personal physician to George Washington.

37. "The History of HMS," Harvard Medical School, 2019, https://hms.harv ard.edu/about-hms/history-hms.

38. Some today undermine Benjamin Franklin's Christianity, but in his writings Franklin consistently expressed belief in the Christian God and often cited this God as his motive for creating do-good organizations in society. Franklin was raised as a Puritan and wrote that he was profoundly shaped in his social work by the writings of Christian thinker and pastor Cotton Mather. See Walter Isaacson, *Benjamin Franklin: An American Life* (New York: Simon & Schuster, 2003), 486; and Roger Olson, *The Mosaic of Christian Belief: Twenty Centuries of Unity and Diversity* (Downers Grove, IL: InterVarsity, 2009), 61.

39. Rossiter Johnson, ed., *Biographical Dictionary of America* (Boston: American Biographical Society, 1906), https://archive.org/stream/biographicaldict 01johnuoft#page/n209/mode/1up.

40. Nicholas Kristof, "He's Jesus Christ," *New York Times*, June 27, 2015, https://www.nytimes.com/2015/06/28/opinion/sunday/nicholas-kristof-hes-jesus -christ.html.

41. Knez Walker, Ashley Louszko, and Pavni Mittall, "What It Is Like Being the Only Doctor in War-Torn Sudan's Nuba Mountains," ABC News, April 12, 2018, https://abcnews.go.com/International/doctor-war-torn-sudans-nuba-mount ains/story?id=54370334.

42. "Dr. Tom Catena," Sudan Relief Fund, accessed May 29, 2019, https://sd nrlf.com/our_team/dr-tom-catena/.

43. Walker, Louszko, and Mittall, "What It Is Like Being the Only Doctor."

44. "Dr. Tom Catena."

45. Kristof, "He's Jesus Christ." See also "Dr. Tom Catena"; and *The Heart of Nuba* (a documentary about Dr. Tom), https://theheartofnuba.com.https://www .nytimes.com/2015/06/28/opinion/sunday/nicholas-kristof-hes-jesus-christ.html

Chapter 9 The Evil of Slavery

1. Isaiah 42:1.
2. Mark 12:31 KJV.
3. Luke 4:18.

4. Outline of the sermon "Cooperative/Noble Competition," based on Luke 22:24, the King Center, Atlanta, GA, https://thekingcenter.org/contact-us/.

5. Montgomery Bus Boycott speech, Holt Street Baptist Church, Montgomery, AL, December 5, 1955.

6. Address to the first Montgomery Improvement Association (MIA) Mass Meeting, Holt Street Baptist Church, Montgomery, AL, December 5, 1955. "Justice runs down like water, and righteousness like a mighty stream" is from Amos 5:24.

7. Sarah H. Bradford, *Harriet: The Moses of Her People* (New York: Geo. R. Lockwood and Son, 1886), 24–25, http://docsouth.unc.edu/neh/harriet/harriet .html.

8. In her final words, Tubman referenced the churches that made up the Underground Railroad network to help slaves escape. Then she quoted Jesus about the heaven he promised to all who believe in him. "To the clergyman she said 'Give my love to all the churches' and after a severe coughing spell she blurted out in a thick voice this farewell passage that she had learned from Matthew: 'I go away to prepare a place for you, and where I am ye may be also.' She soon afterward lapsed into a comatose condition and death came at 8:30 o'clock last evening. Those present when she died included Rev. and Mrs. Smith and Miss Ridgeway, the colored nurse." Harriet Tubman obituary, *Auburn Citizen*, March 11, 1913, http://www.harriettubman.com/memoriam2.html.

9. John 14:3 RSV.

10. Frederick Douglass, *The Life and Times of Frederick Douglass: From 1817–1882* (Hartford, CT: Park Publishing, 1881), 63. Available at https://books .google.com/books?id=X8ILAAAAIAAJ.

11. Christina Snyder, "Indian Slavery," American History, *Oxford Research Encyclopedias*, December 2014, https://doi.org/10.1093/acrefore/97801993291 75.013.5.

12. David R. James, "Slavery and Involuntary Servitude," in *Encyclopedia of Sociology*, ed. Edgar F. Borgatta and Marie L. Borgatta (New York: Macmillan, 1992), 4:1792; and Christina Snyder, *Slavery in Indian Country: The Changing Face of Captivity in Early America* (Cambridge: Harvard University Press, 2010), chap. 1.

13. Snyder, "Indian Slavery."

14. Seymour Drescher and Stanley L. Engerman, eds., *A Historical Guide to World Slavery* (New York: Oxford University Press, 1998), ix. On the horror of slavery as a global norm in pre-Christian civilizations, including present-day Sudan and Mauritania, see also Marvin Harris, *Cannibals and Kings: Origins of Cultures* (1977; repr., New York: Vintage, 1991), 234–35; Toby Wilkinson, *The Rise and Fall of Ancient Egypt* (London: Bloomsbury, 2010); Rodney Stark, *How the West Won* (Wilmington, DE: Intercollegiate Studies Institute, 2014), 1–32; Ronald Segal, *Islam's Black Slaves: The Other Black Diaspora* (New York: Farrar, Straus & Giroux, 2001); James Walvin, *Atlas of Slavery* (New York: Routledge, 2014); W. M. S. Russell, *Man, Nature, and History: Controlling the Environment* (New York: Doubleday, 1969), 99; Raymond Dawson, *Imperial China: The History of*

Human Society (London: Hutchinson, 1972), 62; Milton Meltzer, *Slavery: A World History* (Boston: Da Capo Press, 1993); and Page duBois, *Slavery: Antiquity and Its Legacy* (Oxford: Oxford University Press, 2010).

15. Walter Scheidel, "Human Mobility in Roman Italy, II: The Slave Population," *Journal of Roman Studies* 95 (2005): 64–79, 170.

16. Richard Hellie, "Slavery: Sociology," *Encyclopaedia Britannica*, 2019, https://www.britannica.com/topic/slavery-sociology.

17. David Eltis and Stanley Engerman, eds., *The Cambridge World History of Slavery: Volume 3, AD 1420–AD 1804* (Cambridge: Cambridge University Press, 2011).

18. Galina I. Yermolenko, *Roxolana in European Literature, History and Culture* (Farnham, UK: Ashgate Publishing, 2010), 111.

19. Robert Davis, *Christian Slaves, Muslim Masters: White Slavery in the Mediterranean, the Barbary Coast and Italy, 1500–1800* (London: Palgrave MacMillan, 2003).

20. Nicole Hallet, "China and Antislavery," *Encyclopedia of Antislavery and Abolition* (Santa Barbara, CA: Greenwood Publishing Group, 2007), 1:154–56.

21. Hellie, "Slavery: Sociology."

22. Hugh Thomas, *The Slave Trade: The Story of the Atlantic Slave Trade: 1440–1870* (New York: Simon & Schuster, 1997). See also "Slave Voyages," Emory Libraries and Information Technology, accessed June 23, 2019, https://www.slavevoyages.org/voyage/database.

23. Mia Bay, *The White Image in the Black Mind: African-American Ideas about White People, 1830–1925* (New York: Oxford University Press, 2000); and Karl Jacoby, "Slaves by Nature? Domestic Animals and Human Slaves," *Slavery and Abolition* 15 (1994): 88–99.

24. Susan Alt, "Unwilling Immigrants: Culture, Change, and the 'Other' in Mississippian Societies," in *Invisible Citizens: Slavery in Ancient Pre-State Societies*, ed. Catherine M. Cameron (Salt Lake City: University of Utah Press, 2008), 205–22.

25. Snyder, "Indian Slavery."

26. Snyder, *Slavery in Indian Country*, chap. 1.

27. Philemon 16.

28. This material originally appeared in "Images of the British Abolitionist Movement," Online Library of Liberty, last modified April 13, 2016, http://oll.libertyfund.org/pages/images-of-the-british-abolitionist-movement?q=slavery#.

29. Mark 12:31 KJV.

30. See Luke 4:18.

Chapter 10 The End of Open Slavery

1. Luke 4:18.

2. Theodore Dwight Weld, *The Bible against Slavery*, 3rd ed. (New York: The American Anti-Slavery Society, 1837). Available at https://archive.org/details/bibleagainstslav00weldthe/page/n8.

3. John Rankin, *Letters on American Slavery*, 5th ed. (Boston: Isaac Knapp, 1838). Available at https://archive.org/details/lettersonamerica1838rank/page/n4.

4. *Real Christianity* by William Wilberforce has been published and printed multiple times from 1797 to the present. Available at https://archive.org/details/practicalview_realchristianity_1902_librivox.

5. George B. Cheever, *The Guilt of Slavery and the Crime of Slaveholding, Demonstrated from the Hebrew and Greek Scriptures* (Boston: John P. Jewett & Company, 1860). Available at http://www.archive.org/stream/guiltofslaverycr0 0chee/guiltofslaverycr00chee_djvu.txt.

6. George B. Cheever, *God against Slavery* (New York: Joseph H. Ladd, 1857). Available at https://archive.org/details/godagainstslaver00chee/page/n6.

7. Frederick Douglass, *My Bondage and My Freedom* (New York and Auburn: Miller, Orton & Mulligan, 1855). Available at https://docsouth.unc.edu/neh/do uglass55/douglass55.html.

8. George Bourne, *A Condensed Anti-Slavery Bible Argument* (New York: S. W. Benedict, 1845). Available at https://archive.org/details/condensedantisla 00bour/page/n4.

9. John G. Free, *The Wrongs of American Slavery Exposed by the Light of the Bible and of Facts*, 2nd ed. (New York: W. Harned, 1851). Available at https ://archive.org/details/antislaverymanua00feej_1.

10. "The two sides of 'The 1688 Germantown Quaker Petition Against Slavery' after conservation in 2007. It was written in iron gall ink and has substantially faded. The document was the first public protest against the institution of slavery and represents the first written public declaration of universal human rights. The original document is nine by fourteen inches. The Signatories are Francis Daniel Pastorius, Garret Hendericks, Derick op den Graeff, and Abraham op den Graeff." See "The 1688 Germantown Quaker Petition against Slavery," Wikipedia, uploaded February 2009, https://en.wikipedia.org/wiki/File:The_1688_Germant own_Quaker_petition_against_slavery.jpg.

11. Matthew 7:12.

12. Matthew Quallen, "Making Animals, Making Slaves: Animalization and Slavery in the Antebellum United States" (honors thesis, Georgetown University, 2016), 4–5, https://repository.library.georgetown.edu/bitstream/handle/10822/1 040660/Quallen_Thesis_Final.pdf;sequence=1.

13. See "First Petition to Parliament" (1783), The Abolition Project, 2009, http://abolition.e2bn.org/abolition_view.php?id=34&expand=1; and "Quakers (Society of Friends)," The Abolition Project, 2009, http://abolition.e2bn.org /people21.html.

14. See "First Petition to Parliament"; and "Quakers (Society of Friends)."

15. Image is from http://abolition.e2bn.org/library/0801/0000/0010/1783YM p1small.jpg.

16. Clarkson, "Essay on the Slavery and Commerce of the Human Species."

17. Image of an original copy of Thomas Clarkson's "Essay on the Slavery and Commerce of the Human Species" (1786), Online Library of Liberty, accessed May 29, 2019, http://oll.libertyfund.org/titles/clarkson-an-essay-on-the-slavery -and-commerce-of-the-human-species.

18. Clarkson, "Essay on the Slavery and Commerce of the Human Species."

19. Richard Hellie, "Slavery: Sociology," *Encyclopaedia Britannica*, 2019, https://www.britannica.com/topic/slavery-sociology.

20. "William Wilberforce," History, BBC, 2014, http://www.bbc.co.uk/histo ry/historic_figures/wilberforce_william.shtml.

21. See the Brussels Conference Act of 1890, in which the European countries insisted on an end to slavery in the African and Muslim world, at https://www .loc.gov/law/help/us-treaties/bevans/m-ust000001-0134.pdf.

22. The full title of Wilberforce's book is *A Practical View of the Prevailing Religious System of Professed Christians in the Higher and Middle Classes of This Country, Contrasted with Real Christianity.*

23. "William Wilberforce," BBC.com, last updated July 5, 2011, https://www. bbc.co.uk/religion/religions/christianity/people/williamwilberforce_1.shtml.

24. Wilberforce, *Practical View of the Prevailing Religious System*, 6th ed. (Glasgow: William Collins, 1837), 237.

25. Photograph of the "Declaration of the Anti-Slavery Convention."

26. Photograph of the "Declaration of the Anti-Slavery Convention."

27. Photograph of the "Declaration of the Anti-Slavery Convention."

28. Photograph of the "Declaration of the Anti-Slavery Convention, Assembled in Philadelphia, December 4, 1833." Woodcut signed by Reuben S. Gilbert, Merrihew & Gunn, printers. Digital file from the Library of Congress, https:// www.loc.gov/item/2008661764/. Also available for high resolution download at https://www.awesomestories.com/images/user/da611dbf41.jpg.

29. Photograph of the "Declaration of the Anti-Slavery Convention."

30. Rodney Stark, *For the Glory of God: How Monotheism Led to Reformations, Science, Witch-Hunts, and the End of Slavery* (Princeton: Princeton University Press, 2003), 343.

31. William T. Alexander, A. M., *History of the Colored Race in America* (Kansas City, MO: Hudson-Kimberly Publishing Company), 427. The title page of this book begins with a Bible verse from Genesis: "And God said, 'Let there be light,' and there was light."

32. Melvin Jameson, "A Friend of Human Freedom: Elijah Parish Lovejoy—the Martyr of Alton," *Standard: A Baptist Newspaper* (Chicago), July 16, 1910, 8.

33. Theodore Wright, "Prejudice against the Colored Man," *The Liberator*, October 2, 1837. This article was based on a speech Wright delivered at the New York State Anti-Slavery Society convention in Utica, NY, September 20, 1837. See "Theodore S. Wright, 'Prejudice against the Colored Man,'" BlackPast, January 24, 2007, https://www.blackpast.org/african-american-history/1837-theodore-s -wright-prejudice-against-colored-man/.

34. Portrait of Rev. Theodore Sedgwick Wright, from a daguerreotype by Plumbe, 1845, lithograph by G. S. W. Endicott, New York. Image courtesy of the Randolph Linsly Simpson African-American Collection, Beinecke Rare Book & Manuscript Library, Yale University.

35. Donna B. Jacobson, "Borderlander of Light: Reverend John Rankin," accessed May 29, 2019, http://www.reverendjohnrankin.org/.

36. Alvin J. Schmidt, *How Christianity Changed the World* (Grand Rapids: Zondervan, 2001), 273.

37. "Forced Labour, Modern Slavery and Human Trafficking," International Labour Organization, accessed May 29, 2019, https://www.ilo.org/global/topics /forced-labour/lang--en/index.htm.

38. "Profits and Poverty: The Economics of Forced Labour," International Labour Organization Report, 2014, https://www.ilo.org/global/topics/forced-la bour/publications/profits-of-forced-labour-2014/lang--en/index.htm.

39. "Every Child Counts: New Global Estimates on Child Labour," International Labour Organization Report, 2002, https://www.ilo.org/ipec/Information resources/WCMS_IPEC_PUB_742/lang--en/index.htm.

40. Agape International Missions, https://agapewebsite.org/.

41. Rapha House, https://www.raphahouse.org; Pastor Jeff Vines's interview with Stephanie Freed, Christ's Church of the Valley, San Dimas, CA, January 19, 2016, https://www.youtube.com/watch?v=zA1d3zDW730.

Chapter 11 Literacy and Public Education

1. Matthew 28:19 KJV.

2. William Harris, *Ancient Literacy* (Cambridge: Harvard University Press, 1989), 328; for a simple summary of *Ancient Literarcy*, see the article "Ancient Literacy," Harvard University Press, accessed June 23, 2019, http://www.hup.har vard.edu/catalog.php?isbn=9780674033818&content=book.

3. Eric R. Eberling, "Massachusetts Education Laws of 1642, 1647, and 1648," in *Historical Dictionary of American Education*, ed. Richard J. Altenbaugh (Westport, CT: Greenwood Press, 1999).

4. Alvin J. Schmidt, *How Christianity Changed the World* (Grand Rapids: Zondervan, 2001), 176–79.

5. Michael D. Waggoner and Nathan C. Walker, eds., *The Oxford Handbook of Religion and American Education* (Oxford: Oxford University Press, 2018), 170.

6. In 1948, Americans self-identified their religion for a Gallup poll that has been taken annually ever since. In that year, 69 percent of Americans identified as Protestant Christian, and 22 percent identified as Catholic Christian for a total of 91 percent Christian. See a listing of survey results for every year, from 1948 to 2018, in "Religion," Gallup.com, accessed June 23, 2019, https://news.gallup .com/poll/1690/religion.aspx.

7. The Industrial Revolution, in its various phases, was launched by a generation of students who inherited the knowledge and tools of the Scientific Revolution and who were taught by Christian universities, their educational offspring, their graduates, or the public education that resulted from them. For some late examples, consider Thomas Edison, whose early scientific thinking was shaped by the book *A School Compendium or Natural and Experimental Philosophy* by Richard Green Parker, who was a graduate of Harvard and also the son of a Christian clergyman. The Wright brothers, fathers of modern aviation, were raised by a Christian pastor who was himself a college professor

of theology. Dozens more examples exist from each phase of the Industrial Revolution.

8. See "Ye Ole Deluder Satan Law," implemented by the Puritan Christians in the early American colonies. Many, like John Harvard, were Cambridge graduates. It was a revolutionary law in its requirement that any village with more than one hundred residents had to provide education to its children, teaching them to read the Bible and the Christian-influenced *New England Primer*.

9. Robert D. Woodberry, "The Missionary Roots of Liberal Democracy," *American Political Science Review* 106 (2012): 3–30.

10. See Johannes Kepler, *Ad Vitellionem Paralipomena*, 1604, in which the scientist and devout Christian explains the scientific understanding of light and how to adjust focus for the retina. Kepler is well known for his contributions to the invention of modern eyeglasses. Dozens more examples exist.

11. See the discussion in chapter 8 of the role of Johns Hopkins, a devout Christian Quaker, among others.

12. See the discussion in chapter 8 of the devout Christian Edward Jenner, among others.

13. It is well accepted that one of the most significant breakthroughs for women's rights was the signing of the "Declaration of Sentiments" at Seneca Falls, NY, in 1848. A careful examination of the one hundred original signers reveals that a majority were Christians, with many being Quaker Christians in particular. All had been trained to read and write at institutions founded by Christians. This document and its signers revolutionized women's rights by critiquing what had been the accepted norm for thousands of years in human history. The motivation for many of these activists was their Christian understanding of God, human dignity across both genders, and life—as exhibited in their formal writings, personal writings, and lives. Take, for example, the signers Lucretia Mott, an ordained Christian clergy, and Jane Hunt. See also the discussion in chapter 9 of Harriet Tubman, another devout Christian.

14. Rodney Stark, *For the Glory of God: How Monotheism Led to Reformations, Science, Witch-Hunts, and the End of Slavery* (Princeton: Princeton University Press, 2003), 299–305, 338–65.

15. The conclusion is based on archaeological evidence from major civilizations throughout human history. For proof that slavery was an accepted norm on every continent prior to Christian influence, including North American slavery of Native Americans by other Native Americans, see the list of books in chapter 5, note 2 above.

16. Robert D. Woodberry, "The Medical Impact of Missions" (paper presented at the American Society for Church History, Atlanta, GA, January 5, 2007). See also Robert D. Woodberry, "Religion and the Spread of Human Capital and Political Institutions," in *The Oxford Handbook of the Economics of Religion*, ed. Rachel M. McDleary (New York: Oxford University Press, 2011), 111–31.

17. Henry Charles Shelley, *John Harvard and His Times* (n.p.: Ulan Press, 2012). See also Jeremiah Chaplin, *Life of Henry Dunster: First President of Harvard College* (Charleston, SC: BiblioBazaar, 2008). See also the autobiographical

writings of William Wilberforce, John Rankin, Frederick Douglass, Isaac Newton, Florence Nightingale, and Martin Luther King Jr., among many others.

18. Matthew 5:14.

19. Katie Davis Majors is the author of *Kisses from Katie: A Story of Relentless Love and Redemption* (New York: Simon & Schuster, 2011); and *Daring to Hope: Finding God's Goodness in the Broken and the Beautiful* (Colorado Springs: Multnomah, 2018). Read more from Katie's blog at https://katiemajors.blog/.

20. Amazima Ministries, www.amazima.org (written bio and notes from video interview; description of book *Kisses from Katie*).

Chapter 12 Summary Thoughts on Christian Influence

1. "One in Five Children, Adolescents, and Youth Is Out of School," UNESCO Institute for Statistics, Fact Sheet No. 48 (February 2018), accessed June 23, 2019, http://uis.unesco.org/sites/default/files/documents/fs48-one-five-children-adolescents-youth-out-school-2018-en.pdf .

2. For more information about MCESP, visit https://www.educationformaasai.org/our-mission. Quotations in this profile are taken from a personal interview granted for this book, previously unpublished.

Chapter 13 Did Jesus Actually Exist?

1. 1 Corinthians 15:17, 19.

2. Gary R. Habermas, *The Historical Jesus: Ancient Evidence for the Life of Christ* (Joplin, MO: College Press, 1996), 158; Robert E. Van Voorst, *Jesus Outside the New Testament: An Introduction to the Evidence* (Grand Rapids: Eerdmans, 2000), 39–52, 68–74, 83, 96, 101; Bart D. Ehrman, *Did Jesus Exist?* (New York: HarperOne, 2012), 45, 54; and Lee Strobel, *The Case for the Real Jesus* (Grand Rapids: Zondervan, 2007), 38, 80, 110, 119–20.

3. Habermas, *Historical Jesus*, 190; Van Voorst, *Jesus Outside the New Testament*, 29–38; and Ehrman, *Did Jesus Exist?*, 53.

4. Habermas, *Historical Jesus*, 193; Van Voorst, *Jesus Outside the New Testament*, 12, 15–16, 21, 32, 47, 48, 51, 70, 81–104, 129–34; Ehrman, *Did Jesus Exist?*, 45, 57; and Strobel, *Case for the Real Jesus*, 80, 116–20, 127, 131.

5. Habermas, *Historical Jesus*, 196; and Van Voorst, *Jesus Outside the New Testament*, 20–22.

6. Habermas, *Historical Jesus*, 199; Van Voorst, *Jesus Outside the New Testament*, 23–28; Ehrman, *Did Jesus Exist?*, 51; and Strobel, *Case for the Real Jesus*, 116.

7. Habermas, *Historical Jesus*, 200; and Strobel, *Case for the Real Jesus*, 178.

8. Habermas, *Historical Jesus*, 201; and Strobel, *Case for the Real Jesus*, 178.

9. Habermas, *Historical Jesus*, 203; and Van Voorst, *Jesus Outside the New Testament*, 13, 83, 103–8, 110–11, 114, 116–18, 123–28, 133, 170.

10. Habermas, *Historical Jesus*, 205; and Van Voorst, *Jesus Outside the New Testament*, 122–28.

11. Habermas, *Historical Jesus*, 206; Van Voorst, *Jesus Outside the New Testament*, 58–63; and Strobel, *Case for the Real Jesus*, 119.

12. Habermas, *Historical Jesus*, 207; Van Voorst, *Jesus Outside the New Testament*, 53–57; and Strobel, *Case for the Real Jesus*, 119.

13. Habermas, *Historical Jesus*, 209.

14. Habermas, *Historical Jesus*, 210.

15. Habermas, *Historical Jesus*, 211.

16. Habermas, *Historical Jesus*, 213.

17. Habermas, *Historical Jesus*, 230; and Strobel, *Case for the Real Jesus*, 117, 124–26.

18. Habermas, *Historical Jesus*, 231; and Strobel, *Case for the Real Jesus*, 37, 103, 124.

19. Habermas, *Historical Jesus*, 233.

20. Habermas, *Historical Jesus*, 234.

21. Habermas, *Historical Jesus*, 235; and Strobel, *Case for the Real Jesus*, 38, 130, 171–72, 180, 185, 190–91.

22. Van Voorst, *Jesus Outside the New Testament*; Habermas, *Historical Jesus*; Ehrman, *Did Jesus Exist?*; Rice Broocks, *Man Myth Messiah* (Nashville: W Publishing Group, 2016); and Strobel, *Case for the Real Jesus*.

23. Habermas, *Historical Jesus*, 158; Van Voorst, *Jesus Outside the New Testament*, 39–52, 68–74, 83, 96, 101; Ehrman, *Did Jesus Exist?*, 45, 54; and Strobel, *Case for the Real Jesus*, 138, 80, 110, 119–20.

24. Tacitus, *The Annals*, 15.44.

25. Habermas, *Historical Jesus*, 193; Van Voorst, *Jesus Outside the New Testament*, 12, 15–16, 21, 32, 47, 48, 51, 70, 81–104, 129–34; Ehrman, *Did Jesus Exist?*, 45, 57; and Strobel, *Case for the Real Jesus*, 80, 116–20, 127, 131.

26. This translation of Josephus from the Arabic is by Professor Schlomo Pines of the Hebrew University in Jerusalem, as quoted by James H. Charlesworth in *Jesus within Judaism: New Light from Exciting Archaeological Discoveries* (New York: Doubleday, 1988), 95. See also Flavius Josephus, *The Works of Flavius Josephus*, trans. William Whiston, 4 vols. (Grand Rapids: Baker, 1974).

27. Habermas, *Historical Jesus*, 199; Van Voorst, *Jesus Outside the New Testament*, 23–28; Ehrman, *Did Jesus Exist?*, 51; and Strobel, *Case for the Real Jesus*, 116.

28. Pliny, *Letters*, trans. William Melmoth, ed. W. M. L. Hutchinson, vol. 2 (Cambridge: Harvard University Press, 1935), X:96.

29. Lucian, *The Death of Peregrine*, in *The Works of Lucian of Samosata*, 4 vols., trans. H. W. Fowler and F. G. Fowler (Oxford: Clarendon, 1949), 4:11–13.

30. Habermas, *Historical Jesus*, 199; Van Voorst, *Jesus Outside the New Testament*, 23–28; Ehrman, *Did Jesus Exist?* 51; and Strobel, *Case for the Real Jesus*, 116.

31. Habermas, *Historical Jesus*, 190; Van Voorst, *Jesus Outside the New Testament*, 29–38; and Ehrman, *Did Jesus Exist?*, 53.

32. Habermas, *Historical Jesus*, 201; and Strobel, *Case for the Real Jesus*, 178.

33. Habermas, *Historical Jesus*, 230; and Strobel, *Case for the Real Jesus*, 117, 124–26.

34. Clement of Rome, *Corinthians*, 42.

35. Philippians 4:3.

36. Habermas, *Historical Jesus*, 231; and Strobel, *Case for the Real Jesus*, 37, 103, 124.

37. Ignatius, *Trallians*, 9.

38. Van Voorst, *Jesus Outside the New Testament*; Habermas, *Historical Jesus*; Ehrman, *Did Jesus Exist?*; Broocks, *Man Myth Messiah*; and Strobel, *Case for the Real Jesus*.

39. 1 Corinthians 15:17, 19.

40. John 20:29 NLT.

Chapter 14 What Is the Actual Impact of Jesus's Life?

1. Matthew 16:15–16.

2. "You will be my witnesses in Jerusalem, and in all Judea and Samaria, and to the ends of the earth" (Acts 1:8).

3. "He has anointed me to proclaim good news to the poor. He has sent me to proclaim freedom for the prisoners and recovery of sight for the blind, to set the oppressed free" (Luke 4:18).

4. "Then Jesus came to them and said, 'All authority in heaven and on earth has been given to me'" (Matthew 28:18). "He will reign over Jacob's descendants forever; his kingdom will never end" (Luke 1:33).

5. See "The Future of World Religions: Population Growth Projections, 2010–2050," Pew Research Center, April 2, 2015, http://www.pewforum.org/2015/04/02/religious-projections-2010-2050/.

6. Figures listed from Instagram on the day I wrote this chapter in October 2018.

7. Conrad Hackett and David McClendon, "Christians Remain World's Largest Religious Group, but They Are Declining in Europe," Pew Research Center, April 5, 2017, https://www.pewresearch.org/fact-tank/2017/04/05/christians-remain-worlds-largest-religious-group-but-they-are-declining-in-europe/.

8. I chose these names based on Clive James's book *Fame in the 20th Century* (New York: Random House, 1993).

9. Hackett and McClendon, "World's Largest Religious Group."

10. Demographic Study, "Mapping the Global Muslim Population," Pew Research Center, October 7, 2009, https://www.pewforum.org/2009/10/07/mapping-the-global-muslim-population/.

11. Frank Jacobs, "Map of Saintly Place-names in Europe," Big Think, December 10, 2017, https://bigthink.com/strange-maps/a-map-of-saintly-place-names-in-europe.

12. "List of Biblical Place Names in North America," Wikipedia, last edited May 16, 2019, https://en.wikipedia.org/wiki/List_of_biblical_place_names_in_North_America.

13. "List of Places Named after People in the United States," Wikipedia, last edited April 27, 2019, https://en.wikipedia.org/wiki/List_of_places_named_after_people_in_the_United_States.

14. "Number of International and United States Starbucks Stores from 2005 to 2018," Statista, 2019, https://www.statista.com/statistics/218366/number-of-international-and-us-starbucks-stores.

15. "Number of McDonald's Restaurants in North America from 2012 to 2018, by Country," Statista, 2019, https://www.statista.com/statistics/256040/mcdonalds-restaurants-in-north-america/; and McDonald's Corporation Form 10-K, United States Securities and Exchange Commission, 2016, http://d18rn0p25nwr6 d.cloudfront.net/CIK-0000063908/62200c2b-da82-4364-be92-79ed454e3b88.pdf.

16. "List of Mosques in the United States," Wikipedia, last edited May 9, 2019, https://en.wikipedia.org/wiki/List_of_mosques_in_the_United_States; and "Number of Mosques to Rise to Nearly 4 Million by 2019," Islamic Republic News Agency, July 29, 2015, http://www.irna.ir/en/News/81699685.

17. Kent Shaffer, "Q&A: How Many US Churches Exist?" Church Relevance, December 15, 2008, https://churchrelevance.com/qa-how-many-us-churches-exist/. See also Rebecca Randall, "How Many Churches Does America Have? More Than Expected," *Christianity Today*, September 14, 2017, https://www.christianity today.com/news/2017/september/how-many-churches-in-america-us-nones-non denominational.html; and Greg Stier, "Over 300,000 Churches in America: Do We Really Need More Church Plants?" *Christian Post*, February 16, 2016, https:// www.christianpost.com/news/church-planting-growth-pastors-evangelicals -ministry-america-157730/. The exact number of church buildings in the world is impossible to calculate, but one expert estimates the number to be about thirty-seven million churches. Even if there are less than half that many, Jesus wins the most structures built in his honor by a long shot. See "How Many Christian Churches Are There in the World?," Quora, accessed May 29, 2019, https://www.quora.com /How-many-Christian-churches-are-there-in-the-world.

18. "List of Cathedrals," Wikipedia, last edited January 3, 2019, https://en .wikipedia.org/wiki/Lists_of_cathedrals.

Chapter 15 The Surprising Influence of Jesus

1. John 8:12 NLT.

2. This quotation is popularly attributed to H. G. Wells.

3. Jaroslav Pelikan, *Jesus through the Centuries: His Place in the History of Culture* (New Haven: Yale University Press, 1999), 1.

4. Pelikan, *Jesus through the Centuries*, 1.

5. Michael Luzzi, "A View of Jesus' Impact on Culture," *New York Times*, December 1, 1985.

6. C. S. Lewis, *Mere Christianity*, rev. ed. (1952; repr., New York: HarperCollins, 2009), 52.

Chapter 16 What Does Jesus's Influence Mean for Me?

1. Matthew 11:28–30.

2. Acts 1:8 NLT.

3. "Global Christianity—A Report on the Size and Distribution of the World's Christian Population," Pew Research Center, December 19, 2011, http://www.pew forum.org/2011/12/19/global-christianity-exec/.

4. Matthew 11:28–29.

5. John 3:16.

Chapter 17 Empirically Measuring Jesus's Claims

1. Mark 9:24 RSV.

2. Mark 9:24 RSV.

Conclusion

1. John 13:35.

2. See Matthew 7:16 and John 1:14.

3. John 6:35.

4. See Revelation 3:16.

5. John 14:6.

6. Romans 10:9–11 NLT.

Appendix B: Baselining in Investigations

1. See John Dickerson, "Inhumanity Has a Price," *Phoenix New Times*, December 20, 2007, and related stories in the same publication.

John S. Dickerson is an award-winning journalist, a millennial, and a bestselling author. His writing has appeared in the *New York Times* and *USA Today*, among others. Tom Brokaw (NBC News) and Christiane Amanpour (CNN and ABC News) have named him winner of the Livingston Award for Young Journalists. Now convinced that Jesus launched the greatest movement for social good, John has given his life to join the cause. Today he serves as lead pastor at Connection Pointe Christian Church in Indianapolis. Learn more at JohnSDickerson.com.

Also Available from
JOHN S. DICKERSON

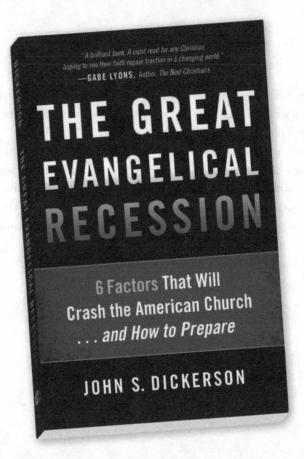

In *The Great Evangelical Recession,* award-winning journalist and pastor John Dickerson identifies six factors that are radically eroding the American church and offers biblical solutions to prepare us for spiritual success, even in the face of alarming trends.

To learn more about
John S. Dickerson's speaking and writing, visit

JOHNSDICKERSON.COM

 @JohnSDickerson

LIKE THIS
BOOK?
Consider sharing it with others!

- Share or mention the book on your social media platforms. Use the hashtag **#JesusSkepticBook**.

- Write a book review on your blog or on a retailer site.

- Pick up a copy for friends, family, or anyone who you think would enjoy and be challenged by its message!

- Share this message on Twitter, Facebook, or Instagram:
  I loved #JesusSkepticBook by @JohnSDickerson @ReadBakerBooks

- Recommend this book for your church, workplace, book club, or class.

- Follow Baker Books on social media and tell us what you like.

ReadBakerBooks

ReadBakerBooks

ReadBakerBooks